D0375096

A REPUBLIC DIVIDED

A

REPUBLIC

DIVIDED

The Annenberg Democracy Project

OXFORD
UNIVERSITY PRESS

OXFORD

UNIVERSITY PRESS

Oxford University Press, Inc., publishes works that further
Oxford University's objective of excellence
in research, scholarship, and education.

Oxford   New York
Auckland   Cape Town   Dar es Salaam   Hong Kong   Karachi
Kuala Lumpur   Madrid   Melbourne   Mexico City   Nairobi
New Delhi   Shanghai   Taipei   Toronto

With offices in
Argentina   Austria   Brazil   Chile   Czech Republic   France   Greece
Guatemala   Hungary   Italy   Japan   Poland   Portugal   Singapore
South Korea   Switzerland   Thailand   Turkey   Ukraine   Vietnam

Published by Oxford University Press, Inc.
198 Madison Avenue, New York, New York, 10016
http://www.oup.com/us

Library of Congress Cataloging-in-Publication Data
A republic divided / the Annenberg Democracy Project.
p. cm.—(Institutions of American democracy)
Includes bibliographical references and index.
ISBN 978-0-19-532527-0
1. United States—Politics and government—2001—   2. Democracy—United States—Public
opinion.   3. Separation of powers—United States—Public opinion.   4. Public opinion—
United States.   I. Annenberg Democracy Project.
JK275.R47   2007
320.973—dc22
2007000240

1 3 5 7 9 8 6 4 2
Printed in the United States of America
on acid-free paper

CONTENTS

DIRECTORY OF CONTRIBUTORS

Joel D. Aberbach (Coeditor of *The Executive Branch*)

Distinguished Professor of Political Science and Public Policy; Director, Center for American Politics and Public Policy, University of California, Los Angeles

Professor Aberbach's research ranges widely over topics in American and comparative politics, with emphasis on legislative–executive relations and broader issues of executive politics and policymaking. His books include *Keeping a Watchful Eye: The Politics of Congressional Oversight* (Brookings, 1990), *In the Web of Politics: Three Decades of the U.S. Federal Executive* (Brookings, 2000), coauthored with Bert A. Rockman, and *Institutions of American Democracy: The Executive Branch* (Oxford, 2005), coedited with Mark A. Peterson and winner of the 2006 Richard E. Neustadt Award for best reference book on the American presidency. He is currently cochair of the Research Committee on Structure and Organization of Government of the International Political Science Association. In 2005 he was elected a fellow of the National Academy of Public Administration. He has also been a fellow at the Center for Advanced Study in the Behavioral Sciences and the Swedish Collegium for Advanced Study in the Social Sciences, a visiting fellow at the University of Bologna's Institute of Advanced Studies, and a senior fellow at the Brookings Institution in Washington, D.C. He is currently (2006–7) the John G. Winant visiting professor of American Government at the University of Oxford and fellow of Balliol College.

Kathleen Hall Jamieson (Coeditor of *The Press*)

Elizabeth Ware Packard Professor of Communication, Annenberg School for Communication; Walter and Leonore Annenberg Director, Annenberg Public Policy Center, University of Pennsylvania

An expert on political campaigns, Dr. Jamieson has received numerous teaching and service awards, including the Christian R. and Mary F. Lindback Award. She is the recipient of many fellowships and grants, including support from the Pew Charitable Trusts, the Ford Foundation, the Robert Wood Johnson Foundation, the MacArthur Foundation, and the Carnegie Corporation of New York. Dr. Jamieson is a fellow of the

American Academy of Arts and Sciences and a member of the American Philosophical Society. She is the author, coauthor, or editor of 15 books, including *The 2000 Presidential Election and the Foundations of Party Politics* (Cambridge, 2004), *The Press Effect* (Oxford University Press, 2003) and *Everything You Think You Know About Politics ... and Why You're Wrong* (Basic Books, 2000). During the 2004 general election, Jamieson regularly appeared on *NOW* with Bill Moyers and *The NewsHour* with Jim Lehrer.

Bruce W. Hardy

Senior Research Analyst, Annenberg Public Policy Center, University of Pennsylvania;
Doctoral Student, Annenberg School for Communication, University of Pennsylvania

Bruce W. Hardy's research focuses on political communication with emphasis on American presidential campaigns, deliberative democracy, and the press. He has published in academic journals such as *Public Opinion Quarterly* and the *Journal of Communication.*

Patrick E. Jamieson

Associate Director, Adolescent Risk Communication Institute, Annenberg Public Policy Center, University of Pennsylvania

Dr. Jamieson's research focuses on smoking and suicide prevention in American youth as well as media portrayals of risky and pro-social behaviors. His work has been published in *Pediatrics,* the *Journal of Adolescence,* and the *Journal of Communication.* He is the author of *Mind Race* (Oxford University Press, 2006).

Kevin T. McGuire (Coeditor of *The Judicial Branch*)

Associate Professor, Political Science, University of North Carolina at Chapel Hill

Dr. McGuire is an expert on judicial politics, constitutional law, and American government and politics. His research on the Supreme Court has won awards from the Law & Courts Section of the American Political Science Association, and he is a former Fulbright Scholar at Trinity College, Dublin. Currently, he is a coeditor of the University of Virginia Press's Series on Constitutionalism and Democracy. His books include the introductory textbook, *Understanding the U.S. Supreme Court* (McGraw-Hill, 2001).

Mary E. McIntosh

Principal and President, Princeton Survey Research Associates International, Washington, D.C.

Dr. McIntosh's research focuses on comparative political sociology, with an emphasis on issues of democratization and transitional societies. Her research includes hundreds of domestic and international surveys on socio-political issues and numerous journal articles featuring this research.

Mark A. Peterson (Coeditor of *The Executive Branch)*

Professor, Public Policy and Political Science, University of California, Los Angeles

Dr. Peterson is a scholar of American national institutions, focusing on the interactions among the presidency, Congress, and interest groups, as well as on national health care policy-making. Former chair of the Department of Public Policy and past editor of the

Journal of Health Politics, Policy and Law, he has been a guest scholar at the Brookings Institution and, as an American Political Science Association Congressional fellow, worked as a legislative assistant in the U.S. Senate. He is chair of the National Advisory Committee for the Robert Wood Johnson Foundation's Scholars in Health Policy Research Program. His writings include *Legislating Together: The White House and Capitol Hill from Eisenhower to Reagan*. With Joel Aberbach he coedited *Institutions of American Democracy: The Executive Branch*, recipient of the 2006 Richard E. Neustadt Award for the best reference on the presidency. A past recipient of an Investigator Award in Health Policy Research from the Robert Wood Johnson Foundation, currently he is completing a book, *Stalemate: Opportunities, Gambles, and Miscalculations in Health Policy Innovation*.

Paul J. Quirk (Coeditor of *The Legislative Branch*)

Phil Lind Chair in U.S. Politics and Representation, University of British Columbia

Dr. Quirk has written on a wide range of topics in American politics, including Congress, the presidency, presidential elections, public opinion, regulatory politics, and public policy-making. He has published in the *American Political Science Review*, the *American Journal of Political Science*, the *Journal of Politics*, and served on the editorial board of several major journals. His books are *Industry Influence in the Federal Regulatory Agencies*, *The Politics of Deregulation* and *Deliberative Choices: Debating Public Policy in Congress*. His awards include the Louis Brownlow Book Award of the National Academy of Public Administration and the Aaron Wildavsky Enduring Achievement Award of the Public Policy Section of the American Political Science Association.

Daniel Romer

Director, Adolescent Risk Communication Institute, Annenberg Public Policy Center, University of Pennsylvania

Dr. Romer studies the political socialization of adolescents and young adults with particular attention to the role of mass media and civics education. His edited volume, *Reducing Adolescent Risk: Toward an Integrated Approach*, presents an overview of research-based strategies to encourage successful transition to adulthood among adolescents. He is also coauthor of *Capturing Campaign Dynamics: 2000 and 2004*, an introduction to the use of the National Annenberg Election Survey.

PREFACE

American democracy is distinctive and, we believe, durable, in part because it is built on five resilient institutions: its three branches of government, a constitutionally protected free press, and universally available public schools. To assess the health of these pillars of our system and recommend ways to improve their prospects, the Annenberg Foundation Trust at Sunnylands convened five commissions. Each produced a scholarly volume of essays making sense of the past, present, and future of one institution. At the helm of this project until his death in spring 2006 was Jaroslav Pelikan, Sterling Professor of History Emeritus at Yale University. A provocative essay by Professor Pelikan introduced each of the first five volumes.

In this, the sixth and final volume in the project, editors who superintended the creation of the earlier books offer a collective report on the well-being of the American democratic system. Our work here is informed by six major surveys, the first of their kind, recording the views of both the elites who have managed these institutions and the public whom they serve.

This enterprise was a joint project of the Annenberg Foundation Trust at Sunnylands, the Annenberg Public Policy Center of the University of Pennsylvania, and Oxford University Press. Even under the most difficult of circumstances, the tireless staff at Oxford University Press provided editorial oversight with grace and good humor. Joyce Garczynski, Annette Price, and Laura Kordiak of the Annenberg Public Policy Center staff scheduled planes, trains, and automobiles; booked hotel rooms; and ensured that ten commission meetings went off with fewer hitches than any of us would have imagined.

We have other debts as well. The project was made possible by the vision and support of Mrs. Leonore Annenberg and the trustees of the Annenberg Foundation Trust at Sunnylands. The collective effort reflects the contributions of 112 scholars and practitioners. To one of them we are particularly grateful, and it is to his memory that we dedicate this final book in the Institutions of

American Democracy series. From its formative to its final stages, Jaroslav Pelikan breathed life into this undertaking. We celebrate his life and mourn his passing.

Kathleen Hall Jamieson
Philadelphia
December 2006

INTRODUCTION

The institutions of democracy in the United States are in a period of exceptional uncertainty. In the aftermath of the 2006 midterm election, they encountered the stresses of both divided government and dramatic political change. The election gave the Democratic Party majority control in both houses of Congress for the first time since the 1994 midterm election inaugurated the so-called Republican Revolution. It also restored a condition of divided party control of the presidency and Congress after four years of unified Republican control, and transformed the political context of the remaining two years of the George W. Bush presidency. Notwithstanding initial promises of bipartisan cooperation from both sides, the nation braced for a period of intense conflict between the executive and legislative branches.

The issues that motivated this book, however, predate the 2006 election and are broader and deeper than the return of divided government. To a remarkable degree, the basic rules of the game in American government have been up for grabs. At the center of the turmoil is an extraordinary conflict over the powers of the presidency. In its 2006 decision in *Hamdan v. Rumsfeld*, for example, a sharply divided Supreme Court struck down President George W. Bush's plan to try suspected terrorists, long held at the military's Guantánamo Bay detainment camp, before special military commissions Bush had created for this purpose. Developed without authorization by Congress, the plan denied detainees in the "war on terror" some of the rights that defendants have enjoyed for the entire history of American civilian and military law. Commentators compared the *Hamdan* decision to the leading decisions that checked expansive claims of presidential power in the twentieth century, such as the 1952 Steel Seizure case, in which the Court struck down Harry S. Truman's claim of presidential power in seizing control of the nation's steel mills to avert a strike during wartime, and the 1974 Nixon tapes case, in which it rejected President Richard M. Nixon's refusal to turn over audiotapes of White House conversations sought by Congress in the Watergate scandal.[1] In his opinion for the five justices in the majority, Justice John Paul Stevens expressed the fundamental institutional imperative that animated critics of President Bush's plan: "The executive is bound to comply with the rule of law." Justice Stephen Breyer added in a concurring opinion that "the Court's conclusion ultimately rests upon a single ground: Congress has not issued the executive a blank check."

Three justices disagreed—and a fourth, the recently appointed chief justice John Roberts, who recused himself because of prior involvement in the case, had supported the president's position at the circuit-court level. In an angry dissenting opinion, Justice Clarence Thomas called the decision "dangerous" and chastised the majority for disregarding "the commander in chief's wartime decisions." John Yoo, a law professor and former Justice Department official who had helped fashion the administration's expansive legal strategy, wrote in an op-ed article that the decision "ignores the basic workings of our separation of powers and will hamper the ability of future presidents to respond to emergencies."[2] He argued that in protecting the nation's security, the president has broad discretion, regardless of Congress's preferences, conferred directly by the Constitution.

Like his predecessors who had similarly been rebuked by the Court, President Bush said he was "willing" to follow the Court's ruling. But even many citizens were not convinced that he was obliged to do so. Shortly after the *Hamdan* ruling in 2006, a national poll by the Annenberg Public Policy Center, the Annenberg Judicial Independence survey, asked whether, in general, a president who disagreed with the Supreme Court should follow its ruling or rather do what he thought was in the best interests of the country. Only a modest 58 percent majority thought that the president should follow the ruling. When a subsequent question added the condition that the president believed the ruling would prevent him from protecting the country against a terrorist attack, the percentage saying he should do what the Court required dropped to 53 percent (with fully 38 percent saying that it is okay for the president to ignore the ruling). After months of often vituperative debate, the Republican Congress passed the Military Commissions Act of 2006, which, though widely criticized as unconstitutional, gave the president most of the authority he had sought to assert, and rendered moot the question of whether he would obey the Court's decision.

Conflict and uncertainty over rules of the game have also occurred within Congress. Republicans and Democrats have fought pitched battles over legislative rules in both the House and Senate. When in the majority, Senate Republicans threatened to employ a hardball procedural strategy to abolish the filibuster on judicial nominations—a strategy the Democrats called "the nuclear option," to suggest that the resulting resentment and retaliation would destroy the Senate. Republicans argued that they were merely trying to reestablish the constitutionally appropriate practice of ensuring that nominees received an up or down vote on the Senate floor. Their efforts were born of frustration; in fact, the Democrats had used the filibuster to block judicial appointments more extensively than it had ever before been used for that purpose.

Over an even longer period, the news media also have been undergoing transformation—as cable news networks (notably Fox) have all but officially abandoned the notion that news reports should aspire to be nonpartisan and objective. Programming that unabashedly cultivates partisan audiences is on the rise. In addition, the major networks have increasingly emphasized soft news—keeping the citizenry informed about fashion trends, box office successes, and celebrity marriages. The rapid rise of blogs as both independent sources of news and analysis and as self-proclaimed watchdogs of the mainstream media has also begun to alter political coverage and audience expectations. These changes have promoted uncertainty about appropriate practice, as a result of which citizens and professionals often disagree about just which media figures are "journalists." The structure of the industry has also changed. The print and broadcast media have come to be dominated by a handful of huge conglomerates, raising the issue of corporate intrusion into political debate and of the sacrifice of traditional journalistic values in favor of unadulterated commercialism.

Other institutional conflicts of long standing continue unabated: within the legal community, judges accuse one another of usurping the authority of elected officials, prompting lawyers and politicians to level and contest charges of "judicial activism." National elections have likewise produced discord. The system of campaign finance underwent major reform with the Bipartisan Campaign Finance Reform Act of 2002, an attempt to reduce the influence of private money on elections. But only a few years later it was widely regarded as unsuccessful; if anything, it had enlarged the role of unaccountable private groups. Even the public schools, institutions that although distant from most day-to-day political issues are essential to nurturing a capable electorate, have faced fundamental institutional challenges, as advocates of school-choice programs and privatization have sought to replace governmental administration with competitive markets in education.

In this book we focus on the perceptions of both institutional "insiders" and the public, and a variety of other evidence, to assess the functioning, well-being, and relationships of five of the core institutions of American democracy: the legislative, executive, and judicial branches of national government; and two nongovernmental institutions that are crucial to democracy because they shape the knowledge and understanding of the citizenry: the press and the public schools. We bring to bear the richest collection of survey data that has ever been assembled on these institutions.

Several developments give this inquiry special urgency and significance. First, American engagement in international conflicts and elevated concerns about national security always test the nation's democratic institutions and the vitality of its constitutional arrangements. In the post-9/11 world, the United States faces the extraordinary challenge of dealing with the threat of terrorism, a phenomenon of uncertain scope and unforeseeable duration. The nation must find ways to minimize the risk of future terrorist attacks, cope with the likelihood that such attacks will occur nevertheless, and yet avoid the unnecessary surrender of cherished rights and freedoms while maintaining the institutional means for holding leaders politically and legally accountable. At the extremes, the stakes include preventing both the destruction of major American cities by nuclear blast and avoiding George Orwell's dark vision of a technologically advanced totalitarian society. The American democracy is in perilous times, and only the institutions of that democracy can protect it.

Second, the Bush administration sought to execute a novel and particularly unrestrained doctrine of presidential power. Its roots go back to the Reagan and Nixon administrations, but it was the governing principle of the Bush presidency. Under the rubric of the "unitary executive," the administration argued that the president has essentially exclusive power to supervise the departments, agencies, and officials of the executive branch. Rejected by most constitutional scholars, this doctrine seems to overlook the implications of Senate advice and consent, the ability of Congress to specify administrative organization and practices by statute, and the authority of the courts to determine the meaning of statutes and judge the constitutionality of legislative and executive action. Moreover, based on its interpretation of "the executive power" and the "commander in chief" roles in the Constitution, the Bush administration posited that the president can act with autonomy in military and foreign affairs, largely unfettered by either congressional or judicial checks. What is more remarkable, from the standpoint of American constitutional law, the administration cited the unitary-executive doctrine in defending its use of presidential signing statements, unprecedented in both frequency and scope, to claim to invalidate provisions of law. Rather than employing the veto power—provided, subject to congressional override, by the Constitution—President Bush instead simply announced his opinion that part of a statute that he had signed was unconstitutional and that he and executive branch officials, therefore, would reserve the right to not enforce it.

Third, recent American politics have seen virtually unprecedented levels of ideological polarization between the Republican and Democratic parties. Through much of the twentieth century, reflecting the legacy of the Civil War, the two parties had been divided partly by regional traditions rather than political beliefs. Both in Congress and among presidents, moderate members of each party—of which there were many—were often disposed to collaborate with the other party and to set aside partisan electoral concerns for the sake of solving national problems. In the early twenty-first century, however, the parties were more severely polarized than at any time since the first decade of the twentieth century. Animated by sharply different visions of American society and the role of government, and with few moderates remaining in their ranks, Republican and Democratic officeholders had a hard time finding significant matters on which they could agree. In particular, they were willing, for partisan advantage, to abandon institutional norms that ensured mutual accommodation or protected the competence or integrity of decision processes. In the House of Representatives, for example, the Republican leadership in 2005 removed a chair of the Ethics Committee who had vigorously pursued an investigation of House majority leader Tom DeLay (DeLay ultimately was forced to resign his seat anyway, as he faced trial on criminal charges).

Fourth, after the Republicans won control of the Senate in the 2002 midterm election, giving them the presidency and majorities in both houses of Congress, they implemented, by American standards, remarkably disciplined and assertive one-party rule. They were able to do so, moreover, even though their electoral victories were quite narrow. The electorate has been almost evenly divided between Republicans and Democrats. The 2000 presidential election, for example, was decided by a hair's breadth; the victor, George W. Bush, lost the popular vote while winning in the electoral college, thanks to a disputed victory by a few hundred votes in Florida. The outcome of the 2004 presidential election was settled by 2 percent of the vote in the pivotal state of Ohio.[3] The margins of party control for the Republican majorities in three Congresses from 2001 to 2006—that is, the number of seats that would have to change hands for the other party to gain control (for example, three seats if the party balance is 220–215) ranged from zero to five seats in the Senate and from five to fifteen seats in the House—were the narrowest in a generation; they resulted, moreover, from elections in which the national vote for Republican candidates averaged just under 50 percent in both House and Senate races.[4]

Despite their narrow victories, the Bush administration and the Republican Congress pushed divisive partisan policies on domestic issues and maintained an aggressive, unilateralist foreign policy. They made relatively few concessions to Democrats or moderates. Rarely in American politics has so much policy change turned on such small differences in electoral outcomes. In the past, major policy enactments generally required either bipartisan support or a sweeping electoral victory by one party. Now, with much riding on small partisan gains or losses in the next election, the electoral stakes are perceived as extraordinary. On many accounts, the parties have responded by dealing with almost every issue as an opportunity for electioneering. The results of the 2006 election promised to reinforce these tendencies. The election gave the Democrats a fairly narrow sixteen-seat margin in the House,[5] and a very narrow two-vote margin (51–49) in the Senate.

As a result of all these circumstances, American democratic institutions are in an unstable, contentious, and even precarious state in the early years of the twenty-first century. The most critical issues are probably those regarding the separation of powers. In criticizing President Bush's demand for legislative endorsement of his planned secret military tribunals, Republican senator Lindsay Graham said sternly, "there are three branches of government, not one."[6] Most Republicans, however, supported the administration's positions on separation-of-powers issues. Perhaps more than at any time since the Civil War, the political system lacks consensus about the fundamental structures of government. The 2006 election shifted the balance of power in conflicts about the separation of powers; but it did nothing to moderate the conflicting views. After the 2006 Democratic takeover of Congress, it was unclear whether, if Congress acted to bar military action against Iran in the dispute over its effort to acquire nuclear weapons, the administration would feel obliged to comply.

The ability of the American public to hold leaders accountable for the management or performance of governmental institutions is also in doubt. Our 2006 Annenberg Judicial Independence survey found that one-third of a national sample could not name any of the branches of government. Most Americans have very limited information relevant to the tasks of citizens. Nearly all general-public respondents in our 2004 Annenberg Congress and Executive Branch survey knew that Dick Cheney was vice president, and about 95 percent recognized Edward Kennedy as a prominent figure in the nation's capital. After more than a decade of Republican majorities in both the House and (apart from the 107th Congress) the Senate, about three-quarters of the respondents said correctly that the Republican Party currently controlled Congress. But most were unaware of the sharp partisan conflict that is, by most accounts, both the hallmark and the central institutional problem of the contemporary Congress. Only one-third of the respondents said that "the Democrats and the Republicans agree with each other less now than in the past"—if anything, an understatement of the reality—and half that number said that the two parties agree more than in the past.

Citizens' lack of information about the nation's institutions is potentially consequential: We find that the more-educated survey respondents are far more likely than the less educated to understand and endorse the central tenets of the constitutional system. For example, respondents who lack a college education were as likely as not to endorse the unsupportable claim that the founders' intended to subordinate Congress and the judiciary and give the president "the final say." The existence of such misinformation about the nation's constitutional system among a substantial fraction of the public raises serious questions about the ability of the public to stand up for that system against reckless, radical, or even antidemocratic institutional change—especially in a time of international and domestic peril.

Several problematic features of electoral processes present further barriers to accountability. Because of the failure of campaign finance reform, American election campaigns are awash in private contributions that create the appearance of and the potential for conflicts of interest. These campaigns are often dominated by independent groups that broadcast messages for which the candidates do not take responsibility. In many of the states, the reliance on private money extends to judicial elections—with contributions to judges' reelection campaigns coming from the very lawyers who practice before them. In the absence of a sweeping partisan tide, as in 2006, elections for the House of Representatives reveal precious few competitive seats—a situation that has reduced losses by incumbents to fewer than ten (out of 435 seats) per election in recent elections. The preponderance of House members, both Republican and Democrat, occupy safe seats. It is hard for the public to hold government accountable when there is only a remote chance of turning out the governing party. Even when elections are reasonably competitive—as in presidential and many senatorial elections—the content of the campaign often undermines accountability. Campaign advertising sometimes features vicious personal attacks and misleading claims about issues. News coverage is mostly about the horse-race aspect of the campaign—what strategies the candidates are using, and who is winning and why—rather than substantive issues. Discussion in the campaign is then about the campaign itself, not about governing.

Difficulties in performance and compromised accountability are likely to produce a loss of trust. The 2004 Annenberg Congress and Executive Branch survey occurred shortly after the presidential election, when the United States was promoting the election of a new government in Iraq, and before the steep decline in approval of the war in 2005 and 2006. By summer 2006, under pressure of a deteriorating situation in Iraq and Republican ethics scandals, trust in Congress and the president had declined—with only 41 and 45 percent, respectively, trusting these institutions to operate in the best interests of the American people. In the long run, such low levels of trust may undermine public support for the maintenance of the constitutional system, or sap public resistance to measures that would drastically change that system.

We address these issues of polarization, rules of the game, performance, trust, and the health of democratic institutions in the following chapters. Our discussion begins with the nongovernmental institutions that educate and inform American citizens. In Chapter 1, "The Role of Public Education in Educating for Democracy," Daniel Romer, Patrick E. Jamieson, and Bruce W. Hardy focus on the role of the schools as a critical provider of civics values and knowledge, as well as career skills. They show that the partisan divide that characterizes current politics is also evident in debates about the schools. Starting with the Reagan administration, conservative critics have focused on a "crisis" in American public education, a theme that has continued into the twenty-first century. Although most of this criticism has been directed toward the schools as developers of the workforce, civics education has also come under fire for tilting too far in a liberal direction. The press has adopted the crisis theme with considerable enthusiasm, to the point where we find in a national survey of parents that those who rely on press coverage of school issues, as opposed to their own experience, have less favorable views of their schools. Despite the crisis rhetoric, and the profound failures of schools in some, mainly inner-city, areas, most Americans are moderately satisfied with their local schools. Americans also recognize the importance of the public schools as agents of civic socialization. Evidence suggests that the schools have performed reasonably well in achieving this goal over the past four decades. Critics who lay a large share of the blame for the problems of American society and politics upon the public schools, in general, appear to be off the mark.

While it remains true that those who read newspapers are more likely to be politically knowledgeable, Chapter 2 argues that the press's ability to perform important democratic functions is impaired by a corporate model that sacrifices substance for profits at too many turns and by public doubts about the extent to which the press performs its traditional functions. In "The Effectiveness of the Press in Serving the Needs of American Democracy," Kathleen Hall Jamieson, Bruce W. Hardy, and Daniel Romer show, for example, that while reporters believe that they correct serious mistakes in their work, the public has serious doubts that they do. That finding is troubling because those who perceive that the press is failing the public are more likely to believe that the press's First Amendment protections can properly be abridged.

Citizens' perceptions of the institutions of democracy, especially their trust or lack of trust in them, is the focus of a bridging chapter between Section I's discussion of democratic citizens and Section III's focus on democratic government. In Chapter 3, "Understanding the Public's Relationship to Government," Mary McIntosh argues that political trust is complex, and that, contrary to the traditional view of trust as an outcome of good governance, trust is both a cause and a consequence of such. The chapter also demonstrates that political trust varies depending on whom you ask. For example, political elites have more trust in government than does the public. And Americans who identify with the party in power are more trusting of the government, although each party's views on the appropriate level of government power are sometimes in conflict with their views on trust—with Republicans, for example, taking a more restrictive view of government even if they trust a Republican Congress and president.

Moreover, trust varies depending on how you ask about it. The trust question used in the Annenberg Institutions of Democracy surveys—focusing on whether people "trust the government to operate in the best interests of the American people"—reports a higher level of trust than the standard trust measure used in the American National Election Studies. The chapter closes with an analysis of what shapes the public's trust in government. For one thing, Americans express more trust in government when they perceive that government as operating efficiently. Unfortunately, from this standpoint, reforms to make government more efficient would encounter resistance on partisan as well as constitutional grounds. In any case, we know that trust can rebound. Although trust was quite low twice before in the recent past—namely 1980 and 1994—it increased substantially in the succeeding periods—suggesting that what can be lost in the minds of the public can also be regained.

With Chapter 4, we begin our assessment of the three branches of the national government with an examination of the separation of powers. After establishing a contemporary baseline for understanding the American system of checks and balances by reviewing the historical evolution of the nation's constitutional arrangements, Mark A. Peterson, in "The Three Branches of Government: Powers, Relationships, and Checks," shows that a majority of the public possesses a rudimentary understanding of separation of powers that is consistent with how the system has emerged in the modern era. In addition, the public's perspectives on attributes of governance and policymaking that derive from separation-of-power arrangements—such as recognizing the inevitable presence of political conflict, the importance of deliberation, and the value of accommodating diverse interests—are reasonably consistent with the views expressed by the insiders who work directly in or with the institutions of government. But education matters greatly. Americans who have been exposed to no more than primary and secondary education are substantially more likely to admit ignorance about central features of the governmental system and, as noted earlier, to be flat wrong in their understanding of checks and balances.

In many ways, Congress is at the center of some of the problematic developments in the American political system. As Paul J. Quirk shows in Chapter 5, "The Legislative Branch: Assessing the Partisan Congress," the U.S. House and Senate, despite public suspicions and comedians' predictable jokes to the contrary, are populated by talented, energetic individuals—both the members and their staff. Difficulties arise, however, from the increasing ideological polarization of the senators and representatives. In the House during the 108th Congress, in 2003–4, every Republican was more conservative than any Democrat; every Democrat more liberal than any Republican. The polarization matters, because how Congress works—far from being fixed by the Constitution, statutes, or other enduring rules—is subject to dramatic variation from one period to another. In the increasingly partisan and ideologically conflicted Congresses of recent years, many of the norms and practices that, for most of the twentieth century, helped Congress provide careful deliberation and bipartisan accommodation have been profoundly compromised, if not abandoned. Staff members of both parties have had serious concerns about the institution's ability to perform effectively—for example, by resisting pressure from organized groups and deliberating carefully. Democratic staff, in particular, perceived an institution that made up the rules as it went along to serve the interests of the majority party. Congress manifestly has failed to legislate means of maintaining electoral processes that can command consensus and respect and enhance the legitimacy of the outcomes. The Democratic majorities elected in 2006 in both the House and Senate claimed that their approach would be more open and bipartisan. But most of the same pressures for party performance that shaped the Republican approach may also affect that of the Democrats.

Meanwhile, the public holds a relatively dim view of Congress as an institution. Yet it is virtually oblivious to the intensified partisan conflict that underlies Congress's greatest difficulties in our era. The public is an ally for reforming Congress mainly if the reform agenda concerns lobbying, ethics, and in some circumstances, campaign finance. As Congress moves away from its traditional consensus building and bipartisanship, a new specter emerges—the potential for unremitting, vicious partisan conflict in a period of divided party control of Congress and the presidency. The last two years of the Bush presidency would test the effectiveness of divided government under conditions of intense partisanship and daunting policy challenges, especially in bringing an end to the Iraq war.

Political polarization is severe even within the executive branch. In Chapter 6, after a general introduction to the people and politics of the branch, Joel D. Aberbach analyzes the wide partisan gulf in opinions that exists both within the executive branch and among the public at large. Drawing on the Annenberg surveys of political appointees and career civil servants in the executive branch and of the general public, "The Executive Branch in Red and Blue" shows how deeply opinion is divided along partisan lines. This division goes beyond the well-known and increasingly strong relationship between party identification and liberal or conservative positions on substantive political issues. It extends even more strongly to issues about executive power that define the nature of the American political system. This partisan divide appears among those who serve, or have recently served, as political appointees; among those at the top of the career civil service hierarchy; and, to a lesser extent, among the general public. It goes beyond the inevitable tensions between career civil servants and presidential administrations because it represents markedly different ideas about how the nation should be governed. Republicans and Democrats differ sharply on such issues as the role of the president and the limits of presidential power. Officials of the executive branch themselves differed about whether they trusted that branch to operate in the best interests of the American people. Such severe differences on fundamental issues and evaluations of how the system works represent potential dangers to the stability and perceived legitimacy of these institutions.

Chapter 7, Kevin T. McGuire's "The Judicial Branch: Judging America's Judges," underscores the basic confidence that the U.S. Supreme Court engenders among the public. Americans generally believe that the Court is essential to democratic government and see its policies as central to their lives. In light of these important functions, the Court's ability to maintain a high level of trust is significant. Nevertheless, the Supreme Court is perhaps the least known and least understood branch of the federal government. The public reveals not only considerable uncertainty about the Court's membership but its decision making and policies as well. Substantial numbers, for instance, do not understand the Court's fundamental power of judicial review. Despite this lack of awareness, Americans still regard the justices as neutral arbiters of the law. A good many Americans—especially the highly educated—believe that the Court's members make decisions based strictly on legal considerations and without influence of personal bias. One segment of that highly educated cohort, the legal community, reveals particular faith in the independence of the judiciary. As one of the Court's principal constituencies, lawyers have a strong faith in the ability of judges to make fully informed legal policy and to do so in ways that are beneficial to society.

Looking across the three branches of government in Chapter 8, "The Three Branches of Government: Comparative Trust and Performance," Mark Peterson finds a public circumspect about the functioning of almost every feature of American national government. In early 2005 bare majorities trusted the elected institutions—Congress and the presidency—to serve the best interests of the American people, and even that limited level of confidence fell several percentage points in a subsequent survey only eighteen months later. The public's relatively greater trust in the judiciary—the branch of government most removed from democratic processes—is thus ironic. Although citizens' views do not suggest serious institutional failure, the public does not believe that any institution of government is particularly effective at performing its job, and it is deeply divided by party in its assessment of President Bush. Compared with the public, the insiders who serve in or interact with the three branches of American national government are more likely to trust that these institutions work in the people's interest. They more readily recognize the difficulties of policymaking in this system. For both the public and insiders, Congress—presumably the most democratic of these institutions of democracy—is currently the most problematic.

In the volume's conclusion, we bring to a close the Annenberg Institutions of American Democracy project by speculating about the long-term implications of the developments we have examined. Recognizing the enormous uncertainties concerning those implications, we consider alternative scenarios for Congress, the courts, the executive branch (including the presidency), the press and media, and the public schools. In doing so we focus on the divides we have isolated, and the sometimes surprising areas of agreement, between institutional elites and the public, and between those on opposite sides of the political aisle. In an uncertain time, we close the book by asking, How resilient are the institutions of democracy in the United States? Is this period of exceptional institutional turmoil evidence of serious vulnerability? What is required to sustain these institutions and the democracy they serve?

Notes

1. The cases are *Youngstown Sheet & Tube Co. v. Sawyer*, 343 U.S. 579 (1952) and *United States v. Nixon*, 418 U.S. 683 (1974).
2. John Yoo, "The High Court's *Hamdan* Power Grab," *Los Angeles Times,* July 7, 2006.
3. President Bush had the narrowest margin of victory in the popular vote over the candidate of the major opposition party (2.86 percentage points) of any reelected president in U.S. history.
4. Vote percentages by party in the 2000, 2002, and 2004 House and Senate elections reported in "Statistics of the Presidential and Congressional Election," compiled for each election year by the Office of the Clerk, United States House of Representatives, http://clerk.house.gov/members/electioninfo/elections.html.
5. At the time of this writing, two House races in the 2006 election had not yet been decided.
6. Carl Hulse, Kate Zernike, and Sheryl Gay Stolberg, "How 3 G.O.P. Veterans Stalled Bush Detainee Bill," *New York Times*, September 17, 2006, sec. 1, 1.

A REPUBLIC DIVIDED

DEMOCRATIC CITIZENS

1

THE ROLE OF PUBLIC EDUCATION
IN EDUCATING FOR DEMOCRACY

Daniel Romer, Patrick E. Jamieson, and Bruce W. Hardy

Universal education has been called "the cornerstone of our democracy" and "America's noble experiment." Traditionally, the nation has "relied upon government schools as a principle purveyor of deeply cherished democratic values" (Ravitch and Viteritti 2001, 5). Education is deemed so important to the welfare of the United States that it is compulsory for those between the ages of six and sixteen. Furthermore, forty state constitutions specifically note the importance of "civic literacy among citizens" (Gibson and Levine 2003, 11), and most states require some form of civics education in the high school curriculum (Niemi and Junn 1998).

The schools also serve as the gateway to employment, by providing students with the literacy and technical skills needed to perform their functions as future workers. In this chapter, we consider public education in its role both as great civic socializer and trainer of the future workforce. Of particular interest is the functioning of this institution as seen by both the public and its internal leadership of administrators and teachers. We begin by examining the historical role of the schools as the vehicle for entry into the civic and economic life of the nation. We then examine evidence suggesting that the public schools have retained their efficacy in instilling democratic values since the mid-twentieth century and that their effectiveness in developing academic skills has been improving. Despite this evidence, the public's evaluation of the schools has been heavily influenced by a widely publicized reform agenda and a focus by the press on the failures of public education, to the exclusion of its successes. This chapter presents results of the Annenberg Institutions of Democracy Public Schools survey (see appendix for survey details); these results indicate widespread consensus about the goals of the

3

schools. However, impressions of school performance are heavily influenced by the "crisis" rhetoric of the reform movement as communicated in the press. Although there is considerable room for improvement, the schools have not declined as a vehicle for either democratic socialization or workforce development. Furthermore, the press is implicated in the ability of the schools to assume their role as civic educator, and improvements in the press's ability to reach and educate young people will have a bearing on how well young people are socialized for citizenship.

The Schools as Civic Educator

The notion that the state should use public education to inculcate its values in the young is a long-lived one. Writing in *Politics*, Aristotle noted that "the citizen should be moulded to suit the form of government under which he lives" (542). The belief that education and citizenship are bound together is a pervasive one as well. As the nonprofit and nonpartisan Center for Civic Education asserted in 1996, the schools "can and should provide effective civic education through both formal and informal means from the earliest grades through high school" (7).

In keeping with this mission, the schools have played an important role in assimilating newcomers to the country. This activity was especially evident in the turbulent Gilded Age and Progressive Era (1880s to 1920), which saw an unprecedented influx of non-English-speaking immigrants and the growth of urban populations. As noted by Reuben (2005), "Progressive Era educators saw inclusive public schools as essential in a democratic polity that included immigrants and their children. They envisioned schools as helping different groups assimilate into American culture and society." This objective included the teaching of basic "academic" skills such as the three R's, and providing students with a greater understanding of U.S. history and the rights and responsibilities of citizenship. To meet this need, states opened "comprehensive" high schools that could educate as well as socialize adolescents to become future workers and citizens.

Despite widespread acceptance of the role of public schools as the training ground of democratic citizenship, the process by which educators implemented this program was frequently plagued by controversy. History and social studies texts that emphasized inequalities in American society were often met with resistance. These disputes were particularly heated during the 1950s, when the House Un-American Activities Committee investigated the practices of teachers who used progressive texts (Reuben 2005). A later example of controversy regarding civics education involved the attempt, in the early 1990s, to develop national guidelines for the teaching of American history (Nash, Crabtree, and Dunn 1997). Critics of this effort, such as Lynne Cheney, as chair of the National Endowment for the Humanities, received national attention by arguing that the

4

guidelines gave too much deference to cultural difference and not enough attention to traditional historical figures (Reuben 2005).

The Schools as Developer of the Workforce

Another strain of contention, which developed during the Reagan administration, focused on the ability of young people to compete in the international marketplace of skilled workers. The release of a federally sponsored report, *A Nation at Risk: The Imperative of Educational Reform,* began a national movement to increase the effectiveness of the public schools as trainers of the future labor force. This agenda spawned the standards movement and its focus on testing to assess the quality of school performance. Such tests, often conducted across the globe, showed that U.S. students were below average compared with students in other industrialized countries. Other tests, such as the SAT, used by American colleges and universities in their admissions procedures, also showed declining performance, which was attributed to erosion in public school standards. A new organization, the National Assessment Governing Board, was created by Congress in 1988 to develop and administer the National Assessment of Educational Progress (NAEP), an achievement test administered to students in grades four, eight, and twelve. The results of this test, known as the "The Nation's Report Card," often found that only a minority of the nation's students could be labeled "proficient" in important academic subjects such as reading and mathematics.

Business leaders, under the aegis of organizations such as the Business Roundtable, also entered the policy arena of school reform when they began to examine educational practices and make recommendations for improving the quality of instruction. Other organizations also challenged the supremacy of the public school model by suggesting that parents begin their own publicly funded (charter) schools or that the government provide vouchers for students to move to better-performing (public or private) schools, or, in the extreme, that parents homeschool their children. These developments served to question the fundamental ability of public schools to meet the challenges of the contemporary work world.

Concerns about the ability of schools to prepare the future workforce were compounded by the continued inability of the schools to reduce the performance gap between white and nonwhite students. Despite the long-standing role of the public schools as assimilators of ethnic groups into the American mainstream, this goal was not being met with regard to African American and Latino youth (Galston 2005). Many of these youths attended urban schools where education was underfunded as compared with the wealthier suburbs. Efforts to reduce these disparities by integrating urban and suburban schools proved largely unsuccessful (Frankenberg, Lee, and Orfield 2003). These stubborn problems fueled the national conversation about the failures of the public schools to meet the challenges of the nation's educational needs.

Reform Agenda and Crisis Rhetoric

The conclusion that America's schools were failing in their academic mission was accompanied by increased rhetoric aimed at mobilizing public opinion to devote more resources to education. As seen in Figure 1, the press was acutely sensitive to this agenda and increasingly featured stories that described the schools as in "crisis." In the decade beginning in 1995, the number of stories in the nation's newspapers about schools in crisis grew dramatically before declining in 2004.

Some of these stories focused on the poor quality of urban schools. For example, in October 2003 Bob Herbert wrote in the *New York Times*, "You'll find these noisy, chaotic classrooms in almost any of America's big cities, not just New York. They are ruthlessly destructive, and scary to students and teachers alike. They are places where childhood dreams all too frequently expire." An article in the *New York Post* noted, "It's no secret that the New York City public school system is in crisis, but new inspection reports . . . show some schools are a complete disaster" (Campanile 2003).

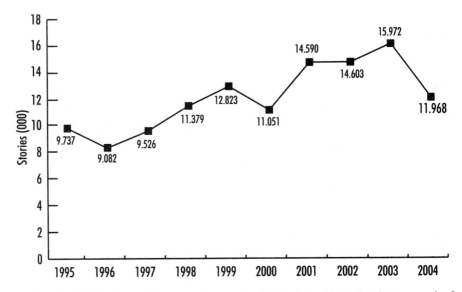

Number of stories (in thousands) per year that contained "schools" and "crisis" within ten words of each other. Stories about violence and colleges were excluded. SOURCE: NewsBank.

Figure 1 Newspaper Reporting on Crisis in Schools

Other stories focused on the quality of the schools in general. For example, "States See Wide Range in Teacher Quality," read the headline of one article run by the Associated Press (Feller 2003). A story in the *New York Times* in 1995 quoted an education official lamenting the "crisis of confidence in the schools that's often exacerbated by the [poor condition of the] buildings themselves" (Applebome 1995). Even in the wealthy environs of Palm Beach, Florida, stories contained discussions of dire conditions in the schools:

> "It's astounding to me that there isn't more of an outcry over this," said Shelley Vana, president of the Palm Beach County Classroom Teachers Association. "We've accepted crisis here as the norm." Almost every one of the 150 schools in the district needs at least one teacher, while some need as many as six. One school in Riviera Beach, Mary McLeod Bethune Elementary, needs 11. Principals say the national teacher shortage has hit the school district hard. To ease the crisis, the state and school district offer incentives to lure potential teachers into the classroom. (Solomon 2000)

In this context, it is not surprising that candidate George W. Bush focused on improving educational standards for the nation's schools as part of his 2000 presidential campaign. His signature No Child Left Behind program was passed with bipartisan support in 2001 and went into effect in 2002. The program sent federal financial support to the states for educational improvements in teacher standards and curriculum. As part of the effort, states were obligated to institute testing regimes that would grade elementary and middle schools on improvement in the basic academic subjects of math, science, and reading. The professed aim of the program was to raise the educational performance of nonwhite and poor students who had in the past been "left behind" by weak schools that failed to bring such students into the mainstream of American life. Bush's political skill in gaining approval of this program from voters and the Congress may well have been aided by his appeal to the traditional mission of the schools as the great vehicle for assimilation into American society.

Public Education Improves

The rising calls for improved educational performance yielded notable successes even before Bush's educational initiative took effect. In a summary of what it termed "good news about American education," the Washington, D.C.–based Center on Education Policy (2005) noted that on many indicators, the nation's education system had registered significant gains since the 1980s. For example, the percentage of students completing a core academic high school curriculum of four years of English and three years of mathematics, science, and social studies increased dramatically, going from a low of 14 percent in 1982 to 57 percent in 2000. Achievement in the early grades also increased, especially in math and reading, as assessed by the NAEP, and SAT scores started to rise despite increasing proportions of young people taking the tests. Furthermore, gaps between white and nonwhite students declined. Although both groups were seen as improving, nonwhite rates of improvement were stronger in math and reading.

Return of Civics Concerns

In the context of concerns about the competitiveness of the American workforce, the civic mission of the schools receded somewhat from the national agenda. At the same time, voting rates of young people declined, as did their interest in politics. Whereas 60 percent of college freshmen felt it important to follow politics in 1966, only 34 percent felt this way early in the new century (Galston 2003). Use of informational print media such as newspapers also declined during this period. Although about 44 percent of eighteen- to twenty-five-year-olds reported reading a newspaper every day in 1972, only about 18 percent did so in 2000 (Olander 2003). However, the fundamental purpose of schools as socializing agents of America's future citizens was not forgotten. Concerns about the civic disengagement of young people and their declining interest in politics led to new initiatives to reinvigorate civics education in the schools. A report sponsored by the Carnegie Corporation and the Center for Information & Research on Civic Learning & Engagement, titled *The Civic Mission of Schools* (Gibson and Levine 2003), focused attention on the potential role that schools might play in reengaging young people to become active citizens as well as breadwinners.

Analyses of the effects of civics education in the public schools show that such a focus does have an impact on student outcomes. Although early studies suggested that civics education had little or no effect on student understanding of the U.S. political system (e.g., Langton and Jennings 1968), later research indicated that as little as one semester of civics increases student outcomes as assessed by the NAEP. In an elaborate study of civics learning based on the 1988 NAEP, researchers concluded that "the civics curriculum has an impact of a size and resilience that makes it a significant part of political learning" (Niemi and Junn 1998, 145). This analysis found that civics classes affected students' knowledge of citizens' rights and state and local government, as well as their understanding of the structure and functions of the federal government.

Although international tests of math and science skills tend to find that American students perform less well than students in other industrialized countries (Ginsburg et al. 2005), an international study of twenty-eight democracies found that fourteen-year-old American students perform at a higher level in civics knowledge and skills compared with their counterparts in other democracies (Torney-Purta, Richardon, and Barber 2004). In interpreting media materials such as political cartoons, U.S. students perform considerably better than others. They also outperform students in other countries in such skills as separating fact from opinion in news stories and campaign leaflets. Hence, it is reasonable to conclude that in the domain of civics skills and knowledge, the U.S. education system performs at least as well as other democracies and, with respect to some skills, even better.

Despite the alarm voiced over the academic deterioration of the schools and the decline in young people's interest in politics, there has been little evidence that the pubic schools have been responsible for the disengagement of young people from politics. However, to assess this possibility, we examined the extended survey research conducted since the 1960s by the American National Election Studies (ANES), a federally funded program to analyze voting and public opinion in national elections. Two questions that have appeared in these surveys are (a) "Which party has control of the House of Representatives?" and (b) "Which party is more conservative?" These items were used by the researchers Michael Delli Carpini and Scott Keeter (1996) to assess changes over time in political knowledge for different age cohorts. In an analysis conducted for this chapter, we examined correct performance on these questions for two age groups: those between eighteen and twenty-five and those over twenty-five. In addition, this analysis separated those respondents who had completed only a high school education from those who had progressed to college and further education.

As seen in Figure 2a, with the exception of 1996, there was a stable discrepancy between the age groups among those with only a high school degree. As one would expect, holding education constant, older respondents were better able to answer these questions than younger respondents. However, those who completed only high school across the years from 1964 to 2004 displayed about the same level of proficiency. Furthermore, the discrepancy between age groups remained about the same. This suggests that across this period, high-school-educated youth were performing at about the same level in regard to these civics-knowledge indicators. Figure 2b shows the same time trends for persons with some post–high school education. As one would expect, additional education beyond high school increases performance and reduces the discrepancy between age groups. However, this comparison also suggests little change in these civics-education indicators over the forty-year time period. Aside from a spike in 1996, young people under age twenty-five performed at about the same level of proficiency across this time span.

Based on these fragmentary but reliable estimates of young people's civics knowledge over the period during which critics claim school performance has deteriorated there is little evidence that civics knowledge has been affected. Apparently, the decline in young people's interest in and engagement with politics has roots other than in the schools.

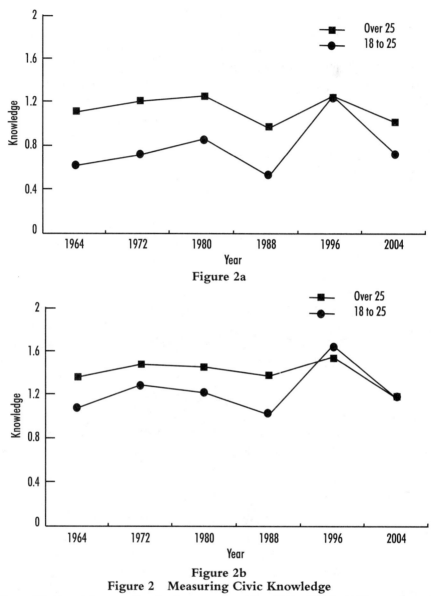

Figure 2a

Figure 2b
Figure 2 Measuring Civic Knowledge

Mean political knowledge scores (from 0 to 2 correct answers) from 1964 to 2004 for ANES respondents who (2a) only completed high school vs. those who (2b) obtained some education past high school. Results are shown for two age groups: those over age 25 vs. those 18 to 25.

The Public's Views of the Mission and Performance of the Public Schools

The renewed interest in the civic function of schools raises the question of how well the public sees the schools performing their long-standing dual missions of building academic skills and good citizenship. Has the increasing concern about academic-skill building for a competitive economy overshadowed the traditional role of the schools as civic socializer? This section examines how the general public and the professionals who run the schools (administrators and teachers) view the fundamental purpose of public education. The discussion focuses on the performance of the public schools in the eyes of the public and how the public comes to form its impressions of school success. The role of the press as the purveyor of news about school performance as well as the primary source of information for effective democratic participation is given particular attention.

To determine how the public, parents, public school teachers, and administrators see the purposes and performance of public schools, the Annenberg Public Policy Center fielded the Annenberg Public Schools survey in 2003. Specifically, the study included four nationally representative telephone surveys of 201 public school administrators; 608 K–12 public school teachers; 800 parents of school-age children; and 802 individuals from the population at large.

School Objectives

After stating that "there are many different perspectives regarding the things public schools should do," survey interviewers asked respondents how important they considered various roles for the schools. Table 1 shows the percentages of the public at large that regarded the function as absolutely essential or very important.

It is not surprising that the public views the three R's as the most important function of the schools. The teaching of reading, writing, and arithmetic was the earliest goal of public schooling and one of the areas in which schools have traditionally performed well. As one historical study asserted in the 1990s, "Schools are doubtless the most important mediating institutions in the development of literacy, that is, they translate economic, political, and religious mandates for literacy into actual training. . . . Literacy rates are generally correlated with school enrollment rates" (Kaestle et al. 1991, 6).

Second in public importance is a purpose rooted in the notion that America is a land of opportunity. The public schools, said respondents, should ensure that everyone has a chance to succeed in life (have a successful career). These two perceived top priorities for the schools, academic and job skills, reflect the extent to which the promises articulated by Horace Mann, considered the father of American public education, retain currency. Education is seen as increasing the productivity of workers and their earnings (see Tyack and Hansot 1982, 55).

There is also agreement in the general population that public education should prepare young people for the responsibilities of citizenship in the United States and that students should learn the unique characteristics of American democratic values. Teaching young people about right and wrong can also be seen as part of this comprehensive function of schooling.

TABLE 1

Views of the Public at Large Regarding the Functions of Public Education

Public School Function	% Considering function absolutely essential or very important
Teach reading, writing, and arithmetic	99
Prepare students for their future careers	87
Teach children the difference between right and wrong	86
Teach children about the values of America, such as freedom and democracy	86
Teach computer literacy	85
Teach the importance of active citizenship	80
Instill a strong sense of patriotism	70
Provide sex education	59

Historically, public schools have played an important role in assimilating immigrants into the national culture. "For many generations of immigrants," write Diane Ravitch and Joseph Viteritti, "the common school was the primary teacher of patriotism and civic values" (2001, 5). Since the children of immigrants (both foreign- and U.S.-born) make up an increasing percentage of the K–12 population, tripling from 6 percent in 1970 to 20 percent in 2000 (Fix and Passel 2003), we asked whether the presence of immigrants in general in schools affected public school quality. More held that immigrants hurt school quality (37 percent) than thought that their presence helped (27 percent). A large number didn't see any effect (31 percent).

The public does recognize the important role schools can play in forging a collective identity. More than eight out of ten (85 percent) agreed or strongly agreed that "in order to graduate from high school, students should be required to show that they understand the common history and ideas that tie all Americans together."

Civic Objectives

There is consensus as well about what the public schools should teach students about democracy. Over 50 percent of the public, parents, teachers, and administrators agree that it is absolutely essential or very important that fourth graders:

understand that the rules of the American government are established in a document called the Constitution;

can give an example of a right protected by the Constitution;

understand the meaning of American holidays such as the Fourth of July and Presidents' Day;

can identify important figures in American history such as George Washington.

More than six in ten concur that it is absolutely essential or very important that eighth graders be able to:

understand the idea of separation of powers in American government;

identify all fifty states on a map of the United States;

understand the effects of European settlement of the United States on Native Americans;

understand the role of slavery in the history of the United States.

Finally, at least six in ten regard as absolutely essential or very important to twelfth graders that they:

understand how immigration has shaped America at different points in history;

understand the civil rights movement of the 1950s and 1960s;

can compare and contrast the U.S. economic system with those of other countries;

know what differentiates a "liberal" from a "conservative" and understand current American political debates.

As important as the high percentages favoring these objectives is the fact that there are very few who do not regard them as important. For example, less than 3.5 percent of respondents (parents, the general population, teachers, and administrators) indicated that it is "not very important or not at all important" that twelfth graders "understand how immigration has shaped America at different points in history," "understand the civil rights movement of the 1950s and 1960s," are able to "compare and contrast the U.S. economic system with those of other countries," and know "what differentiates a 'liberal' from a 'conservative' and understand current American political debates."

Perceptions of School Performance

The public perceives that schools are doing reasonably well at meeting important goals. Table 2 compares the importance of various goals with how well the general population, parents, teachers, and administrators think the schools are meeting each.

TABLE 2
Extent to Which Goals Are Perceived as Being Met

Goal	Goal Importance	Perception of Performance	Difference
Read and write	9.7	6.1	3.6
Prepare citizens	8.6	5.5	3.1
Succeed in life	9.1	6.0	3.1
Skilled workforce	8.8	6.0	2.8
Cultural unity	8.3	5.6	2.7
American values	8.3	5.8	2.5

NOTE: Both scales ranged between zero and 10, with 10 meaning absolutely essential and zero meaning not at all important for importance, and 10 meaning very well met and zero meaning not met at all for performance.

The difference between what is and what ought to be is an indicator of areas in which the public sees a need for improvement in K–12 public education. The greatest discrepancy is in reading and writing, followed by preparing for citizenship, succeeding in life, creating a skilled workforce, gaining a cultural understanding of the United States, and learning American values. Despite the discrepancy between goals and performance, the numbers here are useful in showing public perceptions of the schools.

As the Phi Delta Kappa/Gallup Poll has found since 1983, "The public gives the schools high marks, and the grades improve the closer people are to the schools" (Rose and Gallup 2003, 44). So that the various respondent groups' opinions about local school performance could be assessed, they were all asked to consider the following:

> Students are often given the grades A, B, C, D, or FAIL to denote the quality of their work. Suppose the public elementary and secondary schools themselves, in your community, were graded in the same way. What grade would you give your community's public schools—A, B, C, D, or FAIL?

They were then asked to grade public schools in the nation as a whole. Consistent with the findings of Rose and Gallup, the Annenberg Public Schools survey found that the public, parents, teachers, and administrators graded the public schools in their own communities as better, with a grade of B- (Figure 3a), than those in the nation as a whole, where the average grade was about a C (Figure 3b). Not surprisingly, teachers and administrators graded their local schools somewhat

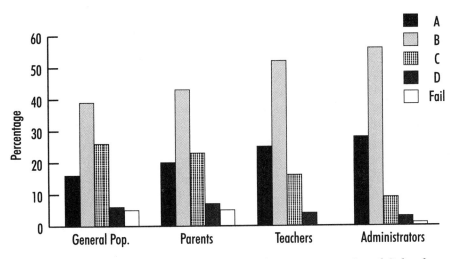

Figure 3a   Grades Assigned by Respondent Groups to Local Schools

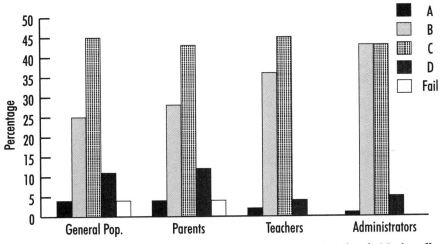

Figure 3b   Grades Assigned by Respondent Groups to Schools Nationally

better than did the general public and parents. Nevertheless, the most frequent grade was a B across all groups, and a majority of the general public and parents graded the local schools with at least a B. In contrast, the most frequent grade for schools nationally was a C across all groups. However, if all of those grading their local schools see the average as B– but cast the schools nationally as C, the perception of the nation's schools is clearly downgraded. This generally unfavorable view of the nation's schools stands in contrast to the finding that about half of parents surveyed think that children today get a better elementary and secondary education than they did when they were in school (51 percent reporting "better," 31 percent "worse," and 17 percent "the same").

News Coverage and Perceptions of School Performance

Unlike the Gallup survey, the Annenberg Public Schools survey asked how respondents arrived at their judgments of "public schools in the nation as a whole." Was the conclusion based on "what you've learned from your own experience, on what you've learned from friends and family, or on what you've seen and heard in the news?" Thirty eight percent of the public, 36 percent of parents, 28 percent of teachers, and 29 percent of administrators responded that their judgment was the by-product of exposure to news.

A focus in news on "the nation's failing schools" and "the crisis in our schools" may account in part for the difference between the grade given local schools and that given schools in the nation as a whole. News sources, such as newspapers, may be driving the perception that the nation's schools on average are worse than local ones. Consistent with this hypothesis, the general population, parents, teachers, and administrators who attribute their perception of the nation's public schools to input from personal experience see the national picture and the local one as more similar than those who report relying on newspaper accounts or the opinions of family and friends. A statistical analysis that took into account demographic differences revealed that people who based their judgment on news sources, such as newspapers, were more likely to believe that nationally, schools were worse than their own local schools. A similar but smaller effect was observed for those who relied on family and friends. Some of the discrepancy may have been rooted in reality. Suburbanites rated their schools higher than did rural or urban residents. However, reliance on news sources more strongly predicted the local versus national difference than did any other factor.

School Reform

Respondents were asked for suggestions to bridge the gaps between goals and realities in their assessments of the public schools. The surveyed groups did not differ significantly in assessment of purpose or performance or in the viable remedies for public school problems. Overall the changes in public schools most favored by the public, parents, teachers, and administrators were the same: ensuring safety and discipline and reducing class size. There was agreement across groups that raising teacher salaries, setting higher academic standards, and ensuring safety and discipline would help some or a lot.

Parents and the Public versus Teachers and Administrators

Parents and the public differed from teachers and administrators in some of the reforms they saw as improving education. The former group favored increased choice in schooling and higher accountability; the latter supported smaller classes and better preschool preparation for children. Specifically, the public and parents were significantly more likely than teachers or administrators to favor providing public tax dollars for parents to use to pay tuition for private or religious schools and to favor requiring students to pass standardized tests in order to graduate. By contrast, teachers and administrators were significantly more likely to favor reducing class size and increasing preschool programs in public schools.

Despite the rhetoric of crisis surrounding public education, the Annenberg survey suggests that the public and parents agree that public education, at least at the local level, performs many of these functions in a satisfactory way. Parents believe that their own local schools are better than schools nationally and that public education has improved since they attended school. The perception that schools nationally are in worse shape than those at home may be driven in part by news coverage that has focused on the shortcomings of the schools. Not only is there widespread consensus on the objectives of public schools, but public schools are perceived to be doing reasonably well at meeting important goals, and there is agreement on what schools should teach future citizens about the United States.

Improving Civics Skills and Understanding

The analysis conducted for this chapter suggests that, compared with other democracies, American public schools perform better than average in educating America's youth about their civic rights and responsibilities. In addition, civics education appears to have been helping young people make the transition to the adult role of active citizenship, and this function has been active to about the same degree since the 1960s, when young people were highly mobilized in opposition to the Vietnam War and engaged in the civil rights movement. However, as noted by the organizations that produced the 2003 report *The Civic Mission of Schools*, there is considerable room for improvement in educating young people to assume the role of responsible citizenship.

The Civic Mission of Schools argued the importance of six components of effective school experiences in the civic development of students:

1. instruction in government with more than just rote learning;
2. discussion of current events, particularly those important to youth;
3. opportunities to apply classroom lessons in a service learning framework;
4. extracurricular community-involvement opportunities;
5. student participation in school governance;
6. simulation of procedures in the democratic process, such as voting.

Tests of educational programs to increase political interest in youth have identified some useful approaches that substantiate these proposals. For example, Kids Voting USA, a public-private civics education program, has been implemented in a number of states, with activities ranging from elementary

17

school children accompanying their parents to the voting booth to high school students engaging in various community-service projects surrounding political issues of interest to their friends and families. These activities encourage hands-on approaches to political involvement that supplement the standard academic curriculum and help engage young people in the political process (McDevitt 2005).

Johanek and Puckett (2005) review several other school-based approaches that might increase civic engagement in young people. One of these, the Student Voices program sponsored by the Annenberg Public Policy Center, applies most of the components that are recommended in *The Civic Mission of Schools*. Tests of the program indicate that students who participate for two semesters (with ten sessions in each semester) display enduring effects over a period of two years post high school (compared with those who take regular civics classes), including greater sense of efficacy toward participation in politics, greater interest in and following of politics, and greater knowledge about the issues in subsequent elections (Pasek et al. 2006a). This program is particularly noteworthy in that it increases political engagement among urban and minority youth, who have traditionally been more disaffected from politics.

Studies of young people's understanding of current politics indicate that in addition to current schooling, use of news sources, such as newspapers, national television news, and the Internet, increases civic knowledge (Pasek et al. 2006b). The Student Voices program relies heavily on this premise by encouraging students to follow an election using a variety of news sources to help identify where the candidates stand on issues of concern to the students' community. Merrow (2005) also notes that the press has an important role to play in encouraging young people to become active citizens. Declining newspaper use among young people and the population in general poses a challenge to this agenda. However, young people's use of the Internet may be able to compensate for this decline and may provide an opportunity for the press to continue its role as purveyor of civic knowledge.

As noted by Richard Niemi and Jane Junn (1998), schools will not be able to carry the burden of educating young people for citizenship on their own: "Schools, even if greatly improved, still operate in the environment that surrounds them, and changes in schools must be matched by changes in the home and in society at large if we are to significantly upgrade students' knowledge levels. Schools alone cannot do it, but neither can we do without them" (146).

References

Amadeo, Jo-Ann, Judith Torney-Purta, and Carolyn H. Barber. 2004. *Attention to Media and Trust in Media Sources: Analysis of Data from the IEA Civic Education Study*. College Park, Md.: Center for Information & Research on Civic Learning & Engagement.

American National Election Studies. Ann Arbor, Mich. www.electionstudies.org.

Applebome, Peter. 2005. "Record Cost Cited to Fix or Rebuild Nation's Schools." *New York Times*, December 26, A1.

Aristotle. 1952. *The Works of Aristotle*. Vol. 2, *Politics*. Great Books of the Western World. Chicago: Encyclopedia Britannica.

Campanile, Carl. 2003. "Schools of Shame—City's Sorry Six Go from Bad to Worse." *New York Post*, August 11, 4.

Center for Civic Education. 1996. *The Role of Civic Education: A Report of the Task Force on Civic Education*. Second Annual White House Conference on Character Building for a Democratic, Civil Society. Washington, D.C., May 19–20, 1995. www.civiced. org/whpaper.html.

Center on Education Policy. 2005. *Do You Know the Latest Good News about American Education?* www.cep-dc.org/pubs/LatestGoodNews/LatestGoodNewsAug05.pdf.

Delli Carpini, Michael X., and Scott Keeter. 1996. *What Americans Know about Politics and Why It Matters*. New Haven, Conn.: Yale University Press.

Feller, Ben. 2003. "States See Wide Range in Teacher Quality." Associated Press, October 20.

Fix, Michael, and Jeremy S. Passel. 2003. *U.S. Immigration—Trends and Implications for Schools*. Washington, D.C.: Urban Institute.

Frankenberg, Erica, Chungmei Lee, and Gary Orfield. 2003. *A Multiracial Society with Segregated Schools: Are We Losing the Dream?* Cambridge, Mass.: Civil Rights Project, Harvard University.

Galston, William A. 2005. "The Politics of Polarization: Education Debates in the United States." In *The Public Schools,* ed. Susan Fuhrman and Marvin Lazerson, 57–80. Institutions of American Democracy. New York: Oxford University Press.

Gibson, Cynthia, and Peter Levine, eds. 2003. *The Civic Mission of Schools*. New York and College Park, Md.: Carnegie Corporation and Center for Information & Research on Civic Learning & Engagement.

Ginsburg, Alan, et al. 2005. *Reassessing U.S. International Mathematics Performance: New Findings from the 2003 TIMSS and PISA*. Washington, D.C.: American Institutes for Research.

Herbert, Bob. 2003. "Failing Teachers." *New York Times*, October 24, A23.

Johanek, Michael C., and John Puckett. 2005. "The State of Civic Education: Preparing Citizens in an Era of Accountability." In *The Public Schools,* ed. Susan Fuhrman and Marvin Lazerson, 130–59. Institutions of American Democracy. New York: Oxford University Press.

Kaestle, Carl F., et al. 1991. *Literacy in the United States: Readers and Reading since 1880*. New Haven, Conn.: Yale University Press.

Kids Voting USA. Tempe, Ariz. www.kidsvotingusa.org.

Langton, Kenneth P., and M. Kent Jennings. 1968. "Political Socialization and the High School Civics Curriculum in the United States." *American Political Science Review* 62, no. 3, 852–67.

McDevitt, Michael, et al. 2003. *The Civic Bonding of School and Family: How Kids Voting Students Enliven the Domestic Sphere*. CIRCLE Working Paper 07. University of Maryland: Center for Information & Research on Civic Learning & Engagement.

Merrow, John. 2005. "Youth, Media, and Citizenship." In *The Public Schools*, ed. Susan Fuhrman and Marvin Lazerson, 188–208. Institutions of American Democracy. New York: Oxford University Press.

National Commission on Excellence in Education. 1983. *A Nation at Risk: The Imperative for Educational Reform.* www.ed.gov/pubs/NatAtRisk/index.html.

Nash, Gary, Charlotte Crabtree, and Ross E. Dunn. 1997. *History On Trial: Culture Wars and the Teaching of the Past.* New York: Knopf.

Niemi, Richard G., and Jane Junn. 1998. *Civic Education: What Makes Students Learn.* New Haven, Conn.: Yale University Press.

Olander, Michael. 2003. *Media Use among Young People.* College Park, Md.: Center for Information & Research on Civic Learning & Engagement.

Pasek, Josh, et al. 2006a. *Schools as Incubators of Democratic Participation: Building Long-Term Political Efficacy through Civic Education.* Philadelphia: Annenberg Public Policy Center.

Pasek, Josh, et al. 2006b. "America's Youth and Community Engagement: How Use of Mass Media Is Related to Political Knowledge and Civic Activity among 14 to 22 Year Olds." *Communication Research* 33, no. 3, 115–35.

Ravitch, Diane, and Joseph P. Viteritti, eds. 2001. *Making Good Citizens: Education and Civil Society.* New Haven, Conn.: Yale University Press.

Reuben, Julie A. 2005. "Patriotic Purposes: Public Schools and the Education of Citizens." In *The Public Schools,* ed. Susan Fuhrman and Marvin Lazerson, 1–24. Institutions of American Democracy. New York: Oxford University Press.

Rose, Lowell C., and Alec M. Gallup. 2003. "The 35th Annual Phi Delta Kappa/Gallup Poll of the Public's Attitudes toward the Public Schools." *Phi Delta Kappan,* www.pdkintl.org/kappan/k0309pol.pdf.

Solomon, Lois K. 2000. "District Needs Hundreds of Teachers." *(South Florida) Sun-Sentinel,* November 12, B1.

Torney-Purta, Judith, Wendy K. Richardson, and Carolyn H. Barber. 2004. *Trust in Government-Related Institutions and Civic Engagement among Adolescents: Analysis of Five Countries from the IEA Civic Education Study.* College Park, Md.: Center for Information & Research on Civic Learning & Engagement.

Tyack, David, and Elisabeth Hansot. 1982. *Managers of Virtue: Public School Leadership in America, 1920–1980.* New York: Basic Books.

2

THE EFFECTIVENESS OF THE PRESS IN SERVING THE NEEDS OF AMERICAN DEMOCRACY

Kathleen Hall Jamieson, Bruce W. Hardy, and Daniel Romer

Thomas Jefferson was of two minds about the utility of reading newspapers. At one point he wrote, "Were it left to me to decide whether we should have a government without newspapers, or newspapers without a government, I should not hesitate a moment to prefer the latter. But I should mean that every man should receive those papers and be capable of reading them."[1] At another, he complained to a friend, "The man who never looks into a newspaper is better informed than he who reads them, inasmuch as he who knows nothing is nearer the truth than he whose mind is filled with falsehoods and errors."[2]

The newspapers to which Jefferson was referring in both instances were highly partisan, pervasively opinionated, and made little, if any, effort to accurately represent the views of the other sides on the controversies of the day. However, when each side had its own press, as was the case for the major political parties, there was in fact a clash of ideas between them even if most who could read consumed only the papers that reinforced their partisan presuppositions.

When the founders guaranteed freedom of the press, they did so in a world of partisan media filled with polemical pamphlets and political papers. As the journalism historians Michael Schudson and Susan Tifft note, during this time it was "more troublesome for printers to be neutral than to be partisan; nearly everyone felt compelled to take sides."[3] It was not until the mid-twentieth century that the norms of objectivity, balance, fairness, and related ethics "became consolidated."[4]

As implemented, these concepts meant that "journalists could claim to be 'neutral' simply by proclaiming to support neither of the political parties and to be 'impartial' by giving an equal amount of attention to both parties."[5]

Jefferson's conflicted views reveal the strengths and weaknesses of the partisan model. When advancing the case for the new nation, as the *Federalist Papers* did, for example, one can imagine the founder from Virginia and third president reflecting the first of the expressed sentiments. However, when he was the object of attack, as he was when Yale president Rev. Timothy Dwight took him on, one can imagine him thinking the second. Dwight's aspersions included the notion that if Jefferson were elected, "the Bible will be burned, the French 'Marseillaise' will be sung in Christian churches, [and] we may see our wives and daughters the victims of legal prostitution; soberly dishonored; [and] speciously polluted."[6]

Early in the nation's history, the party in power tested the relationship between government and freedom of speech and the press, with the outcome ultimately on the side of freedom. The Sedition Act of 1798 made it a federal crime to "write, print, utter or publish . . . any false, scandalous and malicious writing . . . against the government of the United States."[7] At the time, Jefferson, a Republican, serving as vice president under the Federalist John Adams, vigorously opposed passage, believing the act unconstitutional under the First Amendment. The Federalist secretary of state, Timothy Pickering, used the act to prosecute opposition Democratic-Republican newspapers in the election of 1800. Among the twenty-five journalists convicted under the act was Benjamin Franklin's grandson, Benjamin Franklin Bache, publisher of Philadelphia's *Aurora*.[8]

Jefferson was among those who had enshrined the First Amendment in the Bill of Rights. That decision put in place a constitutional protection for the press. In his inaugural address in 1805 Jefferson included these words:

> The artillery of the press has been leveled against us, charged with whatsoever its licentiousness could devise or dare. These abuses of an institution so important to freedom and science are deeply to be regretted, inasmuch as they tend to lessen its usefulness and to sap its safety. . . . Our fellow-citizens looked on, cool and collected; they saw the latent source from which these outrages proceeded. . . . The public judgment will correct false reasoning and opinions on a full hearing of all parties; and no other definite line can be drawn between the inestimable liberty of the press and its demoralizing licentiousness. If there be still improprieties which this rule would not restrain, its supplement must be sought in the censorship of public opinion.[9]

Whether or not one considers the press the fourth branch of government,[10] the outcome in this early test of press freedom bolstered the First Amendment guarantee and gave the press "a central role in a political and social process, that of communication."[11] Indeed, as the political communication scholar Timothy Cook suggests, "the American news media today are not merely part of politics; they are part of government."[12]

As Jefferson's inaugural indicates, the "marketplace of ideas" notion had taken root by 1800. The press scholars Robert Schmuhl and Robert Picard attest that "the media (broadly defined) are now considered the primary 'marketplace of ideas' in the United States, the forum in which truth, falsehood, and every expression in between compete for acceptance and approval."[13]

The notion that truth will emerge in the clash of competing claims antedated Jefferson. "Let Truth and Falsehood grapple," argued John Milton in *Areopagitica*, "who ever knew truth put to the worse in a free and open encounter."[14] In this country, founder Benjamin Franklin tied the clash of ideas specifically to the press in his 1731 "Apology for Printers," when he argued that "both Sides ought equally to have the Advantage of being heard by the Publick."[15] The concept was embodied in the metaphor of the marketplace in a dissenting opinion by Supreme Court justice Oliver Wendell Holmes Jr., who wrote that "the best test of truth is the power of the thought to get itself accepted in the competition of the market."[16]

Those who challenge the assumptions underlying this model argue that there is no such thing as "truth," that deception may well win out in a contest with its opposite, and that both the public's interest in civic knowledge and its capacity for making sense of political debate are severely constrained. Notably, the English philosopher John Stuart Mill doubted that the truth would necessarily triumph in its contest with falsity. In the twentieth century, Isaiah Berlin came down on Mills's side, asking, "Are demagogues and liars, scoundrels and blind fanatics, always, in liberal societies, stopped in time, or refuted in the end?"[17] Whatever the limitations of the metaphor and the model underlying it, "the concept of the marketplace of ideas as a means of protecting democracy and the public interest is now accepted as a major tenet of Western society."[18]

Even within the marketplace model, there are different views of the appropriate functions of the press. This chapter examines how well the press is performing four functions that can be considered central. First, how effective is it at informing? Specifically, since the press tells citizens much of what is known of Congress, the executive branch, the courts, and the public schools, what does it say about them and how adequate and accurate are the accounts? Second, the press both sets an agenda, telling the public what to think about, and frames the ways in which the public considers these matters. Are the interests of democracy advanced by the ways in which the press is performing these agenda-setting and framing functions? Third, the press acts as a watchdog, asking critical questions and scrutinizing government and other institutions. Performing this role requires that the press stand in for the public. Does it? And if so, how well? Finally, the press creates a forum in which issues are debated and political actors and groups communicate. According to the scholars Gabriel de Tarde, Jürgen Habermas, and Elihu Katz and Paul Lazarsfeld,[19] news media provide the tools for deliberative democracy and political action. But how well are these representing and deliberation-producing functions being executed?

Before undertaking this four-part analysis, however, this chapter makes the argument that what constitutes the press is a changing notion. Specifically, there are many ways other than the press or news media through which the public gets news. At the same time, the reemergence of the partisan press has caused public confusion and journalistic anxiety about what is and is not a news medium and who is and is not a journalist. The contention presented here is that both *detached* and *partisan* journalism serve important functions in a democracy and that each has strengths and limitations. The discussion also focuses on how negative perceptions of the press undercut its ability to serve the needs of democracy. Those who perceive the press to be deficient in performing its informing function are more likely to believe that in a time characterized by heightened threats to national security, as in the early twenty-first century's "war on terror," government should have a right to censor the press. In other words, one serious consequence of a perception of poor press performance may be increased risk that the press's First Amendment protection from government will be jeopardized, making it less able to represent the public, hold government accountable, set an issue agenda, and inform. The detached press's ability to correct this perception may be limited by the fact that journalists in this tradition do not acknowledge the existence of the problem.

The discussion begins by looking at how "news" is defined and delivered in the twenty-first century, and then offers a distinction between those media that adopt balance, fairness, and objectivity as norms, and the partisan media. The media landscape is changing, and with it so too are the ways in which the media inform, set agendas, hold government and powerful institutions accountable, and foster debate. Throughout this chapter, data are drawn from the Annenberg Institutions of Democracy Media survey, the methodology of which is described in the appendix.

The Changing Face of News

Discussions of how well the media, or the press, are doing are often confused by the absence of a clear notion of what is being talked about. There is no dispute, however, about the fact that the amount of available news and the ease with which it can be accessed have increased dramatically. Thanks to the Internet, the average user now has increased access to media and an unprecedented capacity to create news sites in the form of blogs (Web logs). Somewhere between 92 and 128 million people in the United States went online for news in 2004.[20] Meanwhile, Google News, which permits wide-ranging searches of news sources, averaged 6 million unique viewers a month in the first ten months of 2004. Among other things, this means that Google has become a packager of news, a news outlet.[21]

There also is useful information about government and public policy in venues as varied as prime-time television drama, as fans of *The West Wing* were particularly aware, and in contemporary satire, in particular *The Daily Show* with Jon Stewart. As the press scholar Robert Entman argues:

> Media not bound by the canons and practices of traditional journalism can serve the core democratizing functions of news, the functions that help citizens hold government to account. These news functions involve illuminating four areas of knowledge vital to effective demo-cratic citizenship:
>
> 1. Policy (specific public policy issues)
>
> 2. Power (the actions of individuals [especially public officials] and groups exerting political power)
>
> 3. Ideology (the philosophical perspectives that shape decisions on allo-cating wealth, status, and other valued resources)
>
> 4. Self-interest (individuals' own political interests and stakes in policy issues and elections, and their roles in society).[22]

Employing a similar line of reasoning, the press theorist Barbie Zelizer argues that "Dan Rather, Matt Drudge, and Jon Stewart—a professional broad-cast journalist, an Internet scoopster and columnist, and a popular television satirist—all convey authentic news of contemporary affairs to a general public, despite the questions raised about whether they are all journalists and all do jour-nalism."[23] A 2004 survey, for example, found that almost one in three respondents reported "sometimes or regularly getting election news from late night TV."[24]

While one might associate the venues of Stewart and Drudge with journal-ism, they are not traditionally considered "news media." Although many forms of media are constitutionally protected, it is what will be called here the "detached" media to which scholars are usually referring when they speak about "the press."

Detached versus Partisan Media

However, if one identifies the functions that Stewart and Drudge serve, one finds that Drudge does in fact inform (it was he, after all, who broke the Clinton-Lewinsky scandal), and Stewart not only informs but, better than many traditional news outlets, holds political leaders accountable for their statements and inconsis-tencies. In the world as it is segmented here, Rather falls into the definition of detached journalism rooted in the values of objectivity, fairness, and balance;

Drudge parses into the partisan model in which news stories are more likely to be framed, spun, and slanted so that certain political agendas are advanced; and Stewart is difficult to categorize. When Rather falters over the documents that he offered as proof that incumbent president George W. Bush slighted the requirements of service in the National Guard, the then CBS anchor and *60 Minutes Wednesday* host fails by the standards of detached journalism. The report was selective in its use of evidence and failed to satisfy the tests of evidence required to establish the credibility of the offered documents. As a result, Rather is hoist on the charge that he is a partisan masquerading as a champion of the detached, "objective," balanced, fair model.

A brief review of the specifics: On the September 8, 2004, segment of *60 Minutes Wednesday,* CBS anchor Dan Rather presented four documents (known as the Killian documents) purportedly taken from the personal files of the late Lieutenant Colonel Jerry B. Killian, commander of the 111th Fighter Interceptor Squadron. Then-lieutenant George W. Bush served under Killian from May 1968 to October 1973. With the military records of Bush and John Kerry, both presidential candidates in the 2004 election, under scrutiny at this time, these documents were presented as new information on the service record of President Bush that supported the allegation that Bush received preferential treatment while in the Texas Air National Guard. The segment created a controversy, originating in the blogosphere, that centered on the authenticity of these documents. Almost two weeks after the *60 Minutes Wednesday* segment aired, CBS News president Andrew Hayward issued a statement saying that CBS could not establish the documents' authenticity. Was airing of the documents an honest mistake or an outcome of liberal bias on the part of Dan Rather and CBS News?

When asked this question, the public and the press responding to the Annenberg Media survey differed. The journalists surveyed did not fault the ethical standards of CBS News. Seventy-six percent of journalists polled said that a major reason CBS ran the story was because it believed the report was accurate; 53 percent of the public felt CBS believed the report to be accurate. On the other hand, 40 percent of the public agreed that a major reason the story aired was that CBS News and Dan Rather are liberals who dislike President Bush. Twenty-nine percent of the public felt that liberal bias was a minor reason for the story being broadcast. Only 10 percent of journalists believed that liberal bias was a major reason, with 31 percent believing it to be a minor reason.

If the public perceives the detached press as biased, and concludes that it is practicing a form of political advocacy, then all four functions of the press are simultaneously undercut. It can't inform because it will not be believed, it cannot scrutinize because the motivation behind the scrutiny will be suspect, it cannot foster debate because it is no longer viewed as independent and objective, and it cannot represent because it is seen as the surrogate for those on one side of the argument. Note how different the scenario would have been had a blogger not tied to a major news organization done what Rather did or if the conservative radio-talk-show host Rush Limbaugh had made similar charges against a Democrat. The standards to which the partisan and detached media are held are different because one is presumed to aspire to balance, objectivity, and an airing of all sides while the other is assumed to selectively use evidence, offering evidence from the other side only when it can be refuted.

Although in general the public expressed confidence that journalists aspire to and do succeed at fair and objective reporting, 69 percent felt that liberal bias was either a major or minor reason in the decision by CBS News to run the story on President Bush's military service. A sizable majority of the public expressed the understanding that political biases play a part in the news they receive.

Even as it consumes partisan media, the public continues to demonstrate that it values the model based on the objectivity ideal. According to survey data, the public finds partisan journalism less informative than its nonpartisan cousin. Fifty-five percent of those surveyed said that they learn more from the coverage of journalists who do not openly express their political views, compared to 35 percent who reported that they learn more from the coverage of journalists who make their political views clear. Almost the same margin was produced when the public was asked which format they enjoyed more. Fifty-seven percent said they enjoy coverage from journalists who do not express their political views, as compared to 35 percent who said that they enjoy coverage from media figures expressing clear political views.

One might read these findings and say, Each to her own. The fact that citizens can choose from a range of approaches increases the likelihood that they will consume news at all.[25]

Unsurprisingly, detached journalists, who were the ones interviewed in the Annenberg Media survey, viewed their partisan competitors with a blend of anxiety and hostility.[26] Most (80 percent) said that news with a decidedly political point of view is bad for the American people. Liberal (84 percent) and moderate (84 percent) journalists were more likely to feel this way than conservative journalists (64 percent), a finding that is not surprising given that the advocacy media, as argued here, are largely conservative.

The public, on the other hand, reflected more mixed views. Slightly over half (53 percent) said that news coverage with a partisan point of view is bad. This view was dependent on age. In fact, a majority (54 percent) of young people, ages eighteen to twenty-nine, said that it is good if some news organizations have a decidedly partisan view.

Different Media, Different Roles

This discussion adapts a perspective on the detached versus partisan or adversarial news media suggested by the press scholar James Curran. The assumption is made that "the media are not a single entity" and, as a result, "there should be a division of labor in which different sectors of the media have different roles, practice different forms of journalism, and make different contributions to the functioning of the democratic system."[27] This view makes it possible to ascribe one set of functions to the core media of society, the detached or objective media, and another to the partisan or advocacy media. In this conception, the detached media are accountable to one set of expectations and standards and the advocacy media to another.

Thus the partisan or advocacy media (such as blogs and talk radio)[28] are seen as having one set of roles, and the detached media (for Curran, mass television channels and monopoly local dailies) as having another. Where the detached media aspire to objectivity, privilege accuracy, and ascribe to fair and balanced journalism, the partisan or advocacy media are case makers who work from unveiled ideological assumptions. The objectivity norm assumes that "journalists should be politically neutral and separate from attachments to political parties and organized social groups."[29] "Partisan media are essentially propagandistic, advancing at best partial truths. Balanced media report 'multiple truths' advanced by rival spokespersons."[30]

It is important to note that the public believes that it gets news from the partisan media. Sixty-five percent of those who reported listening to or watching shows such as *The Rush Limbaugh Show*, *The O'Reilly Factor*, and *Hardball* said that a major reason they do so is to help them keep up with the news. This finding holds across demographic groups. Men and women, older and younger, less well educated and better educated equally said they watch these programs to keep up with the news. When asked if "listening to people who mostly think like I do" is a major reason for tuning in, 28 percent of the public agreed. However, 44 percent said that a major reason they tune in is to listen to people who have different points of view. It would seem that people are getting what they see as news as part of a mix that includes heavy doses of explicit opinion.

Perceptions of Journalists

Where they exist, the differences between journalists' perceptions of who is and who is not a journalist and the public's can be explained in part at least by the assumption that journalists are more likely to see those who adopt the norms of objectivity and balance, in other words those in the detached camp, as journalists, where the public is more likely to grant that label as well to those who embrace one-sided positions and selectively marshal evidence to support that side. Ninety-seven percent of the journalists polled expressed the belief that it is important for the American public to distinguish those who are journalists from those who are not. However, 85 percent of journalists reported that it is not easy to make such a distinction. The basis for such a distinction, it seems clear, is in acceptance of objectivity, fairness, and balance as norms.

Journalists and the public hold similar views when it comes to well-known individuals on network television who espouse the detached model. Ninety-one percent of journalists and 79 percent of the public agreed in our survey that Peter Jennings is a journalist (the survey was conducted before Jennings's death in August 2005). Ninety-two percent of journalists and 64 percent of the public thought the same of *60 Minutes'* Mike Wallace. Eighty percent of journalists and 42 percent of the public agreed that NBC's Brian Williams is a journalist. Ten percent said they did not know whether Peter Jennings is a journalist or not; 20 percent expressed uncertainty about Mike Wallace; and 38 percent did not know if Brian Williams is a journalist. (See Table 1.)

Moving to news and entertainment shows, the hosts of which are more often seen as interviewers than reporters, the public is more likely than journalists to view these individuals as journalists. This may be because the public sees their interviews and interview styles as part of the detached model, where, by contrast, journalists set these shows off from straight news shows because the bulk of their content focuses on "soft" topics such as family relations, cooking tips, and health advice. Specifically, 48 percent of the public and 49 percent of journalists considered then-*Today* cohost Katie Couric a journalist, while only 26 percent of journalists and 37 percent of the public viewed CNN talk show host Larry King the same way. Twenty-three percent of the American public surveyed said they were unsure whether Katie Couric was a journalist or not. Fifteen percent expressed uncertainty about whether the designation applied to Larry King.

The public and journalists hold divergent views on who is a journalist and who is not when it comes to people who host political talk shows. Only 3 percent of the journalists surveyed considered Rush Limbaugh to be a journalist, compared to 55 percent of the public who said that he is not. Of those asked, 18 percent did not know if Rush Limbaugh is a journalist or not. Importantly, Limbaugh does not consider himself a journalist. Why does an increased percentage of the public, as compared to journalists, feel this way? Limbaugh deals almost exclusively with political topics and comments on news throughout his show. It is likely that the partisan nature of his comments pushes him outside the definition of journalist held by those journalists sampled, all of whom fall into the detached model themselves, but the substantive focus on news and public affairs places him within that definition for a third of the public.

Twelve percent of journalists and 40 percent of the public agreed that Bill O'Reilly is a journalist. Of those asked, 27 percent were undecided. *Hardball's* Chris Matthews was the exception to this pattern, with the public and journalists in closer agreement. Thirty-three percent of the public and 49 percent of journalists expressed the understanding that Matthews is a journalist. Of

TABLE 1

Perceptions of Media Figures as "Journalists"

Who is a journalist?			
Personage	**Yes**	**No**	**Don't know**
Peter Jennings	79%	11	10
Mike Wallace	64	16	20
Katie Couric (then of *Today* show)	48	29	23
Brian Williams	42	19	38
Bill O'Reilly	40	33	27
Larry King	37	48	15
Chris Matthews	33	27	40
Bob Woodward	30	17	53
Rush Limbaugh	27	55	18
George Will	19	19	62

Survey of the general public, conducted from March 3 to April 5, 2005.

How close does this person come to your idea of what a journalist is?					
Personage	**Very close**	**Somewhat Close**	**Not too close**	**Not close at all**	**Don't know/no answer**
Peter Jennings	44%	44	8	1	3
Mike Wallace	58	33	5	3	1
Katie Couric (then of *Today* show)	11	37	28	21	3
Brian Williams	30	42	10	8	10
Bill O'Reilly	1	10	19	65	5
Larry King	6	20	34	38	2
Chris Matthews	10	36	28	19	7
Bob Woodward	72	21	4	0	3
Rush Limbaugh	1	2	13	82	2
George Will	20	41	21	13	5

Survey of journalists, conducted from March 7 to May 2, 2005.

the public who were asked this question, 40 percent were undecided. Note that a higher percentage of surveyed respondents listened to these individuals for news than considered them journalists, a finding that admits to the possibility that at least part of the public reserves the label "journalist" for those whose prime responsibility is news and who adhere to the ideal of objectivity, while at the same time absorbing content that they define as news from partisan nonjournalists.

Blogging and Other Challenges to Traditional Media

As an aide to Speaker of the House Dennis Hastert observed, "Blogging is the new talk radio."[31] The fact that bloggers perform news functions is clear. Traditional news reporters in the room for a one-hundredth birthday party for Senator Strom Thurmond failed to recognize the news value of Senator Trent Lott's praise of the elderly senator's 1948 presidential run, a run predicated on the need to maintain racial segregation. Not so bloggers Joshua Micah Marshall and Glenn Reynolds, who watched the event on C-SPAN. They propelled the remark into a controversy that led to Lott's decision that he would not seek a return to his position as Republican majority leader in the Senate. The perceptive bloggers informed the mainstream media and the public of the remark, held Lott accountable for it, participated in the national debate about the meaning of the remark, and did so from a position untied to either political party.

As noted earlier, blogs made news by performing a fact-finding function when they cast doubts on the authenticity of documents used on the CBS program *60 Minutes Wednesday*. And it was the online magazine *Salon* that demonstrated that the *New York Times* was mistaken in its identification of the subject of an iconic photograph from the Abu Ghraib prison scandal, a hooded man standing with outstretched arms on a box. The exposé on that Web news site prompted a correction of the original story by the *New York Times* in March 2006.

Blogging appears to be here to stay. "By the end of 2004," reports Lee Rainie, head of the Pew Internet and American Life Project, "blogs had established themselves as a key part of online culture: 7% of U.S. internet users say they have created blogs and 27% say they are blog readers."[32] Among other things, this means that the adage that freedom of the press belongs to those who own one is now upended. And blogs are attracting audiences in their own right. The Annenberg Media survey found that 28 percent of the public and 52 percent of journalists turn to blogs for news. And 4 percent of surveyed journalists write their own blogs.

Scholars are beginning to conceptualize blogs as a new form of journalism.[33] As Melissa Wall suggests, blogs can best be thought of in a postmodern context because of the de-emphasis on objective reporting and data gathering and an emphasis on a more active role by the author.[34] When a member of the public becomes a blogger, the reader has become a writer. Most bloggers, however, do not see their Web writings as a new form of journalism. Sixty-five percent of bloggers polled by the Pew Internet and American Life Project in 2006 said that their postings were not a form of journalism, yet a majority (57 percent) linked to original sources or (56 percent) spent time verifying facts that they wanted to include in their posts.[35] Basically, what this suggests is that although bloggers do not consider themselves journalists, they practice a vetting process in order to ensure some objectivity and maintain credibility. And in this sense bloggers do resemble the image of a journalist. On the other hand, this same study by Pew found that bloggers are not posting in order to meet the four functions of the press outlined in this chapter. The most cited reason for a person to blog was self-expression.[36] Therefore, the objectivity of journalism loses out to personal preferences and self-selection. Hence, one should not be overly celebratory, rejoicing that bloggers are the new watchdogs for public interests.

That said, discussion of the *60 Minutes Wednesday* case and of other incidents of Web journalism tend to foreground the power of bloggers. And indeed, bloggers could be thought of as "para-journalists."[37] In today's news environment the notion of the traditional audience as the "receiver" is becoming increasingly outdated. There is a new "active" audience providing direct feedback, within a very short period of time, to the mass media. With channels for instant feedback, the audience can exert pressure on traditional media. In this sense, bloggers are both a new form of press and a monitor of the traditional media. In this role, bloggers are opinion leaders mediating opinion from the public to the major news organizations.

The New Partisan Press

Along with the appearance of bloggers, since the mid-1980s the number of outlets that convey information from a specific identifiable ideological point of view has multiplied. Speaking of the rise of right-of-center talk radio and Web sites as well as the Fox News Channel, the conservative organizer Paul Weyrich noted in fall 2003, "There are 1,500 conservative radio talk show hosts. . . . You have FOX News. You have the Internet, where all the successful sites are conservative. The ability to reach people with our point of view is like nothing we have ever seen before."[38]

The top-rated political talk radio host in the nation is Rush Limbaugh. Media reports place his listenership between 14.5 and 20 million listeners. In 2004, *Talkers Magazine* put Limbaugh's audience at 14.75 million and Sean Hannity's at 13 million, on six hundred stations.[39] To set Limbaugh's audience in perspective, the Annenberg Institutions of Democracy Government survey conducted in fall 2003 found that more than two in ten Americans (26 percent) listen every week to National Public Radio (NPR), which adopts the detached, balanced, objective model of journalism; one in ten say the same about Rush Limbaugh (10 percent), whose show embodies the partisan mode. The same survey found a third of Americans (32 percent) saying that they listen to talk radio weekly, with a majority of Americans (54 percent) reporting that they listen to talk radio at least once a month.

At the same time, Fox News Channel, which blends the detached model in its hard news and the partisan model in its political talk formats, has a higher average number of viewers than any of the other cable outlets. In December 2004, Nielsen Media Research figures showed that "FOX averaged 1.67 million viewers in primetime compared with CNN's 855,000, MSNBC's 374,000, Headline News' 212,000 and CNBC's 161,000."[40]

Conservatives acknowledge that the frame of the news on Fox is conservative. "Watch Fox for just a few hours," writes Brian Anderson, "and you encounter a conservative presence unlike anything on TV. Where CBS and CNN would lead a news item about an impending execution with a candlelight vigil of death-penalty protesters, for instance, at Fox 'it is de rigueur that we put in the lead why that person is being executed,' senior vice president for news John Moody noted. . . . Fox viewers will see Republican politicians and conservative pundits sought out for meaningful quotations, skepticism voiced about environmentalist doomsaying, religion treated with respect, pro-life views given airtime—and much else they'd never find on other networks."[41] "Conservatives will almost always defend Fox's claim to be 'fair and balanced,'" writes conservative direct mail consultant Richard Viguerie, "but they find it hard to do so without a smirk or smile on their face. . . . They proudly want to claim Fox as one of their own—it's one of the movement's great success stories."[42]

Comparison of Press Models

In the marketplace of ideas, the partisan and objective media play both different and similar roles. Each performs an accountability function. Until the rise of talk radio and the blogosphere, the main critiques of the mainstream detached media came from scholars and those individuals who disagreed with the way they were portrayed in mainstream news. Now the mainstream detached media critique the partisan media and vice versa with a healthy regularity.

The strength of the detached media resides in their ability to enable "divergent viewpoints and interests to be aired in reciprocal debate. Their central democratic purpose is . . . to mediate between social groups, rather than to champion exclusively one group and set of concerns."[43]

The downside of the detached media, or better put, their vulnerability, comes from the assumptions associated with "objective reporting." Objective reporting can, as work by Stephen Hess has consistently shown,[44] "lead journalists to rely on established power holders and legitimated holders of knowledge as sources of news and comment, and unconsciously internalize assumptions that are 'uncontroversial' within the prevailing framework of thought."[45] As suggested earlier, an objective stance helps the press inform the public. Still, journalistic objectivity may issue from a less noble motivation than promoting democracy. Gaye Tuchman argued that journalists preempt criticism of their work by "emphasizing 'objectivity,' arguing that dangers can be minimized if newsmen follow strategies of newswork which they identify with 'objective stories.' They assume that, if every reporter gathers and structures 'facts' in a detached, unbiased, impersonal manner, deadlines will be met and libel suits avoided."[46] In this sense, providing truths to the public becomes a secondary outcome, eclipsed by journalists' concern for not catching flack from senior editors, other news outlets, and public officials' attorneys.

At the same time, the norm of balance and the desire to be perceived as detached can mean that when dealing with controversial subjects "of a highly partisan nature" journalists become "reluctant to be perceived as taking sides," leaving such stories unresolved, "and the public is never quite sure whose 'spin'—if anyone's—is located in closer proximity to the truth."[47]

By contrast to the establishment-friendly detached media with their reliance on official sources, partisan or adversarial media "are often more ready to voice maverick or dissenting opinions than mainstream media because they cater to minorities and are unconstrained by the 'fair and balanced' norms of objective journalism."[48] In the process, "they can also provide liberating access to alternative ideas and arguments."[49] In other words, the strength of the partisan media counterbalances the weakness of the detached media.

A common concern is that the reemergence of partisan news media will increase the likelihood that partisans hear only one side of the debate. If this occurred, it could minimize deliberation and increase polarization. Arguments that partisan journalism may be polarizing the electorate because individuals are self-selecting news that is consistent with their own points of view are not borne out by the evidence, however. Results of the Annenberg Media survey show that more individuals turn to partisan news outlets to hear different points of view than to hear similar views. But why? Is it because these individuals want to be informed on all sides of an issue? Or are liberals listening to Rush Limbaugh so that they can heartily disagree with all he is saying? Either way, decades of research have suggested that exposure to diverse viewpoints leads to better-informed opinions and higher levels of political knowledge.[50]

At the same time, evidence from the National Annenberg Election survey from 2004 reveals that both Limbaugh listeners and Fox viewers were more, not less, likely than those of comparable educational level and ideological bent to view presidential general-election debates. Decades of scholarship tie debate viewership to increased issue knowledge.[51] And on a detailed survey of uncontested facts from that election, Limbaugh's listeners scored above those of comparable educational background and ideological persuasion who were nonlisteners.

Harkening to the era of the partisan press, the partisan media also inform and contribute to public debate by taking the world of raw fact and cascading opinion and fashioning from it coherent ideological interpretations. Rush Limbaugh performs the role of leader for conservatives in a fashion reminiscent of the early-nineteenth-century alliance between party and partisan press.[52]

Although it is difficult to disentangle the effects of the patronage apparatus tied to partisan newspapers, some scholars believe that the partisan press "may well have been critical to party efforts to raise voter turnout."[53] In the twentieth century, that alliance between the print press and the parties was severed with the rise of nonpartisan or "objective" journalism. Now, it can be argued, partisan and objective journalism coexist, performing different functions for democracy.

As de facto conservative party leader, Limbaugh translates the elements of Reagan conservatism for listeners. In his role as party leader, Limbaugh reinforces a set of coherent rhetorical frames that empower his listeners to act as conservative opinion leaders, and enable him to mobilize party members for action, hold the Republican Party and its leaders accountable, and occasionally help screen candidates for the party's nomination. He also translates the content of the news media from a conservative perspective.

The downside of partisan media occurs when these outlets circulate "scurrilous information about public figures that has no foundation in truth."[54] Also, as the media scholar James Hamilton notes, "The low cost of entry to placing information in the Internet has had many effects on news. The ability of news outlets, and columnists such as Matt Drudge, to post instantly during any time of the day has extended news cycles and created additional pressure on traditional news outlets to run with breaking news. The lack of large investment in sites means that news provided may not be heavily edited or screened, which can give rise to a spread of rumor and gossip."[55]

Four Functions of the Press[56]

Function One: Informing

There is no serious dispute that in the buzzing, blooming, information-saturated world of the twenty-first century, informing the public is a central press function. "Media are normatively expected to provide diverse and pluralistic content that includes a wide variety of information, opinions, and perspectives on developments that affect the lives of citizens," writes the media economics scholar Robert Picard.[57] The Supreme Court justice William O. Douglas put it well when he said, "The press has a preferred position in our constitutional scheme, not to enable it to make money, not to set newsmen apart as a favored class, but to bring fulfillment of the public's right to know."[58] Journalists agree. "The purpose of journalism is to provide people with the information they need to be free and self-governing" write the veteran journalists Bill Kovatch and Tom Rosenstiel.[59] "Only great newspapers," observe the *Washington Post's* Leonard Downie Jr. and Robert G. Kaiser, "systematically provide the factual information, interpretation and commentary that make the American system work."[60] "The country's democracy may belong directly or indirectly to its citizens, but the democratic process can only be truly meaningful if these citizens are informed."[61]

One scholarly finding speaks well of the informing power of newspapers and the value of education. Among the consistent predictors of knowledge of public affairs and civics knowledge are education and newspaper reading.[62] This finding was replicated in the Annenberg Media survey as well.

It would appear that a solid majority of the public continues to trust the press. Also reassuring is the fact that research has shown that news media use is promoting civic activity among young people. A 2006 study conducted by the Annenberg Public Policy Center clearly confirmed that news media use was positively related to political awareness and civic activity in a national sample of American youths, ages fourteen to twenty-two.[63] Specifically, this study found that young people's use of the Internet to gather news, book reading, and watching national television news are related to political engagement and are a source of social capital.

How well do detached journalists believe that they are upholding the ideals to which they aspire in informing the public, including balance, objectivity, and accuracy? Journalists recognize that the norm of balance can readily be perverted into a form of reporting in which political arguments or standpoints are covered only in terms of counterarguments and opposing standpoints. This problem manifests itself most clearly when one side in a political campaign engages in a higher level of deception than the other. What do reporters do in such circumstances? The Annenberg Media survey asked, "In a political campaign, if one side is using deceptive tactics more often than the opponents, do most journalists usually report the greater use of deception by one side, just report that both sides are using deception, or avoid the matter completely?" A majority of the journalists (58 percent) surveyed believe that most journalists report that both sides are using deception. Of those journalists, 79 percent believe that by failing to point out that one side is more deceptive, journalists are suggesting that both sides are engaged in a similar amount of deception. This admission is a tacit acknowledgment that journalists are failing at their role as campaign watchdog and that in this circumstance, striving for balance in informing the public can compromise this other important democratic function.

Are news media accurately reporting facts? Journalists think so. In fact, 86 percent of the journalists polled expressed the belief that news organizations get the facts straight. Only 11 percent of journalists believed that their stories and reports are often inaccurate. The public, however, does not hold the press in such high regard. Specifically, only 45 percent of the public, according to the Annenberg survey, think that news organizations get the facts straight, with 48 percent saying that stories and reports are often inaccurate.

The informing function presupposes not only that the press gets it right but that when it gets it wrong, it corrects its mistakes. Here there is a serious disjuncture between the perception of reporters and that of the public. Forty-one percent of the public, versus only 3 percent of journalists, expressed the belief that when a "serious" mistake is made, most news organizations try to cover it up. Seventy-four percent of journalists surveyed said that most news organizations try to promptly report that a mistake was made, but only 30 percent of the public feel this way.

Results from another part of the survey, however, show that the public still has some regard for the press's capacity to correct its errors. The public expressed the belief that the news media handled two recent controversies well. For example, a majority of the public (58 percent) felt that CBS News and Dan Rather did a good job of addressing mistakes made in the airing of the *60 Minutes Wednesday* broadcast on President Bush's National Guard record. A lesser percent of journalists (52 percent) felt this way. And when the *New York Times* reporter Jayson Blair was found to be plagiarizing and fabricating news stories, 61 percent of the public who had read or heard about Blair's activities believed that the *Times* did a good job of addressing the situation. Eighty percent of the journalists polled felt the same way.

What about objectivity? Almost all of the journalists in the Annenberg survey sample expressed the belief that their fellow reporters strive for objectivity. Specifically, 94 percent of the journalists surveyed think their colleagues try to report the news objectively, without regard to their own political views. Although less than half of the American public thinks that news organizations get their facts straight, the public is generally confident in journalists, but to a lesser degree than are the journalists themselves. Almost two-thirds of the public surveyed believed that journalists try to report objectively and fairly. Similarly, 91 percent of journalists and 63 percent of the public believed that journalists succeed in being objective.

Pointing to waning levels of political knowledge held by Americans,[64] many scholars have concluded that the news media are failing. These scholars call for the media to supply higher-quality news coverage and devote more time to the issues. However, as Thomas Patterson and Philip Seib rightly point out, "Although it is impossible to watch television news or read the typical newspaper without concluding that the quality of information could be higher, it is less certain that raising the level would produce a markedly better informed public."[65] These authors believe that the problem resides in an oversaturated news-media environment. There is too much information for the average citizen to comprehend and retain. The political scientist John Zaller calls this the "Full News" standard for the quality of news. This standard, driven by the notion of objectivity, posits that the news should provide "basic information necessary to form and update opinions on all of the major issues of the day."[66] In other words, it should provide all the news of the day in an unbiased fashion. Zaller argues that such a standard is actually too demanding on the average citizen in that it requires continual monitoring of current events. Along these same lines, the news scholar W. Lance Bennett has suggested that the news is too fragmented and superficial to be useful to the average citizen.[67] There are too many facts reported, without any coherent in-depth linkage.

Scholars offer a final indictment of the way in which the press covers politics. When reporters focus on political strategizing, as three decades of studies suggest is the case,[68] they pervert their informational role, exposing political manipulation rather than focusing on viewpoints and platforms. In revealing the strategies behind political rhetoric, they may be trying to increase the transparency of the campaign process, but without an accompanying analysis of the issues, this form of reporting makes it difficult for voters to know whom to believe. By emphasizing strategy over substance in political campaigns, the press sunders the link between campaigning and governance, activates cynicism, and depresses voter learning.[69] Reporting only the facts and not the values that underscore political debate can be problematic and leads to the depiction of political conflict as political gaming.[70] In other words, debate on substantive issues gets framed in the news media as a conflict between political parties, and the embedded values and beliefs that are at the heart of the debate are not discussed. Reporting of simple facts that focus on political behavior of political leaders during a political conflict distances some citizens from politics.[71]

News reporting focusing on the political issues instead of the political conflicts surrounding the debate does have measurable consequences. In a study of the media effects of reporting on the health-care-reform debate of 1993–94, Cappella and Jamieson found that "strategic" coverage activated cynicism and depressed learning about the substance of the debate.[72] At the same time, by focusing on the conflict between two plans rather than the areas of agreement shared by all seven actually at play, the press reports made it more difficult for the public to perceive commonality among the alternatives.[73] Each plan, for example, ensured that health insurance coverage would not be lost when a person switched employers, a notion with broad public support. Had that element of the plans been featured and public opinion on it tested, reform legislation might have been passed in 1994 rather than being delayed until the following Congress.

Strategic coverage activates cynicism about elective politics as well. In a study that exposed audiences to strategic and issues-based coverage of a

Philadelphia mayoral election, Cappella and Jamieson found that those exposed to strategic coverage of the election concluded that the candidates were unlikely to keep their promises and were simply telling the public what it wanted to hear.[74] Those exposed to issues-based coverage were less likely to report these inferences.

Were the conclusions drawn by those exposed to strategic coverage realistic or cynical? Democrat Ed Rendell was elected mayor in that election. Not only did he keep the central promises he made in the campaign, but later surveys attested to the fact that the public believed that he had. When he ran for reelection, Rendell won in a landslide. And when he ran for governor of Pennsylvania he carried his home city overwhelmingly. Those in the study who had drawn the conclusion that he was simply pandering were proven wrong by his behavior in office. Their response was cynical, not realistic.

Function Two: Setting the Agenda

The journalist, as Cater observed, "can choose from among the myriad events that seethe beneath the surface of government which to describe, which to ignore. He can illuminate policy . . . he can prematurely expose policy and, as with an undeveloped film, cause its destruction. At his worst, operating with arbitrary and faulty standards, he can be an agent of disorder and confusion. At his best, he can exert a creative influence on Washington politics."[75] Here we ask, How effective is the press in bringing important debates to the fore?

It is clear that the media can focus people on some topics rather than others and on some candidate attributes rather than others.[76] "By giving prominence to certain issues, concerns, and proposals, core media in effect privilege them and provide the opportunity for them to win wider support."[77]

For unobtrusive issues such as distant wars and abstractions such as the trade balance and the budget deficit, "the press is the citizenry's principal source of information and enjoys considerable influence."[78] The agenda-setting power of the press can prompt government response. As Martha Kumar and Alex Jones note, "With television pictures aired worldwide in the summer and fall of 1992 showing people suffering from extreme malnourishment in Somalia, President George H. W. Bush responded to calls for help from the United States by sending troops there. Prior to that point, complained at least one official in the State Department, those calling for action had little effect on administration officials."[79]

The consequence of the press's failure to accurately assess the importance of a story can be damaging to the country. In January 2001 a bipartisan U.S. National Commission on National Security chaired by former senators Gary Hart and Warren Rudman warned that "the combination of unconventional weapons proliferation with the persistence of international terrorism will end the relative invulnerability of the U.S. homeland to catastrophic attack. A direct attack against American citizens on American soil is likely over the next quarter century."[80] The report was featured in the *Los Angeles Times*,[81] buried on the inside of a few other papers, and largely ignored by the mass media. Neither Rudman nor Hart was invited to appear on any of the major networks. Nor did an appearance by CIA director George Tenet before the Senate Intelligence Committee who warned that "Osama bin Laden and his global network of lieutenants and associates remain the most immediate and serious threat" to American national security become front-page news.[82] Did it matter? Imagine that the press had made a big deal out of the report and Tenet's testimony. Imagine that President Bush were asked repeatedly how the United States was preparing. Would the country have been better prepared for September 11?[83]

Hindsight is always twenty-twenty, and there is broad agreement among journalists (81 percent) that the news media did a poor job of reporting on the problem of terrorism prior to the attacks on September 11, 2001, including nearly four in ten (37 percent) who believed that the media did a very poor job.

What about coverage of issues in general? According to congressional staff members surveyed, the press is not doing a very good job. As survey findings presented in Chapter 5 indicate, 56 percent of congressional staff members believe that lack of media coverage on public affairs is making it harder for members of Congress to get media attention for their politically important activities.

A major critique of media in general and news media in particular is that they focus on matters that have little to do with the information voters need. "The majority of content in newspapers today is not anything that can be considered 'news,'" writes Picard.[84] "About two-thirds of most newspapers is advertising, and of the remaining editorial matter only about 15 percent is news; the remaining is lifestyle material devoted to topics such as fashion, automobiles, entertainment, homes, sports, and so on." So, as James Hamilton argues, "[in the United States] since the 1970s news coverage has shifted to an increasing emphasis on what people want to know and away from information that they may need as voters."[85] This shift may be producing a paradox, if, as Thomas Patterson argues, the focus on "infotainment" and negative cynical news invites the potential audience to turn away from news entirely.[86]

Function Three: Scrutinize

The third function of the press is that of watchdog over the exertion of power. Watchdog journalism is defined by W. Lance Bennett and William Serrin as: "(1) independent scrutiny by the press of activities of government, business, and other public institutions, with an aim toward (2) documenting, questioning, and investigating those activities, in order to (3) provide publics and officials with timely information on issues of public concern."[87] This assumes that the press stands in for the public, not for corporations who own it, and it presupposes as well that the press is skeptical of claims of government—something demonstrably not true when the press as patriot emerges.

Journalists are aware of their own shortcomings as a watchdog. For example, when asked, "How good a job has the news media done of reporting on the Bush administration's justification for war in Iraq?" a majority of journalists (59 percent) said that the news media had done a poor job. In fact, a little over a fourth of the journalists surveyed (26 percent) said that the press had done a very poor job. These beliefs are dependent on political ideology. Conservative journalists (57 percent) were much more likely than liberal reporters (29 percent) to say that the media did a good job of reporting the Bush administration's justification for going to war in Iraq. Journalists who worked for local news outlets were more positive than national journalists—those who did most of the reporting of the administration's justifications for war. Only a third (33 percent) of the national journalists said they did a good job, compared to 46 percent of the local journalists who said the media did a good job.

Like the informing function, the watchdog function is driven by a notion of objectivity. Much of the information provided to the public is a product of watchdog journalism. Everyday reporting of government happenings and documentation of other political events is watchdog journalism. However, the notion of the press as a watchdog connotes the scrutiny of public institutions and the uncovering of scandal or exposing of hidden activities of government officials and institutions.

Press performance of the watchdog role has come under criticism because of the press's seeming incapacity to pursue critical questions or follow up on controversial stories in a timely fashion. Others have criticized the press for stylizing investigative reporting in the form of television news magazines and adopting an overall cynical tone in reporting.[88] Many of these stories dressed as investigative reporting have little consequence.

Some question the watchdog metaphor and argue that it undermines the public's confidence in the press. A study by Paula Poindexter, Don Heider, and Maxwell McCombs found evidence that the public expects the local newspaper to be a good neighbor instead of a watchdog and would like to see more news coverage on education, health and medicine, and arts and culture.[89] Those who more strongly expect the local newspaper to be a good neighbor feel that television news—not the newspaper—is better suited to handle the role of the watchdog. Poindexter and her colleagues note, "This good neighbor–watchdog dichotomy may be one of the keys to understanding the reason behind the public's increasing disaffection with the press."[90]

Function Four: Represent

The presumption of a free press is that it stands in for the public. The marketplace-of-ideas notion presupposes that the agora is open to all points of view, and that in the clash of competing ideas the public has the wherewithal to make good judgments. All of that is called into question "if commercial media enterprises constrain the marketplace by their size and activities, by limiting who may introduce ideas and information, and by the range and scope of ideas, information, and discussion available."[91] "In the twentieth century, the United States was the only country to develop a primarily commercial broadcasting system."[92] That fact adds to the democratic press equation two elements missing in many other countries: the profit motive and corporate interest.

The press cannot represent the public if it protects the interests of the corporations that own it anymore than the detached press can protect the public if it is a partisan mouthpiece. The basis for concern here is simple. In 2006, five conglomerates owned most U.S. mass media. The interests of those corporations and their owners played an increasing role in American political culture. The big five—Time Warner, Disney, Rupert Murdoch's News Corporation, Viacom, and General Electric—own much of the media in the United States and, as a result, for practical purposes control much of what the American public learns or doesn't learn through media about politics and government.

Because corporations owe their allegiance to their shareholders, their purpose is not serving the public good unless doing so is compatible with the creation of profit margins attractive to shareholders. "Today the business of news is business not news. . . . News has become secondary, even incidental, to markets and revenues and margins and advertisers and consumer preferences," concluded a 2001 study of publicly owned newspapers.[93]

Consolidation has produced a reduction in the number of people editing and reporting news. The Project for Excellence in Journalism's report on the state of journalism in 2004 found, for example, twenty-two hundred fewer full-time editorial employees at newspapers since 1990 and a third fewer correspondents at the networks than in the 1980s.[94] Among other things, that meant an increase in the workload of the remaining employees and a cut in the number of foreign bureaus.

After all is said and done, the desire to achieve profit is a driving force behind news media organizations. Is the profit motive incompatible with the democratic functions examined here? Logically, these two components of news media organizations must conflict from time to time. Most obviously would be a journalist's commitment to objectivity and the revenue generated from advertising. A simple example clearly illustrates this tension: A newspaper journalist finds out that some unfavorable political and business dealings are being practiced by the newspaper's advertising client. The tension between the watchdog role and the need for revenue would surely have some influence on what is reported and how the information is framed.

Journalists are aware of this tension. When asked on the Annenberg Media survey what role the pressure to make a profit should play in journalistic decisions in a news organization, a slight majority (53 percent) said that profit pressures should not influence news decisions at all. Although a majority of journalists were shown to feel this way, it is by no means a consensus. The need to generate revenue is salient. A sizable number of journalists (31 percent) said that profits should have a small influence, and 16 percent of journalists thought that profits should have a moderate or great influence on journalistic decisions. Political ideology does play a role in journalists' views on the optimum influence of profits. Journalists who are self-described conservatives were more likely to accept the profit motive (28 percent) than liberals (12 percent) or moderates (16 percent).

Even though a slight majority of journalists believe that profit pressures should not have an impact, the influence of such pressures is felt by journalists. More than two-thirds (68 percent) said that profit pressures greatly or moderately influenced journalistic decisions. Roughly one-fourth (26 percent) said that the pressure affects news decisions to a small extent, and only a handful of journalists (4 percent) said that the pressure does not influence decisions at all. Interestingly, executives were more likely than staff journalists, editors, and producers to perceive the effect as small or absent. This worrisome finding suggests that the information the public receives is not solely dependent on attempts at objectivity—providing truthful accounts of the day's events—but is to some extent dependent on the commercial business needs of media outlets.

When the Annenberg Media survey asked the journalists about specific effects of profit pressures, over two-thirds agreed that these pressures have reduced the number of stories that take time and money to report. The kind of journalism most likely to be sacrificed in cutbacks of staff and bureaus is watchdog journalism. Investigative work is time- and resource-intensive.

Along these same lines, 56 percent of the journalists surveyed said that profit pressures had increased the number of "quick-and-dirty stories." This may also be due to the fact that profit pressures have led to cutbacks in the number of reporters and editors, without corresponding cutbacks in workload (84 percent of the journalists polled agreed that such was the case). These data suggest that the protector of the public good, the press, is increasingly comprised of overworked, undersupported reporters who may not be able to pursue the stories that increase governmental accountability.

The American public also expresses concern about the influence of profit pressures on the news it receives. A little under three-fourths of the public (72 percent) believe that the quality of news is hurt by news organizations' efforts to make a profit. Seventy-nine percent of those surveyed felt that news media companies that receive substantial advertising revenue from a company would hesitate to report negative stories about that company. However, when focused on the motivations of the journalist as an individual, the public is split, with 49 percent believing that journalists are motivated mainly by the desire for financial and professional success and 42 percent holding that the journalists' main motivation is to inform the public.

Another characteristic of the commercial structure of the press is the increasing corporate mergers and acquisitions of newspapers and television stations. Beginning in the mid-1990s, many locally owned newspapers and television stations were bought by larger corporations or diversified companies. The impact of such buyouts is a cause of concern for many journalists. Specifically, two-thirds of the journalists surveyed believed that the quality of the news suffered because most news organizations were owned by large corporations. Similarly, 68 percent of the journalists surveyed felt that buyouts of locally owned newspapers by larger chains had a negative impact on the quality of news. Journalists (72 percent) believed that concentrated ownership reduces the number of different voices and views the American people hear each day. Executives (46 percent) were less likely to feel this way than staff journalists (79 percent) and editors and producers (69 percent).

Even though journalists believe that corporate ownership has a negative effect on the quality of news, a little under half (49 percent) of the journalists surveyed thought that corporate owners strive to provide factual and timely news, but business realities sometimes get in the way. Thirty-six percent of journalists expressed the belief that corporate owners are more concerned with profit than with providing news, and 12 percent felt that making a profit is the top priority of corporate owners.

What all of this suggests is that journalists, as well as the public, are very aware of the negative influence of profit pressure and corporate media ownership. The ability of the press to meet its democratic responsibilities is clearly limited by the commercial structure of news media systems. Newsmakers are conscious of these limitations and the American public fears that the quality of the information it receives from the press is compromised by profit pressures. Moreover, journalists believe that corporate ownership is limiting the diversity of opinions and the number of voices that are represented in the news.

In sum, due to the commercial structure of the news media, the press cannot completely fulfill its function to provide a marketplace of ideas where all sides of an issue are presented and debated. Consequently, the American public is left with less than ideal tools for democratic participation.

Public Perceptions and Press Censorship

If informing, setting the national agenda, scrutinizing those in power, and standing in for the public to facilitate debate are important ways in which the marketplace of ideas is sustained in a democracy, then we should worry when these functions are not performed as well as they might be. But additional cause for concern can be seen in the possibility that those who believe the press is defaulting on its informing role are more likely to favor censoring the press in a time of heightened national security.

Making this argument requires that we step back for a moment and set the historical context by arguing that in times of war, whether hot or cold, the public becomes more receptive to government censorship of the press, and the government becomes more disposed to muzzle the "fourth estate."

So, for example, in the Sixty-Fourth Congress in 1917 the House passed a piece of legislation that would become the Espionage Act, which included a provision advocated by President Woodrow Wilson that punished anyone who "shall collect, record, publish, or communicate . . . information relating to the public defense calculated to be, or which might be, useful to the enemy." After an outcry by the press, the provision was stripped from the Senate version of the bill by a single vote. As the bill moved into the conference process, President Wilson sent a letter to Congress asserting that "authority to exercise censorship over the press to the extent that that censorship is embodied in the recent action of the House of Representatives is absolutely necessary to the public safety." The Senate version prevailed and the censorship provision failed to become law. Wilson persisted. The next year he pressed for passage of amendments to prohibit "profane, scurrilous, or abusive language about the form of government." This provision became law in the form of the Sedition Act in May 1918. Under the Espionage and Sedition Acts, U.S. newspapers deemed favorable to Germany were punished; socialist papers were banned from the mails. The acts went off the books in 1921 when Congress, now unaffected by war fervor, failed to renew them.[95]

Consistent with the notion that the press comes under attack in times of threat or war, in January 2006 President George W. Bush claimed that America's enemies in the war on terror had been aided by a *New York Times* investigative report showing that the administration had authorized wiretaps of U.S. citizens without court order. This attack on the press occurred in a context in which the public was more disposed than it would otherwise have been to tolerate press censorship.[96]

An April 30, 2006, *New York Times* article observed that the press was operating in "a judicial climate that seems increasingly receptive to constraints on journalists."[97] At a time when *New York Times* reporter Judith Miller was jailed for refusing to reveal a source, public support for government censorship of the press could be seen as having serious consequences concerning the balance of power between journalists and the state. And perceptions of press failures did not help matters. Perceptions of press performance coupled with the war on terror produced a troubling finding in spring 2005, when the Annenberg Media survey was fielded. Those who believed that the press covers up serious errors rather than correcting them were more likely to believe that the government has the right to censor the press in the war on terror. Conservatives and those with lower levels of education were also more likely to hold this view. In other words, one consequence of public perception that the press fails to perform its informing function may well be a willingness to restrict its First Amendment rights in times of war or threat. This willingness is amplified during certain times of crisis that may cause an increased surge of patriotism, or a "rally 'round the flag effect"[98] when citizens are more likely to blindly support policies that may impinge on the basic rights afforded by the Constitution.

As for the public's willingness to censor the press, trust in government is directly related to support for government censorship. This finding is not limited to the public. Trust in government was positively related to support for government restriction on the press in the Annenberg Media survey sample of journalists as well.

On the other hand, individuals who trust the news media are less likely to support government restrictions on the press. Over two-thirds of the public (78 percent) said that they trust the news media a great deal or a fair amount to operate in the best interests of the American people.

Notes

1. Thomas Jefferson, *The Life and Selected Writings of Thomas Jefferson*, ed. Adrienne Koch and William Peden (New York: Random House, 1944), 411–12.
2. Ibid., 581–82.
3. Michael Schudson and Susan E. Tifft, "American Journalism in Historical Perspective," in *The Press*, ed. Geneva Overholser and Kathleen Hall Jamieson, Institutions of American Democracy (New York: Oxford University Press, 2005), 19.
4. Daniel C. Hallin and Robert Giles, "Presses and Democracies," in *The Press*, ed. Overholser and Jamieson, 8.
5. Jean Chalaby, quoted in Hallin and Giles, "Presses and Democracies," 11.
6. Quoted in David Cushman Coyle, *Ordeal of the Presidency* (Washington, D.C.: Public Affairs Press, 1960), 76.
7. United States Congress, *Debates and Proceedings in the Congress of the United States, 1789–1824* (Washington, D.C.: Gales and Seaton, 1834–56), Fifth Congress, 3776–77.
8. Roger Matuz, *The Presidents Fact Book: A Comprehensive Handbook to the Achievements, Events, People, Triumphs, and Tragedies of Every President from George Washington to George W. Bush,* ed. Bill Harris (New York: Black Dog, 2004), 32.
9. Text of Jefferson's complete 1805 inaugural address can be found at www.bartleby.com/124/pres16.html.
10. See Douglass Cater, *The Fourth Branch of Government* (Boston: Houghton Mifflin, 1959).
11. Timothy E. Cook, *Governing with the News: The News Media as a Political Institution,* 2nd ed. (Chicago: University of Chicago Press, 2005), 165.
12. Timothy E. Cook. *Governing with the News: The News Media as a Political Institution* (Chicago: University of Chicago Press, 1998), 3.
13. Robert Schmuhl and Robert G. Picard, "The Marketplace of Ideas," in *The Press*, ed. Overholser and Jamieson, 145.

14. John Milton, *Areopagitica*, 1644. In *Complete Prose Works* (New Haven, Conn: Yale University Press, 1970), 126ff.
15. See Leonard W. Labarce, ed., *The Papers of Benjamin Franklin* (New Haven, Conn.: Yale University Press, 1959), vol. 1, 194–95.
16. The quote comes from Holmes's 1919 dissent in *Abrams v. New York*.
17. Isaiah Berlin, "John Stuart Mill and the Ends of Life," in *Four Essays on Liberty* (London and New York: Oxford University Press, 1969), 187–88.
18. Schmuhl and Picard, "The Marketplace of Ideas," 143.
19. Gabriel de Tarde, *L'Opinion et la foule* [Opinion and the Public], 4th ed. (Paris: F. Alcan, 1922); Jürgen Habermas, *The Structural Transformation of the Public Sphere: An Inquiry into a Category of Bourgeois Society*, trans. Thomas Burger (Cambridge, Mass: MIT Press, 1989); Elihu Katz and Paul F. Lazarsfeld, *Personal Influence: The Part Played by People in the Flow of Mass Communications* (Glencoe, Ill.: Free Press, 1955).
20. Project for Excellence in Journalism, *The State of the News Media 2005*, www .stateofthemedia.org/2005/narrative_online_audience.asp?cat=3&media=3.
21. Ibid.
22. Robert M. Entman. "The Nature and Sources of News," in *The Press*, ed. Overholser and Jamieson, 49.
23. Barbie Zelizer, "Definitions of Journalism," in *The Press*, ed. Overholser and Jamieson, 67.
24. Pew Research Center for the People and the Press, *Cable and Internet Loom Large in Fragmented Political News Universe: Perceptions of Partisan Bias Seen as Growing, Especially by Democrats*, January 11, 2004, http://people-press.org/reports/display.php3?ReportID=200.
25. Thirty-eight percent of the journalists surveyed believed that journalists' accepting information without verifying it is the single most important reason bias slips into reporting. Twenty-nine percent of journalists stated that "strong personal views" is the single most important reason for bias in news reports, and 18 percent credited bias to tight deadlines.
26. National newspapers were selected for the Annenberg survey from the top twenty newspapers ranked by circulation in the *2004 Editor & Publisher International Year Book* and included the *New York Times*, the *Wall Street Journal*, the *Washington Post*, and *USA Today*.

    National broadcast organizations include the national television networks, major national cable television networks, public television, and radio chains with Washington, D.C., bureaus. Local newspapers were selected from the top one hundred local newspapers ranked by circulation, excluding those selected for the national sample, and an additional sample of local newspapers ranked from 101 to 350 in circulation.

    Local television stations were selected from the top fifty media markets and from the fifty-one to one hundred top markets as defined by Nielson Media Research in 2004. Local radio stations were selected from the top fifty markets as well.

    The primary sampling frame for media owners and executives, editors and producers, and staff journalists with each of these organizations was the Leadership Directories' *2005 News Media Yellow Book*. Secondary sampling frames included

Bacon's MediaSource, Editor & Publisher International Year Book, and *Broadcasting and Cable Yearbook.*

Respondents were selected using a two-stage sampling procedure. In the first stage, a random sample was drawn of media organizations. In the second stage, random samples of individuals were drawn by title—owners and executives, editors and producers, and staff journalists—from these organizations. In addition, a random sample of journalists who publish online was drawn. A total of 673 journalists were interviewed.

27. James Curran, "What Democracy Requires of the Media," in *The Press,* ed. Overholser and Jamieson, 128.

28. To Curran's focus on blogs we add partisan political talk radio of the sort practiced by Rush Limbaugh and Sean Hannity on the right and Al Franken on the left.

29. Hallin and Giles, "Presses and Democracy," 7.

30. Curran, "What Democracy Requires of the Media," 130.

31. Quoted in Gail Russell Chaddock, "Their Clout Rising, Blogs Are Courted by Washington Elite," *Christian Science Monitor,* October 27, 2005.

32. Pew Internet and American Life Project, *The State of Blogging,* January 2005, www.pewinternet.org/reports_archive.asp.

33. See J. D. Lasica, "Blogging as a Form of Journalism," in *We've Got Blog: How Weblogs Are Changing Our Culture,* ed. John Rodzvilla (Cambridge, Mass.: Perseus, 2002); and Melissa Wall, "'Blogs of War': Weblogs as News," *Journalism* 6, no. 2 (2005), 153–72.

34. Wall, "'Blogs of War.'"

35. Amanda Lenhart, *Bloggers: A Portrait of the Internet's New Storytellers* (Pew Internet and American Life Project, July 19, 2006).

36. Ibid.

37. Michael Schudson, *The Sociology of News* (New York: Norton, 2003).

38. Quoted in Matt Bai, "Notion Building," *New York Times Magazine,* October 12, 2003, 84.

39. "The Talk Radio Research Project," www.talkers.com/talkaud.html.

40. Michael Learmonth, "Auds Droop at Cable Newsies," *Variety,* December 29, 2004, 1.

41. Brian C. Anderson, "We're Not Losing Anymore," *Wall Street Journal,* November 3, 2003, www.opinionjournal.com/extra/?id=110004245.

42. Richard A. Viguerie and David Franke, *America's Right Turn: How Conservatives Used New and Alternative Media to Take Power* (Chicago: Bonus Books, 2004), 229.

43. Curran, "What Democracy Requires of the Media," 124.

44. See Stephen Hess, *The Government/Press Connection: Press Officers and Their Offices* (Washington, D.C.: Brookings Institution, 1981).

45. Curran, "What Democracy Requires of the Media," 126.

46. Gaye Tuchman, "Objectivity as Strategic Ritual: An Examination of Newsmen's Notion of Objectivity," *American Journal of Sociology* 77, no. 4 (1972), 664.

47. Schmuhl and Picard, "The Marketplace of Ideas," 147.

48. Curran, "What Democracy Requires of the Media," 126.

49. Ibid.

50. See, for example, Jack M. McLeod et al., "Understanding Deliberation: The Effects of Discussion Networks on Participation in a Public Forum," *Communication Research* 26,

no. 6 (1999), 623–54; Dietram A. Scheufele et al., "Social Structure and Citizenship: Examining the Impacts of Social Setting, Network Heterogeneity and Informational Variables on Political Participation," *Political Communication* 21 (2004), 315–38.

51. See, for example, Becker et al., "Debates' Effects on Voters' Understanding of Candidates and Issues," in *The Presidential Debates: Media, Electoral, and Policy Perspectives*, ed. George F. Bishop, Robert G. Meadow, and Marilyn Jackson-Beeck (New York: Praeger, 1978), 126–39; William L. Benoit, David J. Webber, and Julie Berman, "Effects of Presidential Debate Watching and Ideology on Attitudes and Knowledge," *Argumentation and Advocacy* 34 (1998), 163–72; Steven H. Chaffee, "Presidential Debates: Are They Helpful to Voters?" *Communication Monographs* 45 (1978), 330–46; Kathleen Hall Jamieson and Christopher Adasiewicz, "What Can Voters Learn from Election Debates?" in *Televised Election Debates: International Perspectives*, ed. Stephen Coleman (New York: St. Martin's, 2000), 24–42.

52. See Joseph N. Cappella, Joseph Turow, and Kathleen Hall Jamieson, *Call-In Political Talk Radio: Background, Content, Audiences, Portrayal in Mainstream Media* (Philadelphia and Washington, D.C.: Annenberg Public Policy Center, August 7, 1996); Kathleen Hall Jamieson, Joseph N. Cappella, and Joseph Turow, "Rush Limbaugh: The Fusion of Party Leader and Partisan Mass Medium," *Political Communication* 15 (1998), special CD-ROM issue.

53. Paul Starr, *The Creation of the Media: Political Origins of Modern Communications* (New York: Basic Books, 2004), 130.

54. Curran, "What Democracy Requires of the Media," 127.

55. James T. Hamilton, "The Market and the Media," in *The Press*, ed. Overholser and Jamieson, 354.

56. Because the Annenberg Media survey, in asking about the functions of the press, asked about how "traditional," or detached, media are serving those functions, the survey-based analysis presented here focuses on the traditional press.

57. Robert G. Picard, "Money, Media, and the Public Interest," in *The Press*, ed. Overholser and Jamieson, 338.

58. This statement appears in Douglas's dissent in *Branzburg v. Hayes,* 1972.

59. Bill Kovatch and Tom Rosenstiel, *The Elements of Journalism: What Newspeople Should Know and the Public Should Expect* (New York: Crown, 2001), 17.

60. Leonard Downie Jr. and Robert G. Kaiser, *The News about the News: American Journalism in Peril* (New York: Knopf, 2002), 258.

61. Herbert J. Gans, *Democracy and the News* (New York: Oxford University Press, 2003), 1.

62. Steven Chaffee and Stacey Frank, "How Americans Get Political Information: Print versus Broadcast News," *Annals of the American Academy of Political and Social Sciences* 546 (1996), 48–96.

63. Josh Pasek et al., "America's Youth and Community Engagement: How Use of Mass Media Is Related to Civic Activity and Political Awareness in 14- to 22-Year-Olds," *Communication Research* 33, no. 3 (2006), 115–35.

64. Michael X. Delli Carpini and Scott Keeter, *What Americans Know about Politics and Why It Matters* (New Haven, Conn.: Yale University Press, 1996); Norman H. Nie, Jane Junn, and Kenneth Stehlik-Barry, *Education and Democratic Citizenship in America* (Chicago: University of Chicago Press, 1996).

65. Thomas Patterson and Philip Seib, "Informing the Public," in *The Press*, ed. Overholser and Jamieson, 191.

66. John Zaller, "A New Standard of News Quality: Burglar Alarms for the Monitorial Citizen," *Political Communication* 20, no. 2 (2003), 110.

67. W. Lance Bennett, *News: The Politics of Illusion* (New York: Longman, 1983).

68. S. Robert Lichter, "A Plague on Both Parties: Substance and Fairness in TV Election News," *Harvard International Journal of Press/Politics* 6, no. 3 (2001), 8–30.

69. Joseph N. Cappella and Kathleen Hall Jamieson, *Spiral of Cynicism: The Press and the Public Good* (New York: Oxford University Press, 1997).

70. Patterson and Seib, "Informing the Public," 194.

71. Doris A. Graber, *Processing the News: How People Tame the Information Tide* (New York: Longman, 1984).

72. Cappella and Jamieson, *Spiral of Cynicism*.

73. Kathleen Hall Jamieson and Joseph N. Cappella, "Do Health Reform Polls Clarify or Confuse the Public?" *Journal of American Health Policy* 4, no. 3 (1994), 38–41.

74. Cappella and Jamieson, *Spiral of Cynicism*.

75. Cater, *The Fourth Branch of Government*, 7.

76. Maxwell McCombs and Donald Shaw, "The Evolution of Agenda-Setting Research: Twenty-Five Years in the Marketplace of Ideas," *Journal of Communication* 43 (1993), 58–67; Maxwell McCombs, "The Agenda-Setting Function of the Press," in *The Press*, ed. Overholser and Jamieson.

77. Curran, "What Democracy Requires of the Media," 124.

78. McCombs, "The Agenda-Setting Function of the Press," 159–60.

79. Martha Joynt Kumar and Alex Jones, "Government and the Press: Issues and Trends," in *The Press*, ed. Overholser and Jamieson, 231.

80. The United States Commission on National Security/21st Century, *Road Map for National Security: Imperative for Change* (Wilkes-Barre, Penn.: Kallisti), viii.

81. Norman Kempster, "New Anti-Terror Cabinet Agency Urged; Defense: The Plan Calls for An Overhaul of the Government's Approach to Security and Predicts an Attack on American Soil Within 25 Years," *Los Angeles Times*, February 1, 2001, 4.

82. "U.S. Senator Richard Shelby (R-AL) Holds Hearing on Worldwide Threats to National Security," *FDCH Political Transcripts*, February 7, 2001, 4.

83. See Geneva Overholser and Kathleen Hall Jamieson's afterword to *The Press*, 439.

84. Picard, "Money, Media, and the Public Interest," 345.

85. Hamilton, "The Market and the Media," 351.

86. Thomas E. Patterson, "Doing Well and Doing Good" (working paper, Joan Shorenstein Center on the Press, Politics, and Public Policy, Harvard University, December 2000), 3.

87. W. Lance Bennett and William Serrin, "The Watchdog Role," in *The Press*, ed. Overholser and Jamieson, 169.

88. Ibid.

89. Paula M. Poindexter, Don Heider, and Maxwell McCombs, "Watchdog or Good Neighbor? The Public's Expectation of Local News," *Harvard International Journal of Press/Politics* 11 (2006), 77–88.

90. Ibid., 85.

91. Schmuhl and Picard, "The Marketplace of Ideas," 152.

92. Hallin and Giles, "Presses and Democracies," 7.

93. Gilbert Cranberg, Randall Bezanson, and John Soloski, *Taking Stock: Journalism and the Publicly Traded Newspaper Company* (Ames: Iowa State University Press, 2001), 2.

94. Journalism.org, *The State of the News Media 2004: An Annual Report on American Journalism,* www.stateofthenewsmedia.com/2004.

95. See Donald C. Bacon, Roger H. Davidson, and Morton Keller, ed., *The Encyclopedia of the United States Congress* (New York: Simon & Schuster, 1995), vol. 2, 774ff.; Harold Edgar and Benno C. Schmidt Jr., "The Espionage Statutes and Publication of Defense Information," *Columbia Law Review* 73, no. 5 (May 1973).

96. This tolerance actually extends to any infringement of civil liberties. In fact, a CBS/*New York Times* poll that was conducted during this time showed that a majority (53 percent) of the public approved government wiretaps on some phone calls in the United States without getting court warrants, if it was necessary to reduce the threat of terrorism.

97. Adam Liptak, "In Leak Cases, New Pressure on Journalists," *New York Times,* April 30, 2006.

98. See John E. Mueller, *War, Presidents, and Public Opinion* (New York: Wiley, 1973).

THE NEXUS BETWEEN THE PUBLIC AND GOVERNMENT

3

UNDERSTANDING THE PUBLIC'S RELATIONSHIP TO GOVERNMENT

Mary McIntosh

A s democratic citizens, educated by public schools and informed by the media, Americans have a complex and often testy relationship with their democratic government. Ask Americans what comes to mind when they hear the words "the federal government," and an amazing variety of words and images come spilling out, demonstrating the richness of this relationship. Some of these ideas come from what Americans learn in school. So it is not surprising that the Annenberg Institutions of Democracy (IOD) Government survey found that many Americans mention fundamental facts in response to the question, "What comes to mind when you hear the words 'the federal government in Washington'?"

"Three branches of government of the United States."
—Female, age fifty-four

"George W. Bush."
—African American female, age seventy-six

"Congress and the executive branch."
—White male, age thirty-eight

Classroom instruction, of course, goes beyond learning the names of each department and agency or the differences in the lower courts. Students also learn about the function of the federal government and the impact that it has on the daily lives of Americans. The way Americans relate to their government and how they understand it is neither black and white nor simple, but is comprised of numerous shades of gray and complexity. Some respondents allude to these intricacies.

"It is a very complicated situation. There are factions that are sincere in representing the people, but I think there is a lot of influence from lobbyists and big money that may not be in our best interest."

—White female, age fifty-six

"The presidential administration is one part of the federal government and I have low confidence. The rest is made up of career people and I have a pretty high level of confidence."

—African American male, age fifty

Yet, for even more Americans, being prompted to think about "the federal government in Washington" elicits a largely negative response. These citizens are critical of the government's performance, calling it largely wasteful and inefficient. And they also talk about the government's leadership in less than flattering terms.

"Waste of money."

—White female, age twenty-two

"Money. Spends too much on the little stuff."

—White male, age thirty-nine

"Bureaucracy . . . logjam and nothing getting done, especially on unemployment."

—White male, age forty-four

"Bunch of stinking rats, money-hungry thieves and parasites [that] feed off the working man."

—White male, age fifty-seven

"They think for themselves and not for the people overall. It irritates me."
—White female, age sixty-three

Other Americans simply react with distrust, annoyance, or worse.

"I'm suspicious of them. But, as bad as it is they are the best on the planet."

—White male, age seventy-eight

"Legitimate crooks."

—Male, age thirty-one

"Distrust, no faith at all."

—African American female, age fifty-one

"I don't trust them too much. [They] don't seem to be telling the truth."

—Hispanic male, age twenty-five

Answers to this simple question illustrate the wide array of views that Americans have of the federal government. These off-the-cuff remarks show that many Americans' immediate reaction is one of skepticism or even distrust of their government. Yet these comments also reveal views about the government that are as nuanced as they are blunt. People question the government's leadership, performance, power, and integrity. Nevertheless, the American system of government is, for many Americans, "the best on the planet."

And it is not just members of the general public who have doubts about the government. American presidents, including Jimmy Carter and Bill Clinton, have declared that the government cannot solve all problems and that "big government" is a thing of the past.[1] And candidates in the modern era run *for* Congress largely by running *against* the institution itself.[2] The irony of this notwithstanding, this lack of confidence in the federal government speaks volumes about what these leaders think that the government can or should be doing and how well they think the government can do it.

"Government cannot solve our problems, it cannot set our goals, it cannot define our vision."

—Jimmy Carter, State of the Union address, 1978

"Government is not the solution to our problem; government *is* the problem.

—Ronald Reagan, inaugural address, 1981

"The era of big government is over."

—Bill Clinton, State of the Union Address, 1995[3]

This chapter builds on the words of these citizens, exploring how Americans relate to their government and, to a lesser extent, how government leaders relate to the public. A central theme of the chapter is the extent to which Americans trust their government and whether trust in government matters. Using survey data from the Annenberg Institutions of Democracy surveys, the discussion concludes that trust does matter. Trust in government is not just a gauge of the health of American democracy, it shapes Americans' attitudes and affects support for particular government policies and programs. Traditionally, trust is viewed as an outcome of good governance, and its decline since the late 1950s has spawned concern. Trust in government has been found to be both a cause and a consequence.[4]

57

As such, trust can increase or decline in response to government actions and, alternatively, citizens' trust in the government can bolster support for specific government programs. The goal of this chapter is to discuss each of the pieces in this intricate relationship between American citizens and their government.

Trust in Government

There is a long-standing debate about what level of trust is appropriate in a democratic society, beginning with the Federalists and the Antifederalists and the role of the Bill of Rights in the U.S. Constitution. Recall that the Federalists reasoned that government could be trusted and that a Bill of Rights "was superfluous because all power not expressly delegated to the new government was reserved to the people."[5] The dissenting Antifederalists argued that "trusting an all-powerful authority, remote and inaccessible to the people," without stipulating explicit individual liberties and limitations on the power of government, would endanger and subjugate common working people to aristocratic politicians keen on "protecting their own class interests."[6]

Though determining the right amount of trust in the federal government is a normative exercise, this debate remains relevant in the twenty-first century. Some scholars believe that *too much* trust is not healthy for a democracy. They argue that a sizable portion of the public should always be distrustful, in order to keep government accountable. Furthermore, political parties then have an incentive to address the concerns of this distrustful minority.[7] Other scholars believe that *too little* trust is not healthy for a democracy. They contend that a lack of trust can dampen interest in government service and civic participation, undermine the legitimacy of government decisions, and fuel cynicism throughout the political system.[8]

But what does trust in government mean? This is not a trivial question, as scholars have tried to make sense of the causes and consequences of the well-documented decline in trust since the 1970s. Some scholars argue that survey research on trust typically measures *political trust*—specific support for the actions of government or government leaders. Thus, this decline in trust may be a measure of dissatisfaction with specific elements of the political process and not with the constitutional foundations of government per se, or *regime legitimacy*.[9] Others counter that there is a relationship between political trust and regime legitimacy and suggest that declining political trust may signal a threat to the latter.[10]

In addition to the ongoing debate about the various dimensions of trust in government, there is considerable discussion about the different measures of trust.[11] The American National Election Studies (ANES), for example, was one of the first to track public trust in government and provides the longest trend data, spanning roughly five decades.

Yet it is not without detractors. The exact wording of the ANES question is: "How much of the time do you think you can trust the government in Washington to do what is right—just about always, most of the time, or only some of the time?" Many scholars and practitioners have taken issue with the wording of the ANES question. In particular, the vagueness of the reference to "doing the right thing" raises the question: Doing the right thing for whom or for what? Others argue that the three-point response scale, first written during a time of substantial trust in government, is hard to interpret. Although trusting the government "only some of the time" is typically treated as a measure of distrust, it is unclear just how negative this response is. By not providing a balanced response scale that is clearly anchored to positive and negative response options, the ANES question makes it difficult to assess the full range of trust and distrust in government.

Beyond these measurement issues, some worry that the question is overly sensitive to current events. The research on political trust points to a range of factors, including current events, that have been associated with declining political trust. Downturns in the economy and negative evaluations of the nation's economic health have been associated with decreased trust in the government.[12] Social factors, such as rising crime and child poverty, may also result in distrust of the government.[13] Others argue that there is a relationship between decreasing trust and the negative performance of institutions and incumbents.[14] And consistent with the argument of Kathleen Hall Jamieson, Bruce W. Hardy, and Daniel Romer in the previous chapter, decreasing trust has been linked to an increase in political scandals and a greater focus by the media on political misdeeds and corruption.[15] More specifically, Timothy E. Cook and Paul Gronke, among others, conclude that "the ANES trust-in-government is most highly affected by assessments of contemporary political and especially personal economic circumstances" rather than a deep orientation toward trust in government.[16]

Declining Political Trust

While scholars debate how best to measure trust in government and what the measurements reflect, few would argue with the fact that political trust has declined considerably since the 1950s. Of course, political trust has ebbed and flowed since it was first tracked by ANES (see Table 1). In 1958, for example, 73 percent of the public said they trusted the federal government "just about always" or "most of the time" to do what is right. By 1968, a majority still trusted the government but levels had dipped to 61 percent. After Vietnam and Watergate, ANES found that trust had tumbled to 36 percent in 1974. With severe economic stagflation and a hostage crisis in Iran, trust dropped even further, to 25 percent, by 1980. Trust in the government rose in the 1980s, but it never again reached

TABLE 1

Trust in Government, 1958–2003

How much of the time do you trust the government in Washington to do what is right? Would you say just about always, most of the time, or only some of the time?

Source	Date	Always/ most of the time	Some of the time/ never
ANES	11/58	73%	23
ANES	11/64	76	22
ANES	11/66	65	30
ANES	11/68	61	36
ANES	11/70	53	44
ANES	11/72	53	45
ANES	11/74	36	62
ANES	11/76	33	63
ANES	11/78	29	68
ANES	11/80	25	73
ANES	11/82	33	65
ANES	11/84	44	54
ANES	11/86	38	59
ANES	11/88	40	58
ANES	11/90	28	71
ANES	11/92	29	70
ANES	11/94	21	77
ANES	11/96	33	67
Pew	11/97	39	61
ANES	11/98	40	59
ANES	11/00	44	56
Brookings	7/1/01	9	70
Brookings	10/6/01	57	41
Annenberg	11/03	39	59

pre-Watergate levels and dropped back down to 21 percent by the early 1990s. In 2001, in the aftermath of terrorist attacks on American soil, trust in government rose sharply in a classic rally-'round-the-flag response. This increase occurred among virtually all segments of American society regardless of age, gender, race or ethnicity, and party affiliation. By 2003, trust had slid back to pre-9/11 levels.[17]

The decline in political trust does not stop with the federal government. Confidence in other key institutions, albeit with ups and downs along the way, was generally lower in 2005 than when these measures were first tracked for Congress, the presidency, the public schools, and the media in the early 1970s by the Gallup Organization.[18] Confidence in the Supreme Court, by contrast, remained relatively stable. Notably, only the military was more trusted in 2005 than when first measured by Gallup in the early 1970s. In fact, the military garnered more confidence than any of these other institutions, according to Gallup. The Harris Poll, which asks about the "people in charge of running" major institutions, reported a trend similar to Gallup. Harris reported that Americans have greater confidence in the military than in other institutions, and the poll reported similar overall declines in confidence in many major American institutions from 1966 to 2002.

Low levels of trust are also found globally. Trust was low and generally declining in most of the twenty countries surveyed by Gallup International in 2005. Trust in major institutions—national governments, nongovernmental organizations (NGOs), and businesses—to operate in the best interests of their society has generally declined across the board since 2001 when trust in these institutions was first systematically measured by Gallup International.[19] Specifically, from 2004 to 2005, trust in government declined in twelve of the sixteen countries surveyed. The decline spanned the globe from Canada to Mexico to Spain to South Korea. The public's trust in NGOs, which are often viewed as a counterpoint to government, also fell modestly in ten of the sixteen countries surveyed.

Constitutional Crisis?

A decline in trust in government here at home *could* have significant implications for how our government functions. Some scholars believe that if a decline in political trust does in fact signal a threat to regime legitimacy, then we may reach a point where the government's ability to make or change necessary policy will be limited by a lack of public confidence.[20] And if the decline is sustained, some are concerned about an irreversible slide in political participation, decreased political efficacy, and compliance with the law.[21] There is clearly considerable disagreement about how and when this country could reach such a crisis. But it can be posited that a decline in political trust does not suggest a constitutional or regime crisis, for several reasons.[22]

First, Americans on the whole are not outraged at their government. When asked whether they are basically content, frustrated, or angry with the federal government, one-third of the public (32 percent) in the Annenberg IOD Government survey responded that they are content. While half (50 percent) admitted to being frustrated, only one in ten (14 percent) responded that they are angry—hardly an indication of an institutional crisis.

Second, more than two-thirds (69 percent) of the American public affirmed that there are things the government could do to increase the public's trust, while less than one-third (27 percent) responded that people will mistrust the federal government no matter what. Clearly a solid majority of Americans have not given up on their system of government; they believe it can be improved, not that it is inherently flawed.

Third, Americans admitted to the belief that they can make a difference and influence how their government works, which is another mark of confidence in the basic system itself. The Annenberg Government survey (Question 33a) found that three-fourths (77 percent) of the public agreed that "people can make a difference in what happens in Washington," including one-third (34 percent) who strongly agreed.

Finally, another solid show of support for the American system of government is found in a 1997 Pew Research Center survey that asked about the extent to which the government needed major, minor, or no reform. Although 37 percent said the federal government needs major reform, the majority said the federal government is basically sound and needs only some reform (58 percent) or does not need much change at all (4 percent).[23] Taken together, these attitudes do not suggest that a regime-legitimacy crisis is imminent.

Annenberg Measure of Trust

In an effort to address criticism of how the trust question is worded in the ANES measure, the Annenberg Institutions of Democracy surveys asked about trust differently: "Generally speaking, how much do you trust the federal government in Washington to operate in the best interests of the American people?" The Annenberg wording asks about the intensity of trust ("how much") rather than the frequency of trust ("how much of the time") and employs a more balanced scale ("great deal, fair amount, not too much, or not at all") than used in the ANES series ("just about always, most of the time, or only some of the time"). And most important, it avoids the ambiguity of "doing what is right" and instead asks clearly about "operating in the best interests of the American people." An assumption of the ANES question is that the government "does what is right" when it is operating in the best interests of the American people. The Annenberg survey question states this plainly, reducing ambiguity.

The Annenberg trust question, as put to the American people, reveals an overall positive attitude toward the federal government.[24] According to the Annenberg Government survey, a slim majority of Americans (54 percent) trust the federal government "a fair amount" or "a great deal" to operate in the best interests of the American people. But that trust is not strong—just one in ten (11 percent) trust the government a great deal. On the negative side, a sizable minority of four in ten Americans (42 percent) trust the government "not too much" (27 percent) or "not at all" (15 percent).

The Annenberg trust question also addresses the criticism that the ANES question does not measure a range of opinion about the government—from those who do have trust in the government to those who do not trust the government at all. The Annenberg Government survey asked both the Annenberg trust measure and the original ANES measure. Findings show that those who said that they trust the government "only some of the time" on the ANES measure responded as having "not too much," "not at all," or a "fair amount" of trust on the Annenberg measure (see Table 2). In other words, roughly a quarter of those who said they trust the government only some of the time on the ANES measure actually do not trust the government at all. At the same time, a third of the respondents who said they trust the government only some of the time on

TABLE 2
Trust in Government: Annenberg and ANES Measures

	(ANES question) How much of the time do you trust the government in Washington to do what is right?		
	Just about always	Most of the time	Only some of the time [never— volunteered response]
(Annenberg question) How much do you trust the federal government in Washington to operate in the best interests of the American people?			
Great deal	53%	17	2
Fair amount	34	70	33
Not too much	5	10	40
Not at all	5	2	23

the ANES measure expressed a fair amount of trust in terms of the Annenberg measure, which suggests that the "only some of the time" response taps a fairly wide range of attitudes toward the government. This may also help explain why the Annenberg trust measure is higher than the ANES measure—54 percent versus 39 percent responding that they have a great deal or fair amount of trust in government. The ANES measure not only does not differentiate between those who do not trust the government too much and those who do not trust the government at all, it also captures some who have a fair amount of trust in government. Although it is possible that "a fair amount" may not be clearly defined in the minds of some members of the public, the full scale—great deal, fair amount, not too much, not at all—allows for the full range of trust and distrust to be more accurately reflected in the Annenberg question than in the ANES question.

Trust Levels by Institution

This straightforward look at the federal government fails to reveal the complexity and nuance in the public's views about the various components of the government. Specifically, ask Americans about their level of trust in the three branches of the federal government to operate in the best interests of the American people and answers vary from largely favorable (the Supreme Court: 76 percent) to somewhat favorable (the president: 65 percent; Congress: 54 percent). And answers are even more varied and favorable when it comes to most of the major departments and agencies that comprise the federal government. In the Annenberg Government survey, more than three-quarters of Americans said they trust the Department of Defense (78 percent), followed by the Food and Drug Administration (73 percent) and the Federal Bureau of Investigation (70 percent). The Social Security Administration is the least trusted of the six agencies and departments named in the survey. Nevertheless, a majority of nearly six in ten (59 percent) said they trust this agency, which is still higher than trust in the federal government overall (54 percent).

Why would confidence in any individual department or agency generally be higher than in the federal government overall? In part it may be easier for the public to give a more positive rating to an organization with a clear and specific purpose, as compared with a seemingly amorphous entity like the federal government. Moreover, it may be easier for people to accept one agency having jurisdiction over one particular aspect of their lives, but harder to accept that the federal government should oversee all these agencies and multiple aspects of their lives. The important point is that the public does not have a monolithic view of the federal government but differentiates among the government's various components.

Varying Levels of Trust

Just as different institutions inspire different levels of trust, trust levels vary by which members of the public you ask and what aspect of the government you ask about. Levels also vary depending on whether you ask the public or the political elite. This discussion looks at political elites and the public and how their views about government differ. One benefit of this approach is that political elites—presidential appointees, in this case—generally have both access and information not available to the public. But political elites may also have an entirely different set of criteria and expectations about the government, and perhaps an altogether different orientation toward government service and institutions more generally. Contrasted here are how these political elites and the American public view government, with particular focus on their different levels of trust in government. Not surprisingly, trust levels are higher among political elites. What is noteworthy, though, is why these elites think the public distrusts government and, more importantly, what this implies for improving trust in government.

The Public versus Political Elites

Presidential political appointees are the planners, dreamers, and workhorses who conceive of, develop, and execute the programs and policies of the federal government. Consequently, one would expect these political elites to be more trusting of the government, which they personally help to operate, as compared with the public. Indeed, the Institutions of Democracy surveys show this to be the case. Political appointees' trust in the federal government is nearly double the level of the public's (91 percent versus 54 percent, respectively), according to the Annenberg Government survey. Trust in Congress to operate in the best interest of Americans was shared by a solid majority of political appointees (69 percent) but a notably smaller number of the public (54 percent).

A large gap exists not only in the level of trust political appointees hold in government as compared with that of the public but in their respective understandings of why this gap exists. Political appointees believe that they understand how the public feels about issues, and that the government pays the right amount of attention (57 percent), or even too much attention (12 percent), to what the public thinks. The public is divided but respectfully disagrees. Only one-half (50 percent) think that high-level government officials understand what the public thinks about issues facing the country, while one-half (48 percent) think they do not. Moreover, the public and political appointees often see different reasons behind the decisions government officials make.

Political appointees point to a wide array of reasons for why the public distrusts the government. From a list of seven reasons ranging from events such as Watergate and Vietnam to misplaced priorities, political appointees were asked to rate the importance of each reason for the public's lack of trust in government. Remarkably, every one of the seven reasons was considered at least somewhat important by a substantial majority of the political appointees in explaining the public's distrust (see Table 3).

One-half of the political appointees (49 percent) attribute exaggerations of government failures by the media to be a "very important" reason for the public's distrust. As Kathleen Hall Jamieson, Bruce W. Hardy, and Daniel Romer suggested in the last chapter, how the public evaluates trust in government may depend on how and what the media report about the government. If the media focus on mistakes and conflict, the public understandably may not have confidence in the government. The perception that criticizing government is a popular campaign theme, the repercussions of events such as Vietnam and Watergate, and the understanding that politicians make promises they cannot keep are other reasons for the public's distrust that resonate among a substantial number of political appointees.

TABLE 3
Political Appointees' Perceptions of Public Distrust

How would you rate each of the following as reasons for why the public might distrust the government?

Reason	Very important	Somewhat important	Not too important	Not at all important
Media exaggerates government failures	49%	37	10	2
Criticizing government is a popular campaign theme	40	40	15	4
Events such as Vietnam and Watergate	38	42	14	3
Politicians promise too much	36	48	13	2
Government unresponsiveness	26	60	10	1
The government has the wrong priorities	18	54	23	2
Belief that the government is too powerful	17	54	23	3

Recognizing the role of events such as Vietnam and Watergate is noteworthy because there is an inference that the blame rests with the government. Yet the other three reasons related to direct performance by the government (unresponsiveness, misplaced priorities, excessive power) were not considered to be "very important" in the same magnitude. This lack of internal reflection on the part of elites may short-circuit efforts to improve the public's trust levels in the federal government. If political elites do not acknowledge that their perceived unresponsiveness is a major reason that the public distrusts the government, efforts to boost trust in government may be hindered.

Republicans versus Democrats

The country is often described as being divided fifty-fifty or between "red" and "blue" states.[25] Although it is unclear if political parties and activists are driving the polarization or simply responding to a changing environment, the divide has been steadily increasing within Congress as well.[26] While some scholars refute the extent of this polarization when it comes to a broad range of issues,[27] the political divide at the ballot box manifests in measures of attitudes toward the government. The country's partisan division may be a factor in how trust affects government capacity to pursue policies, and affects the public's willingness to trust the government and support certain policies. Namely, Americans who identify with the president's political party tend to have more confidence in the government than those who do not.[28] And for many Americans on either side of the line, trust in the government is related to who holds power more than to the ideology posited by that power.

Reflecting the often close relationship between presidential approval and trust,[29] Americans are most polarized when it comes to trust in the presidency—with nearly all Republicans (91 percent) but half as many Democrats (43 percent) surveyed responding that they trust the president to operate in the best interests of the American people (see Table 4). With a Republican president and Republicans in control of Congress at the time of the Institutions of Democracy surveys, Americans who identified with the Republican Party (73 percent) admitted to having more trust in the federal government to operate in the best interests of the American people than Democrats (42 percent). But approval of Congress has also been linked to trust, often operating in tandem with presidential approval.[30] However, the gap in trust in Congress is narrower, with two-thirds of Republicans (66 percent) and just over half of Democrats (52 percent) reporting trust in Congress. The Supreme Court, however, was shown to enjoy solid support from the public, regardless of political orientation.[31]

Knowledgeable versus Less Knowledgeable

Studies of public opinion consistently find that Americans often lack factual knowledge about government leaders and current issues of importance.[32] But

TABLE 4

Trust in Government Based on Political Orientation

Generally speaking, how much do you trust [political entity] to operate in the best interests of the American people?

% Responding "great deal" and "fair amount"			
	Republican	Democrat	Independent
President George W. Bush	91%	43	61
Federal government	73	42	48
Congress	66	52	45
Supreme Court	79	76	74

there is less agreement about what this means. Do Americans who are knowledgeable about government view it differently than those who are less knowledgeable? In other words, does increased knowledge about the facts and processes of government better enable people to make informed decisions about their government, or are the source of information and the extent of preexisting beliefs more important?[33]

Building on the work of James D. Barber and of W. Russell Neuman, Marion Just, and Ann Crigler, Michael Delli Carpini and Scott Keeter identified and evaluated three types of knowledge in their study of public opinion: (1) knowledge of the key players, parties, and groups in government; (2) knowledge of the institutions and processes of government; and (3) knowledge of substantive and current issues.[34] The Annenberg Government survey includes several questions that measure knowledge of the players and the processes. These questions can be used to examine how Americans who have more knowledge about the government differ in their levels of trust in government from those who have less knowledge.

General knowledge about national politics has been shown to be unrelated to trust—those who know which party has more members in the House of Representatives or can identify which party controls the Senate are as likely to trust the federal government to operate in the best interests of the American people as those who do not have this knowledge.[35] But when asked about specific players in government, Americans who know or recognize specific leaders tend to be more trusting of the government. Those who could correctly identify the position in government held by Vice President Dick Cheney were more likely to trust the government than people who could not name Cheney's position (59 percent versus 40 percent). While partisanship is clearly a factor when it comes to trust in government, with Republicans expressing more trust in a Republican-controlled government and presumably in Vice President Cheney as well, knowledge of Cheney is not entirely partisan—most Republicans (85 percent) and a large majority of Democrats (75 percent) could identify Cheney as vice president.

Although substantially fewer Americans were able to provide an answer when asked about less visible figures, Americans who could correctly identify Bill Frist as the Senate Republican leader, Senate majority leader, Republican leader, or congressional leader were somewhat more likely to trust the government than those who could not identify Frist (66 percent versus 53 percent). However, the pattern did not hold when it came to identifying the then House minority leader, Nancy Pelosi; the secretary of state; secretary of defense; or attorney general.

A less challenging question—whether respondents recognize the names of some people who are prominent in Washington and some who are not—produces mixed findings. Only with respect to people who were recognized by most, Ted Kennedy (95 percent) and John McCain (84 percent), were trust levels different. But trust in government was only somewhat higher among those who recognized Ted Kennedy (56 percent versus 43 percent) and John McCain (57 percent versus 45 percent).

When asked about a different aspect of government—the institutions and processes of government—knowledge is shown to be unrelated to trust. Americans who answered correctly four questions on the Annenberg Institutions of Democracy Judicial Branch survey about the functioning and jurisdiction of the Supreme Court reported having as much trust in the government as those who answered fewer questions correctly. Table 5 details the level of trust among those who answered each question correctly compared to those who answered incorrectly.

The Institutions of Democracy surveys did not ask any questions that measure knowledge of substantive and current issues. It is possible that knowledge of these issues is related to trust. However, the findings here suggest that trust is predicated on something other than knowledge of the players, institutions, and processes of government. The implication, although not tested, is that educating Americans about *who* runs the government and *how* will not turn people into more trusting citizens. Similar to the effect of education on political participation and political efficacy,[36] knowledge of government, although necessary in order for one to be a "good" citizen, is perhaps not sufficient to make one a trusting citizen.

Young versus Old

Younger Americans, when asked how much they trust the government to operate in the best interests of the American people, are more likely to express trust in government than older Americans, though with some variability.[37]

TABLE 5

Trust in Government and Knowledge of the Supreme Court

	Percent of Americans who trust the federal government to operate in the best interests of the American people either "a great deal" or "fair amount"	
	Correct response	Incorrect response
Can the U.S. Supreme Court declare an act of Congress unconstitutional?	59%	66
Do you know if it was the intention of the "founding fathers" for the president, Congress, and the Supreme Court to have different but equal powers or was it that the founding fathers intended each branch to have a lot of power, but the president to have the final say?	61	63
How would you describe the primary role of the Supreme Court—to interpret the U.S. Constitution, to oversee the actions and policies of the federal government, or to ensure that our judicial system runs smoothly and that judges do their jobs?	62	62
If the Supreme Court rules on a decision 5 to 4, does this mean the decision is final, the decision is too close and needs to be sent to Congress, or the decision is too close and needs to be sent back to the lower courts?	61	62

Younger Americans are also more trusting than older Americans when asked about specific agencies and departments of the federal government, such as the Federal Bureau of Investigation, the Environmental Protection Agency, the Food and Drug Administration, the Department of Defense, and the Department of Homeland Security. When asked about the Social Security Administration (SSA), younger people are shown to be generally more trusting than older people, with one notable exception—Americans who are at or near the typical retirement age (sixty-five years of age and older) trust the SSA just as much as young Americans (eighteen to twenty-four years of age). Despite the widespread reporting on the looming crisis facing social security, many of these older Americans are likely receiving their retirement benefits and may have more confidence in the SSA since the agency is actually fulfilling its obligations to them as retirees. Younger Americans, however, are unlikely to fare as well when they reach retirement age, yet they are as trusting of the SSA as those who are currently benefiting. As others have noted,[38] trust in government is predicated on more than experience, even positive experience, with government.

The implications for what young Americans can be taught in classrooms to help them maintain this trust in government cannot be understated. Moreover, the lack of import of the other demographic factors (race, gender, education, or income) in relation to trust in government is quite remarkable given historic issues of discrimination and inequality based on race, gender, citizenship, and income. For example, African Americans (52 percent) expressed having as much trust in the federal government as whites (55 percent), despite the fact that many African Americans remember having lived through segregation and struggles over civil rights. Women (53 percent) reported being as likely to trust the government as men (55 percent), at a time when a woman's right to choose may be in the balance as the makeup of the Supreme Court shifts. This suggests that Americans may be beyond single issues with respect to levels of trust. It also suggests that the Annenberg trust measure, as argued earlier, taps more than current events and measures, to at least some extent, more deep-seated attitudes toward government.

Understanding the Components of Trust

The relationship between the public and government is complex. The discussion thus far has explored appropriate levels of trust, how trust is measured, and how levels of trust can vary depending on what institution is being looked at and who is being asked. The remainder of this chapter continues to explore this intricate relationship between the government and its constituents by examining what shapes the public's trust in government.

Advanced statistical analysis can be employed in exploring what drives public opinion about trust in government (see "Regression Analysis of Trust" in appendix for details). Such an analysis shows that views about the government's leadership and the government's performance shape—to a large extent—the public's trust in government. As discussed previously, it matters whether people think that the political elites in Washington understand how they feel about the issues facing the country. Despite the often-heard debate about the appropriate level of government power or the appropriate size of government, assessments along these dimensions matter somewhat less in shaping public opinion about the government. Partisanship also drives trust, with Republicans, as the party in power when the Annenberg Institutions of Democracy surveys were administered, fairly trusting of government. But this relationship is somewhat conflicted—Americans who want to cut back government programs, a position generally favored by Republicans, are less trusting of the government than those who want to maintain government programs, a position generally favored by Democrats. Finally, age is the only demographic variable in the analysis that affects trust, with younger Americans more likely than older Americans to trust the federal government.

Given the importance of these aspects of government in shaping the public's trust in government, each is examined in greater depth below, starting first with leadership and then government performance, followed by perceptions of the appropriate level of power and size of government.

Leadership

The Annenberg analysis shows that many Americans distrust the government in part because they do not fully trust the individuals who lead it. Some have argued that a wary and cynical public can be traced at least in part to the structure of national politics, and of Congress in particular.[39] But even the president, who holds the highest elected position in U.S. government, is believed by the American people to be honest only sometimes (70 percent). Relatively few Americans express the belief that presidents are always honest (7 percent). At the same time, the public appears to accept the reality that not being forthright comes with the territory of being president of the United States, particularly when it comes to issues of national security, an area in which presidents are, at least initially, given broad support from the American public.[40] In fact more than half (56 percent) of those who think presidents are not always honest believe that presidents are at least somewhat justified in not being completely forthcoming.[41] These Americans who think dishonesty can be justified are also more likely to have a great deal or fair amount of trust in the federal government compared to those who do not find dishonesty by the president justifiable.

The public's concern about truthfulness does not stop at the White House; the perception of a lack of ethical leadership extends to other institutions as well. Our statistical analysis indicates that Americans are more likely to trust the government if they believe federal government officials are trustworthy, the federal government is not corrupt, and federal government officials are ethical. Over half of the public (56 percent) surveyed agreed that federal government officials are trustworthy, but relatively few strongly agreed (9 percent). And a substantial number of Americans expressed the belief that federal agencies in Washington are plagued by corruption. Roughly three in four Americans (73 percent) reported believing that at least a fair amount of corruption exists in federal agencies; fully one in four (25 percent) understood there to be a great deal of corruption. While the public is skeptical about the practices of government and of the potentially corrupting effect of running for elected office, it is less condemning of government workers. Again, illustrating the complexity of views about the government, a majority of the public (66 percent) expressed the view that federal government officials have good ethical and moral practices.

The public's concern about government leaders is fueled in part by a basic question of motivation. Many Americans question the motives of high-level officials, such as presidential appointees, in their decision to serve in government. Although a large majority of the public responded that they think many high-level government officials serve to make America a better place to live (80 percent) and to make a difference (79 percent), just as many believe these individuals serve for selfish reasons—to have power and to make important decisions (84 percent) and to meet important people and to get ahead professionally (80 percent). The public is just as suspicious about why civil servants enter government service. Most Americans surveyed reported that they think civil servants seek government employment more for the job security (76 percent) or salary and benefits (75 percent) than to help the public (16 percent) or to make a difference (19 percent). At the same time, the public expressed the belief that government workers generally try to do a good job (13 percent) but that the government bureaucracy keeps them from doing so (63 percent). These findings are not only informative but show generally that Americans who think government employees—whether high level or civil servants—serve for the public good are more likely than those who think they are motivated by self-interest to trust the federal government.

A fundamental assumption underlying democratic societies is that leaders of democratic institutions understand the wishes or the will of the people even if leaders do not necessarily agree with them. This sense of understanding plays a key role in predicting trust in the federal government in the Annenberg statistical analysis. Just one in two Americans thinks high-level government officials understand how the public thinks about issues facing the country. It is these same Americans who are also more likely to trust the government. Even more (64 percent) expressed the belief that the federal government is removed from "real life" and that people like them have no say about what the federal government does (62 percent). This perceived disconnect between the public and those who govern is even more evident when the public is asked why high-level officials make decisions that do not coincide with public opinion. A slim majority (51 percent) said that this occurs because government officials are catering to the needs of special-interest groups and not to the views of the majority.

Performance

How the public perceives the performance of the government was also an important factor in the advanced statistical analysis. Government performance along four key dimensions plays a large role in shaping views of government. Americans who think the government is doing a good job running its programs and services, helping people who need assistance, being fair in its decisions, and spending its money wisely express more trust in government than those who evaluate the government's performance in a less favorable light.

Americans are moderately positive about the government's running of its programs, being fair in its decisions, and helping those who need assistance—all responsibilities the public expects the government to fulfill.[42] A solid majority of Americans said the government does a good job running its programs and services (64 percent) and being fair in its decisions (64 percent). And nearly as many believed that the government does a good job helping people who need assistance (58 percent). In each of these cases, only one in ten Americans applauded the government for doing a very good job, while the majority evaluated the government's performance in these areas as somewhat good.

Where the public finds notable fault in the government's performance is with how it spends its money. Less than one-third of Americans (31 percent) said that the federal government does a good job spending its money wisely. More than twice as many (67 percent) reported thinking that the government does a bad job of spending its money wisely. Along these lines, nearly half of the public (47 percent) said they are paying too much in taxes considering the services they get from the government. And the public's perception about the government's performance in this area matters—Americans who say the government spends its money wisely are more likely to trust the government than those who say the government does not spend its money wisely (77 percent vs. 44 percent).

The framers of the U.S. Constitution purposely established a deliberative democracy that was not meant to be especially efficient or swift. But this goes against a relatively fast-paced environment to which most people have grown accustomed. Hence, although many Americans do not pay attention to specific government agencies or specific policy issues,[43] the public may nonetheless expect things to work and to work quickly. And that is not what the public thinks is happening, according to the Annenberg Government survey. Nearly two-thirds (63 percent) described the federal government as slow and inefficient in 2003. And the statistical analysis shows it is largely these inefficiencies, not the actual priorities of government, that bother people the most. The public believes the bigger problem with the federal government today is that it runs its programs inefficiently (56 percent), not that it has the wrong priorities (31 percent). In yet another display of deep-seated confidence in the American system of government, the public is not willing to write these inefficiencies off as a problem inherent in the government. The vast majority of Americans (86 percent) think the government can become more efficient.

Perceptions of government performance also vary by specific policy issues, illustrating again the multidimensional view the public has of the federal government. Solid majorities gave the government good marks for ensuring that food and medicines are safe (78 percent) and for protecting the nation against terrorist attacks (73 percent). And just over half said that the government does a good job conserving the country's natural resources (57 percent). On the negative side, majorities believe the government is doing a poor job ensuring access to affordable health care for all Americans (66 percent) and reducing poverty (61 percent). Other issues—caring for the elderly, managing the economy, and promoting honesty and morality—divide Americans more or less in half. As one would expect, those who say the government is doing a good job in these areas are also likely to have greater trust in the government.

Power

The Annenberg statistical analysis also shows that the role of governmental power matters when it comes to trust in government—Americans who say that the government should use its powers more vigorously to promote the well-being of all segments of society are also more trusting of the government. Careful not to repeat what they had learned under British rule, the founding fathers debated extensively the question of how much power government and its leaders should have. Although the Constitution, historical precedents, and past governmental commitments provide some guidance for what the government can and cannot do, what the government *should* do is quite a different matter.

The Annenberg Government survey shows that the American public is more conflicted today about the amount of power government should exercise than it has been in the past. Roughly one-third of respondents said the government has too much power (32 percent) while one-third said it should use its powers more to promote the well-being of all Americans (35 percent). Roughly a quarter of the public (28 percent) responded that they think the government is using about the right amount of power to meet today's needs, compared with a plurality of nearly four in ten (38 percent) in 1964.

The public is equally conflicted about the desired size of the federal government and the reach of its programs.[44] Asked to choose between a smaller government that provides fewer services and a larger government that provides more services, an equal number reported preferring a bigger government with more services (46 percent) as preferring a smaller government with fewer services (46 percent). Those who preferred a bigger government that provides more services, however, were also more likely to have expressed a great deal or fair amount of trust in the federal government.

Public opinion has been shifting in favor of maintaining government programs. When asked to rate themselves on a scale from 1 to 6, with 1 being someone who thinks government programs should be cut back to reduce the power of the government and 6 being someone who thinks that government programs should be maintained, just over half of the American public in 1995 wanted to maintain programs. A decade later nearly two-thirds (63 percent) expressed the belief that government programs should be maintained—and these same Americans were more likely to trust the government than those who would prefer to cut back.

This preference for maintaining the status quo may be daunting in the years to come as Congress and the executive branch increasingly encounter the strain of entitlement spending, all the while expanding the scope and expense of government through the war on terror, military conflicts abroad, and the bipartisan drive for increased pork-barrel spending. Interestingly, those who want to maintain the status quo are more likely to trust the government than those who want to cut back (58 percent vs. 49 percent).

Political Orientation

Both political orientation and views on the role of government were important factors in the Annenberg statistical analysis. As discussed earlier, trust in government is colored by political orientation—Americans who identify with the party in power are more trusting of the federal government to operate in the best interests of the American people. With a Republican in the White House and Republican majorities in the House and Senate at the time the Institutions of Democracy surveys were administered, Republicans (73 percent) were more likely than Democrats (42 percent) to trust the government. However, underscoring the point that trust depends on who you ask as well as on what you ask, the analysis shows that political allegiance is often at cross-purposes with views on the scope of government. Americans who prefer to reduce government power by cutting back government programs—a position typically supported by Republicans—are actually less likely to trust the government. And Americans who instead prefer to maintain government programs—a position typically supported by Democrats—are more trusting of the federal government.

Age

As mentioned earlier, age is the only demographic factor in the statistical analysis that affects trust in government. While it is unclear exactly what is influencing the relationship between trust and age, Americans tend to be less trusting as they grow older. What is clear from the analysis is that other key demographic factors—education, income, gender, and race—are unrelated to trust. This again suggests that political trust in some measure may be tapping into a core set of beliefs about government that cut across the fissures that can often separate Americans on other issues. And it also suggests that more work is needed to determine if this is largely a generational or life-cycle phenomenon, or, as is more likely, a combination of the two.

Consequences of Low Political Trust

It is worth repeating that the type of trust being discussed here is political trust—as measured in the standard ANES survey and the Annenberg surveys and referred to in the literature on trust—and not institutional or regime trust. Initial research on the subject tried to sort out the relationship between declining trust and negative views about the political system.[45] However, as discussed earlier, there is no evidence in the Annenberg surveys or the scholarly literature that indicates the country is in the midst of an institutional or regime crisis.[46]

This leads to an obvious question—Does it really matter that political trust has declined? Aside from *sounding* bad, does declining or low trust actually have negative effects? A growing body of research indicates that low levels of trust may have important political and social effects. Low levels of trust in government may mitigate support for domestic policies and positive views about Congress.[47] And going in the other direction, trust in government has been linked to citizen compliance with the law, support for incumbent political leaders, as well as opposition to term limits for elected leaders. More broadly, the researchers John Brehm and Wendy Rahn find that confidence in the government affects interpersonal trust and civic participation.[48]

In addition to presenting converging evidence on the effects of declining trust, these studies question the conventional approach to studying political trust. The debate on trust in the political science literature has for the most part focused on explaining what has caused the decline in political trust rather than on what effect this decline has caused.[49] By focusing on effects, scholars have been able to link low levels of trust to broader political phenomena. For example, looking at trust as an explanatory variable rather than a dependent variable, Marc Hetherington argues that the decline in trust has significantly affected redistributive policies and suggests that the so-called shift toward conservatism in the United States is actually the result of declining trust rather than a shift in political attitudes.[50] Expanding on Hetherington's approach, Thomas Rudolph and Jillian Evans, using data from the 2000 National Annenberg Election Survey, found that trust—moderated by ideology—may affect a broad range of government policies but that the effect is strongest among conservatives, and that increased trust in government among conservatives often shores up the ideological gap between liberals and conservatives on spending issues.[51]

The Annenberg surveys were not designed to directly test these arguments, particularly regarding change in trust over time as it affects specific government policies, but the surveys can be used to determine whether the basic arguments hold. According to Hetherington, because Americans generally support big government when they perceive a benefit but want limited government when they perceive risks, political trust is necessary for support of policies that require perceived sacrifice. Without at least a certain level of political trust, Americans will not support policies that entail risk or sacrifice, even if they otherwise might favor such policies. Consequently, high levels of trust result in more liberal policy while lower levels result in conservative policy. Hetherington concludes that the trend since the 1960s toward conservative policies in the United States can be explained in large part by declining trust rather than a direct shift or demand for more conservative policies. Rudolph and Evans expand this logic but argue that the relationship holds beyond policies that entail perceived sacrifice.

There are a few questions in the Annenberg Institutions of Democracy Congress and Executive Branch survey that allow these hypotheses to be tested. The public was asked specifically about six issues and whether it was important for the federal government to be responsible for them. In broad terms, three issues have been historically associated with the Democratic Party (conserving natural resources, promoting racial equality, and reducing poverty) and three with the Republican Party (keeping taxes low, protecting the unborn, and promoting stronger moral values). Although specific policy questions would be ideal, these broader measures from the Annenberg surveys provide a reasonable gauge of the public's preferences in these areas.

There is evidence that political trust, moderated by ideology, affects support for government policies. This is particularly clear when it comes to conserving the country's natural resources. Given that the Republican Party generally favors a free-market approach over increased regulation, Republicans should generally be less supportive than Democrats of the federal government having responsibility for conserving natural resources. The survey data found this to be largely true: Although most Republicans (89 percent) and Democrats (94 percent) say conserving natural resources is an important responsibility, Republicans (41 percent) are notably less likely than Democrats (63 percent) to see this as a *very* important responsibility. But the key point is that Republicans who trust the government are somewhat more likely than Republicans who do not trust the government to say it is an important responsibility for the federal government to conserve natural resources (91 percent vs. 80 percent). The logic is that Republicans who trust a Republican-controlled government are more likely to trust that environmental policies will not adversely affect them, whereas Republicans who do not trust the government—even if the government is under Republican control—are less certain.

The argument holds for promoting racial equality as well. Republicans (82 percent) are somewhat less likely than Democrats (90 percent) to say that promoting racial equality is an important responsibility of the federal government, with Republicans (39 percent) less likely than Democrats (51 percent) to say that this is a *very* important responsibility. And when it comes to trust, Republicans who trust the government are much more likely than Republicans who do not trust the government to say that it is an important responsibility for the federal government to promote racial equality (86 percent vs. 69 percent).

For the remaining issue areas, the differences are not statistically significant. However, there is a positive correlation between trust and Republican support for both protecting the unborn and promoting stronger morals.[52] These findings are consistent with the argument that Republicans trust a Republican-controlled government in areas that have been important to Republicans.

Furthermore, it is possible that direct policy questions and a larger sample would produce more robust findings, perhaps presenting additional support for the argument that trust directly affects support for government policies.

There are also a number of other findings in the Annenberg surveys that indicate that current levels of political trust may affect support for public policy. Americans who distrust the government are less likely to approve of the job the government is doing in specific policy areas compared to those who trust the government. People who distrust the government are less likely than those who trust the government to say the government has done a good job fighting poverty (22 percent vs. 46 percent), ensuring that every American has access to affordable health care (22 percent vs. 40 percent), and providing a decent standard of living for the elderly (31 percent vs. 61 percent). And of those who think the government has done a poor job fighting poverty, people who distrust the government are more likely to say that the government is to blame rather than that poverty is an intractable problem, than those who trust the government (60 percent vs. 40 percent). The same holds for ensuring that every American has access to affordable health care (65 percent vs. 47 percent) and providing a decent standard of living for the elderly (70 percent vs. 59 percent).

Political orientation matters here as well. Republicans, who identified at the time of the survey with the party in power, were more trusting of the federal government on these issues and less likely to blame the government for falling short as compared with Democrats. However, it is worth noting that the public in general—Democrats and Republicans alike—have a more favorable view of the government and blame the government less if they trust the federal government to operate in the best interests of the American people.

The context in which Americans are asked about trust also matters. This is evident in the pre-9/11 and post-9/11 measures of trust, when national security became a new basis on which Americans evaluate trust.[53] The context of the war on terror matters in other ways as well. Data from the Institutions of Democracy Congress and Executive Branch survey show that trust in government is related to a somewhat greater willingness to give the president extraconstitutional powers (see Table 6). Although solid majorities of the public oppose rather than support such proposals, the degree of trust Americans have is a factor. For example, over a third of those who expressed trust in government (36 percent) said that they believe that "the president should have the authority without the consent of Congress to take preemptive military action, even if an attack is not imminent." Less than half as many who expressed distrust in government supported this rather extraordinary use of presidential power (15 percent). Likewise, those who said that they trusted the government were more than twice as likely as those who expressed distrust in government (31 percent vs. 15 percent) to agree that "the president should have the authority without the consent of Congress to suspend constitutional protections for certain individuals." And Americans who said that they trust the government were

TABLE 6

Trust in Government and Approval of Expanded Executive Power

	How much do you trust the federal government in Washington to operate in the best interests of the American people?	
	Great deal/ fair amount	Not too much/ not at all
The president should have the authority without the consent of Congress to take pre-emptive military action, even if an attack is not imminent.	36%	15
The president should have the authority without the consent of Congress to suspend constitutional protections for certain individuals.	31	15
The president should have the authority without the consent of Congress to disregard international laws or treaties to which the U.S. is a signatory.	26	13

also more likely than those who distrusted the government (26 percent vs. 13 percent) to believe that "the president should have the authority to disregard international laws or treaties to which the U.S. is a signatory."

While support on these issues is partisan, with Democrats overwhelmingly opposed and Republicans more divided, the public's willingness to grant additional powers to the president appears to depend on how much they trust the government as well as what is being asked of them. In the post-9/11 environment, Americans who trust the government are more likely to cede such authority to the president. And while trust may make a difference, judging by the majorities opposed to these extraordinary powers, there are clearly limits to how far the public is willing to go when it comes to presidential leadership.[54]

But does this have any connection to what happens in Washington? Using data from the Pew Research Center's *Deconstructing Trust* survey, Molly Sonner and Mary McIntosh found that government leaders often misinterpret the public's distrust of government as a lack of enthusiasm for government programs.[55] Consequently, this disconnect between political elites and the public may lead to incoherent or rash policy decisions and perhaps complicate the government's efforts to rebuild trust. Evidence from the Annenberg Government survey of political elites is consistent with this finding. Three-fourths of political elites (77 percent) said that they understand how the public feels and that the government pays the right amount of attention or too much attention to what the public thinks. But only half of the public (50 percent) agrees that political elites understand what the public thinks about the issues facing the country. And as the statistical analysis discussed here clearly points out, a strong predictor of trust is the extent to which the public feels government leaders understand the public's concerns.

Beyond this gap between the views of political elites and the public, low trust does not seem to affect core democratic principles. According to the Annenberg Government survey, trust does not increase voting. However, distrust in government also does not dampen this basic civic responsibility. Where trust does seem to matter is in the satisfaction derived from the voting process itself—Americans who trust the government are somewhat more likely to get a feeling of satisfaction from voting compared with those who distrust the government (63 percent vs. 51 percent). But again, trust does not seem to affect attitudes about bedrock democratic beliefs. Results of the Institutions of Democracy Media survey show that those who place a high level of importance on the basic tenets of liberal democracy—such as freedom of speech, an impartial judicial system, freedom of the press, freedom of religion, and free and honest elections—are no more likely to trust the government to operate in the best interests of the American people than those who do not value these fundamental tenets of democracy.

These nonfindings have led others to wonder if the public's trust in government matters.[56] The Annenberg Institutions of Democracy surveys, however, contribute to a growing literature showing that trust in government is more important than ever and merits more rather than less attention.

Notes

Ken Gaalswyk and Christina An Finkelstein were instrumental in the analysis and writing of this chapter. Both are project directors at Princeton Survey Research Associates International and made substantial contributions to the Annenberg Institutions of Democracy surveys.

1. Donald F. Kettl, "Reforming the Executive Branch of the U.S. Government," in *The Executive Branch*, ed. Joel D. Aberbach and Mark A. Peterson, Institutions of American Democracy (New York: Oxford University Press, 2005).
2. Richard F. Fenno, *Home Style: House Members in Their Districts*, repr. (New York: HarperCollins, 2005); Gary C. Jacobson, "Modern Campaigns and Representation," in *The Legislative Branch*, ed. Paul J. Quirk and Sarah A. Binder, Institutions of American Democracy (New York: Oxford University Press, 2005).

3. Quotes are from Marc J. Hetherington, *Why Trust Matters: Declining Political Trust and the Demise of American Liberalism* (Princeton, N.J.: Princeton University Press, 2005), 1.

4. See Hetherington, *Why Trust Matters*.

5. Roger A. Bruns. "A More Perfect Union: The Creation of the U.S. Constitution," National Archives and Records Administration, www.archives.gov/national-archives-experience/charters/constitution_history.html.

6. Ibid.

7. John H. Aldrich, *Why Parties? The Origin and Transformation of Political Parties in America* (Chicago: University of Chicago Press, 1995); Bernard Bailyn, *The Ideological Origins of the American Revolution* (Cambridge, Mass.: Belknap Press of Harvard University Press, 1992).

8. Margaret Levi, "A State of Trust," in *Trust and Governance*, ed. Valerie Braithwaite and Margaret Levi (New York: Russell Sage, 1998); Samantha C. Luks and Jack Citrin, "Revisiting Political Trust in an Angry Age," paper presented at the Annual Meeting of the Midwest Political Science Association, Chicago, 1997; Gary Orren, "Fall from Grace: The Public's Loss of Faith in Government," in *Why People Don't Trust Government*, ed. Joseph S. Nye Jr., Philip D. Zelikow, and David C. King (Cambridge, Mass.: Harvard University Press, 1997); Seymour Martin Lipset and William Schneider, *The Confidence Gap: Business, Labor, and Government in the Public Mind*, rev. ed. (Baltimore: Johns Hopkins University Press, 1987).

9. Jack Citrin, "Comment: The Political Relevance of Trust in Government," *American Political Science Review* 68, no. 3 (1974), 973–88; Hetherington, *Why Trust Matters*; John R. Hibbing and Elizabeth Theiss-Morse, *Stealth Democracy: Americans' Beliefs about How Government Should Work* (Cambridge and New York: Cambridge University Press, 2002); Joseph S. Nye Jr. and Philip D. Zelikow, "Conclusion: Reflections, Conjectures, and Puzzles," in *Why People Don't Trust Government*, ed. Nye, Zelikow, and King.

10. David Easton defines two types of political support—specific support and diffuse support. Specific support is based on the performance and actions of the government and political leaders. Diffuse support is based on the support for the system of government or regime rather than evaluations of what it or its leaders do. David Easton, *A Systems Analysis of Political Life* (New York: Wiley, 1965).

    Arthur H. Miller and Jack Citrin debated the significance of this distinction in the early 1970s. Miller contended that declining trust as measured by the American National Election Studies (ANES) signaled a lack of trust in the regime and that dissatisfaction with the policies of both political parties was a leading cause. Arthur H. Miller, "Political Issues and Trust in Government, 1964–1970," *American Political Science Review* 68 (1974), 951–72; and "Rejoinder to 'Comment' by Jack Citrin: Political Discontent or Ritualism?" *American Political Science Review* 68 (1974), 989–1001. Citrin disagreed and argued that declining trust instead reflected dissatisfaction with incumbents, caused largely by disapproval of the performance of the administration of the incumbent president. Citrin, "Comment: The Political Relevance of Trust in Government."

    Others contend that diffuse and specific support are not empirically distinct and suggest that confidence in and approval of institutions are so closely linked that it is difficult to assess diffuse support. See Timothy E. Cook and Paul Gronke, "The Skeptical American: Revisiting the Meanings of Trust in Government and Confidence in Institutions," *Journal of Politics* 67, no. 3 (2005), 784–803; Stephen C. Craig, *The Malevolent Leaders: Popular Discontent in America* (Boulder, Colo.: Westview Press, 1993); John R. Hibbing and Elizabeth Theiss-Morse, *Congress as Public Enemy: Public Attitudes toward American Political Institutions* (Cambridge and New York: Cambridge University Press, 1995). For a discussion of possible consequences of declining trust, see Orren, "Fall from Grace."

11. Even the positioning of the trust question in a survey may influence a person's response, as is evident in the Annenberg Institutions of Democracy surveys of 2003 and 2005 in which the public was asked how much trust they have in the news media to operate in the best interests of the American people. When the question appeared at the beginning of the survey in 2003 (Question 2b), less than half (46 percent) said that they had a great deal or fair amount of trust. When the question appeared at the end of the survey in 2005 (Question 49b), after dozens of specific questions about the media and its functioning, more than three-fourths (78 percent) said that they had a great deal or fair amount of trust in the news media.

12. Jack Citrin and Philip Green, "Presidential Leadership and the Resurgence of Trust in Government," *British Journal of Political Science* 16 (1986), 431–53; Stanley Feldman, "The Measure and Meaning of Trust in Government," *Political Methodology* 9 (1983), 341–54; Arthur H. Miller and Stephen A. Borrelli, "Confidence in Government in the 1980s," *American Politics Quarterly* 19 (1991), 147–73.

13. Jane Mansbridge, "Social and Cultural Causes of Dissatisfaction with the U.S. Government," in *Why People Don't Trust Government*, ed. Nye, Zelikow, and King.

14. Ralph Erber and Richard R. Lau, "Political Cynicism Revisited: An Information-Processing Reconciliation of Policy-Based and Incumbency-Based Interpretations of Changes in Trust in Government," *American Journal of Political Science* 34 (1990), 236–53; John T. Williams, "Systemic Influences of Political Trust: The Importance of Perceived Institutional Performance," *Political Methodology* 11 (1985), 125–42.

15. Suzanne Garment, *Scandal: The Crisis of Mistrust in American Politics* (New York: Random House, 1991); Orren, "Fall from Grace."

16. Cook and Gronke, "The Skeptical American," 799. See also Hetherington, *Why Trust Matters*; David W. Moore, "Just One Question: The Myth and Mythology of Trust in Government," *Public Perspective* (January/February 2002), 7–11; Gary Langer, "Trust in Government: To Do What?" *Public Perspective* (July/August 2002), 7–10.

17. An ABC News survey in January 2002 showed that 68 percent of Americans trusted the government in Washington to do what is right (about always/most times) when it came to handling national security and the war on terrorism. But only 38 percent trusted the government when it came to handling social issues like the economy, health care, social security, and education, similar to pre-9/11 baseline levels of trust. See Langer, "Trust in Government: To Do What?"

18. The Annenberg Government survey asked about newspapers and TV news as separate items, not about the media overall. Gallup began asking about newspapers in 1973 and television news in 1993, for which confidence measures in 2005 were lower compared to baseline measures.

19. World Economic Forum, "Full Survey: Trust in Governments, Corporations and Global Institutions Continues to Decline," *GlobeScan Report on Issues and Reputation* (Washington, D.C.: GlobeScan, December 2005). For evidence on the decline in trust in Japan, see Susan Pharr, "Public Trust and Democracy in Japan," in *Why People Don't Trust Government*, ed. Nye, Zelikow, and King.

20. Richard E. Neustadt, *Presidential Power and the Modern Presidents: The Politics of Leadership from Roosevelt to Reagan* (New York: Free Press, 1990); Douglas Rivers and Nancy L. Rose, "Passing the President's Program: Public Opinion and Presidential Influence in Congress," *American Journal of Political Science* 29 (1985), 183–96.

21. Lipset and Schneider, *The Confidence Gap*; Orren, "Fall from Grace."

22. See Derek Bok, "Measuring the Performance of Government," in *Why People Don't Trust Government*, ed. Nye, Zelikow, and King; Moore, "Just One Question."

23. Pew Research Center, *Deconstructing Trust: How Americans View Government* (Washington, D.C.: Pew Research Center for the People and the Press, 1998).

24. It may be difficult to separate measures of diffuse and specific support. (See, for example, Citrin, "Comment: The Political Relevance of Trust in Government"; Cook and Gronke, "The Skeptical American"; Craig, *The Malevolent Leaders*; and Hibbing and Theiss-Morse, *Congress as Public Enemy*.) The Annenberg measure is arguably a closer measure of specific support than of diffuse support.

25. See, for example, James W. Ceaser and Andrew E. Busch, *Red over Blue: The 2004 Elections and American Politics* (Lanham, Md.: Rowman and Littlefield, 2005); Pew Research Center, *Evenly Divided and Increasingly Polarized* (Washington, D.C.: Pew Research Center for the People and the Press, 2004); Larry J. Sabato, ed., *Divided States of America: The Slash and Burn Politics of the 2004 Presidential Election* (New York: Pearson Education, 2005).

26. Barbara Sinclair, "Parties and Leadership in the House," and Steven S. Smith, "Parties and Leadership in the Senate," in *The Legislative Branch*, ed. Paul J. Quirk and Sarah A. Binder, Institutions of American Democracy (New York: Oxford University Press, 2005).

27. See Morris P. Fiorina, with Samuel J. Abrams and Jeremy C. Pope, *Culture War? The Myth of a Polarized America* (New York: Pearson Longman, 2005).

28. Angus Campbell et al., *The American Voter* (New York: Wiley, 1960); John R. Alford, "We're All In This Together: The Decline in Trust in Government, 1958–96," in *What Is It about Government That Americans Dislike?* ed. John R. Hibbing and Elizabeth Theiss-Morse (Cambridge and New York: Cambridge University Press, 2001); Feldman, "The Measure and Meaning of Trust in Government."

29. Alford, "We're All In This Together"; Marc J. Hetherington, "The Effect of Political Trust on the Presidential Vote, 1968–96," *American Political Science Review* 92 (1998), 311–26.

30. Jeffrey L. Bernstein, "Linking Presidential and Congressional Approval During Unified and Divided Government," in *What Is It about Government That Americans Dislike?* ed. Hibbing and Theiss-Morse; Citrin and Green, "Presidential Leadership and the Resurgence of Trust"; Paul J. Quirk and Sarah Binder, "Congress and American Democracy: Assessing Institutional Performance," in *The Legislative Branch*, ed. Quirk and Binder.

31. The Annenberg Institutions of Democracy surveys show a slight drop in trust in the Supreme Court among Democrats from 2003 to 2005. In the Government survey (2003), Republicans (79 percent) and Democrats (76 percent) were equally likely to trust the Supreme Court. Differences in intensity were statistically insignificant—30 percent of Republicans and 23 percent of Democrats trusted a great deal, and 49 percent of Republicans and 53 percent of Democrats trusted a fair amount. In the Annenberg Judicial Branch survey (2005), trust in the Supreme Court overall was similar for Republicans (78 percent) and Democrats (74 percent), but the intensity had changed since 2003—Democrats were less likely than Republicans to have a great deal of trust (30 percent vs. 16 percent), and Democrats were more likely than Republicans to have a fair amount of trust (58 percent vs. 48 percent).

32. Campbell et al., *The American Voter*; Benjamin I. Page and Robert Y. Shapiro, *The Rational Public: Fifty Years of Trends in Americans' Policy Preferences* (Chicago: University of Chicago Press, 1992); John R. Zaller, *The Nature and Origins of Mass Opinion* (Cambridge and New York: Cambridge University Press, 1992).

33. Thomas Patterson and Philip Seib, "Informing the Public," in *The Press*, ed. Geneva Overholser and Kathleen Hall Jamieson, Institutions of American Democracy (New York: Oxford University Press, 2005); Zaller, *The Nature and Origins of Mass Opinion*.

34. James D. Barber, *Citizen Politics: An Introduction to Political Behavior*, 2nd ed. (Chicago: Markham, 1973); W. Russell Neuman, Marion R. Just, and Ann N. Crigler, *Common Knowledge: News and the Construction of Political Meaning* (Chicago: University of Chicago Press, 1992); Michael X. Delli Carpini and Scott Keeter, *What Americans Know about Politics and Why It Matters* (New Haven, Conn.: Yale University Press, 1996): 63–89.

35. By and large, knowledge of key players is also not related to trusting other institutions. Americans who know which party has more members in the House of Representatives have similar levels of trust as those who do not know when it comes to large private businesses (34 vs. 36 percent), the news media (44 vs. 49 percent), religious groups (62 vs. 60 percent), trade unions (46 vs. 41 percent), Congress (55 vs. 53 percent), nonprofit organizations (63 vs. 67 percent), and state government (54 vs. 57 percent).

36. Wendy D. Puriefoy, "The Education of Democratic Citizens: Citizen Mobilization and Public Education," and Clarence N. Stone, "Civic Capacity: What, Why and from Whence," both in *The Public Schools*, ed. Susan Fuhrman and Marvin Lazerson, Institutions of American Democracy (New York: Oxford University Press, 2005).

37. Alford, "We're All in This Together"; Robert J. Blendon et al., "Changing Attitudes in America," in *Why People Don't Trust Government*, ed. Nye, Zelikow, and King; Craig, *The Malevolent Leaders*; Jack Citrin and Samantha S. Luks, "Déjà Vu All Over Again?" in *What Is It about Government That Americans Dislike?* ed. Hibbing and Theiss-Morse.

38. Pew Research Center, *Deconstructing Trust*.

39. E. J. Dionne Jr., *Why Americans Hate Politics* (New York: Simon and Schuster, 1991); Hibbing and Theiss-Morse, *Congress as Public Enemy*; Gary C. Jacobson, *The Politics of Congressional Elections*, 5th ed. (New York: Longman, 2001); Susan J. Tolchin, *The Angry American: How Voter Rage Is Changing the Nation* (Boulder, Colo.: Westview Press, 1996).

40. Samuel Kernell, *Going Public: New Strategies of Presidential Leadership* (Washington, D.C.: Congressional Quarterly Press, 1986); Stephen Skowronek, *The Politics Presidents Make: Leadership from John Adams to George Bush* (Cambridge, Mass.: Belknap Press of Harvard University Press, 1993).

41. Even President George Washington, who according to American lore could not tell a lie, proved to be a master of espionage. President Bill Clinton's admission, after initially denying it, that he had had an affair with intern Monica Lewinsky negatively affected Clinton's personal approval rating but had little effect on his job approval rating. Presidential scholars argue that a charismatic personality or the "personal presidency" in the modern era has made it easier for presidents to communicate directly to the public rather than negotiate or bargain with Congress and other players. A president's use of the bully pulpit, employing increasingly sophisticated communication strategies while talking in a language that Americans can identify with, often results in the public thinking favorably of the president, even if they oppose a particular policy or dispute. See Lawrence R. Jacobs, "Communicating from the White House: Presidential Narrowcasting and the National Interest," in *The Executive Branch*, ed. Joel D. Aberbach and Mark A. Peterson, Institutions of American Democracy (New York: Oxford University Press, 2005). Kernell, *Going Public*; Theodore J. Lowi, *The Personal President: Power Invested, Promise Unfulfilled* (Ithaca, N.Y.: Cornell University Press, 1985); Jeffrey K. Tulis, *The Rhetorical Presidency* (Princeton, N.J.: Princeton University Press, 1987).

42. Page and Shapiro, *The Rational Public.*

43. Delli Carpini and Keeter, *What Americans Know about Politics and Why It Matters*; Zaller, *The Nature and Origins of Mass Opinion.*

44. Campbell et al., *The American Voter*; James A. Stimson, *Public Opinion in America: Moods, Cycles, and Swings* (Boulder, Colo.: Westview Press, 1991).

45. Citrin, "Comment: The Political Relevance of Trust in Government"; Jack Citrin et al., "Personal and Political Sources of Alienation," *British Journal of Political Science* 5 (1975), 1–31. Miller, "Political Issues and Trust in Government" and "Rejoinder to 'Comment' by Jack Citrin."

46. Hibbing and Theiss-Morse, *Stealth Democracy.* For a counterargument, see Orren, "Fall from Grace," and Lipset and Schneider, *The Confidence Gap.*

47. Virginia A. Chanley, Thomas J. Rudolph, and Wendy M. Rahn, "The Origins and Consequences of Public Trust in Government," *Public Opinion Quarterly* 64 (2000), 239–56; Cook and Gronke, "The Skeptical American"; Hetherington, *Why Trust Matters*; Thomas J. Rudolph and Jillian Evans, "Political Trust, Ideology, and Public Support for Government Spending," *American Journal of Political Science* 49 (2005), 660–71.

48. John Brehm and Wendy Rahn, "Individual-Level Evidence for the Causes and Consequences of Social Capital," *American Journal of Political Science* 41 (1997), 999–1023. See also Hibbing and Theiss-Morse, *Congress as Public Enemy*; Pew Research Center, *Deconstructing Trust*; John T. Scholz and Mark Lubell, "Trust and Taxpaying: Testing the Heuristic Approach to Collective Action," *American Journal of Political Science* 42 (1998), 398–417; and Virginia Chanley, Thomas J. Rudolph, and Wendy M. Rahn, "Public Trust in Government in the Reagan Years and Beyond," in *What Is It about Government That Americans Dislike*, ed. Hibbing and Theiss-Morse.

49. Feldman, "The Measure and Meaning of Trust in Government."
50. Hetherington, *Why Trust Matters*.
51. Rudolph and Evans, "Political Trust, Ideology, and Public Support for Government Spending."
52. For Republicans, the positive correlations between trust in the federal government and views on the importance of federal responsibility for all four issues—conserving the country's natural resources, promoting racial equality, protecting the unborn, and promoting stronger morals—are significant at the .01 level (2-tailed).
53. Langer, "Trust in Government: To Do What?"
54. See Scott C. James, "The Evolution of the Presidency: Between the Promise and the Fear," and Joel D. Aberbach and Mark A. Peterson, "Control and Accountability: Dilemmas of the Executive Branch," both in *The Executive Branch*, ed. Aberbach and Peterson, for a discussion of the factors that limit the leadership capability of modern presidents.
55. Pew Research Center, *Deconstructing Trust*; Molly Sonner and Mary McIntosh, "Bureaucrats and Citizens: Misunderstanding Public Cynicism," paper presented at the Annual Meeting of the American Political Science Association, Boston, September 1998.
56. See, for example, David C. King, "The Polarization of American Parties and Mistrust of Government," and Joseph S. Nye Jr. and Philip D. Zelikow, "Conclusion: Reflections, Conjectures, and Puzzles," in *Why People Don't Trust Government*, ed. Nye, Zelikow, and King; Moore, "Just One Question"; Kevin Phillips, *Arrogant Capital: Washington, Wall Street, and the Frustration of American Politics* (Boston: Little, Brown, 1995): and Pew Research Center, *Deconstructing Trust*.

DEMOCRATIC GOVERNMENT

4

THE THREE BRANCHES OF GOVERNMENT: POWERS, RELATIONSHIPS, AND CHECKS

Mark A. Peterson

Who is to be credited when the national government takes beneficial concerted action in response to a policy problem? Who or what bears the blame when it fails to act, or acts ineffectively or perhaps unwisely? In the American system of government, these are not easy questions to answer. The ways in which they are addressed may ultimately determine whether or not citizens trust their government and the people who run it. Moreover, they bring to the fore the potential for a significant divide in the understanding of government performance, and its impediments, between the citizens who are represented by the nation's public institutions and the officials who serve in them. The true health of American institutions of democracy—and the capacity to recognize and rectify real threats to them—can hinge substantially on the particular perspective one brings to these questions and the perceptual lens through which one weighs the evidence. To begin our detailed exploration of public and insider judgments about the functioning of the primary governing institutions in the United States, here we focus on the constitutional roles of, relationships among, and checks upon the executive, legislative, and judicial branches of government.

Those who study the politics and governing institutions of the United States, especially the presidency and Congress, typically conclude that they function roughly as expected and largely according to the basic design established at the founding of the Republic. Scholars may personally lament the substantive policy results in given instances or during specific periods, but rarely view them as either mysteriously derived or perniciously conceived—unless there is, in fact, evidence that public officials have violated constitutional or statutory dictates. Those who toil in government, especially elected officials—and their aides— who hold office for relatively brief periods and bear most direct responsibility for tackling the problems confronting the nation, are often far less sanguine. Effective policymaking, they conclude, is simply too difficult in the American decentralized system. Lloyd Cutler, counsel to President Jimmy Carter, famously wrote that a "particular shortcoming in need of remedy is the structural inability of our government to propose, legislate, and administer a balanced program for governing. In parliamentary terms, one might say that under the U.S. Constitution it is not now feasible to 'form a Government.' The separation of powers between the legislative and executive branches, whatever its merits in 1793, has become a structure that almost guarantees stalemate today."[1]

Media coverage that provides citizens with their primary sources of current information often seems to raise an entirely different set of objections in the face of a policymaking breakdown: It is not the institutions that are problematic. Query students in an undergraduate political science class, already well imbued with their standard civics education, and many can hardly fathom a functioning democracy without U.S. constitutional arrangements (apparently unaware that few of the recognized democracies in the world follow either this country's institutional lead or its written Bill of Rights). As President Carter responded some years ago when asked about Cutler's complaint, "That's a radical change in our government structure that the people of our country would never accept. To say that Canada or Great Britain has a better system than ours would be a blow to American pride."[2] Instead of reflecting on the implications of institutional design, when the government fails to meet specific needs or solve certain problems, or does what it should not do, it is easy for both the media and the public to find fault in the policymakers themselves for displaying incompetence, arrogance, shortsightedness, petty partisanship, self-interestedness, or, worst of all, simple corruption.

With the media's focus on the daily battles, the routine clash of individuals, and the personal auras or deficiencies of the men and women in leadership positions, perhaps they are missing the constitutional forest for the anecdotal trees. Both scholars and policymakers are more likely, as with Cutler, to see the challenges of modern government emerging—for good or ill—from the very heart of the design of American constitutional government: the separation of powers among the three branches and the associated checks and balances by which the various branches are insinuated in the affairs of one another. The noted constitutional scholar Edward Corwin suggested long ago that the U.S. Constitution established "an invitation to struggle."[3] Although inter-institutional cooperation makes more frequent appearances in American policymaking than Corwin's phrase may suggest, such an invitation has indeed often been accepted by officials in the respective institutions of government.[4] National political debate and policymaking are rife with competition, compromise, and even stalemate promoted by the establishment of distinct branches of government that are also infused with the means to influence, even block, the actions of one another.[5] Do the public, with their limited public affairs education and increasing dependence on broadcast news accounts, recognize these implications of the U.S. government's constitutional design, from the potential for frustrating policymaking to fulfilling the protections against abuse of governmental power? Are the public's perceptions fundamentally different from the assessments cast by the men and women who see government firsthand, serving in the executive and legislative branches or working directly with the judicial branch?

How well the constitutional arrangement of government authority works early in the twenty-first century, given the policy challenges the nation confronts, is a matter of evaluation and interpretation by both the officials who attempt policymaking in this institutional setting and the electorate that holds them accountable. Drawing from other volumes in the Institutions of American Democracy series—*The Legislative Branch, The Executive Branch,* and *The Judicial Branch*—as well as other relevant literature, this chapter first describes briefly the constitutional foundations of the separation of powers and the ongoing efforts by presidents, Congress, and the courts to obtain increased institutional advantage in the system of checks and balances. We then turn to the responses provided in several of the comprehensive Annenberg Institutions of Democracy (IOD) surveys, which permit us to ascertain directly the similarities and differences in the assessment of the separation of powers and its effects held by the general public (overall, and among people who are the most educated, or informed, or politically engaged[6]) and by individuals who have immediate professional experience within the institutions themselves. For the public's views, this chapter relies on the two mass public components of the Annenberg Institutions of Democracy Court survey and the Congress and Executive Branch survey. To capture the views of the "insiders," we turn to the Executive Branch survey of senior executive service and political appointees, the Congress survey of congressional staff, and the Courts survey of lawyers (see appendix for survey details).

Returning to the themes that we identified in the introductory chapter, this comparative public and insider appraisal of the separation of powers in American government, in the context of judging the overall health of the nation's democratic institutions, could not come at a more important time. In 2006, as part of what it defined as the "war on terror" and its prosecution of the war in Iraq, the Bush administration continued to push constitutional interpretations that permit "the extraordinary expansion of the powers of the president," striving to be free of both congressional and judicial limitations in war making, the handling of combatants, and intelligence gathering, including domestic spying.[7] In the words of Vice President Dick Cheney, the administration was acting in the belief that "especially in the day and age we live in, the nature of the threats we face, the president of the United States needs to have his constitutional powers unimpaired, if you will, in terms of the conduct of national security policy."[8] The administration also pursued an unprecedented degree of unilateral power in domestic affairs.[9] There was a prominent divide between Republicans and Democrats in Congress with respect to how far the legislature as a constitutionally independent institution should push back against this forthright executive assertion of constitutional authority, but prominent Republican members of Congress expressed their own concerns about too unrestrained a stance on presidential power. Senator Lindsey Graham of South Carolina, for example, commented that President Bush and his administration "have a view of executive authority that basically smothers the other two branches."[10] Noted another Republican senator, Chuck Hagel of Nebraska, "There's a very clear pattern of aggressively asserting executive power, and the Congress has been essentially complicit in letting [the president] do it."[11]

The federal courts ratified some of President Bush's war-related actions, but provided some checks as well, particularly with the 2006 Supreme Court ruling in *Hamdan v. Rumsfeld,* which invalidated the system of military commissions that had been authorized by the president for trying suspected terrorists, and more cases were pending in the sixth year of Bush's presidency. In the meantime, conservatives raised a growing hue and cry about alleged "lawmaking from the bench" by activist judges on social issues like abortion, same-sex marriage, end-of-life decisions, and the role of religion in the public square, prompting congressional initiatives to rein in the courts and judges through threatened impeachment, as well as proposed legislation and constitutional amendments to strip the courts of specific areas of jurisdiction. Commented Tom DeLay, until September 2005 the Republican majority leader in the House of Representatives, "This Congress is not going to sit by and let an unaccountable judiciary make these kinds of decisions."[12]

In the first decade of the twenty-first century the American constitutional system of checks and balances, conceived more than two centuries earlier, was being put to an unusual, perhaps even extraordinary, test. At issue were the meaning of these institutional arrangements, their current practicality and adaptability to modern challenges, and the appropriateness of the strategies used by various policymakers to give advantage to their policy positions. This chapter looks at how citizens and policymakers responded to the challenges of the times.

Separation of Powers: Design and Development

Initially the government of the United States was organized under the Articles of Confederation. A reaction to the perceived excesses of the British monarchy against which the American Revolution had been launched, the Articles offered few authoritative levers of power. Sovereignty rested with the states, and the national government, such that it was, had little authority; new laws required supermajority support to be enacted, and, an executive office of any kind not having been established, both executive and legislative tasks were performed by Congress. This arrangement proved incapable of managing the war debt, promoting the economy, or securing the borders of the new Republic. The U.S. Constitution, unanimously ratified by the states in 1788 and implemented in 1789, "establish[ed] a more nationally oriented and more capable central government . . . invigorating national government by imbuing it with popular sovereignty, establishing a more functional legislature, and unifying the executive responsibilities in a single president," with George Washington the first to serve in that position.[13]

Historical Evolution

The framers, while rejecting the infirmities of the Articles of Confederation, nonetheless retained a deep fear of concentrated government power, the "mischief of faction," and the potential imprudence of an impassioned public.[14] As James Madison argued in *Federalist* 51,

> It may be a reflection on human nature, that . . . devices should be necessary to control the abuses of government. . . . If men were angels, no government would be necessary. If angels were to govern men, neither external nor internal controls on government would be necessary. In framing a government which is to be administered by men over men, the great difficulty lies in this: you must first enable the government to control the governed; and in the next place oblige it to control itself.[15]

Among the protections incorporated into the Constitution to fulfill this obligation was the separation of powers, creating three discrete branches for the legislative, executive, and judicial functions of government. To the framers, the "separate and distinct exercise of different powers of government . . . is admitted on all hands to be essential to the preservation of liberty."[16] No single faction—whether in the minority or majority—and no false and ill-considered whim of the public could take hold of all the instruments of government. But having given independent authority to each of the three branches, there remained the ensuing task of preventing any one of them from growing in dominion over time, threatening the power and sustained capacity of the other branches. To forestall this concern, the Constitution included "checks and balances." In Madison's words, "the great security against a gradual concentration of the several powers in the same department, consists in giving to those who administer each department the necessary constitutional means and personal motives to resist encroachments of the others."[17] Congress legislates, but the president holds the veto power. The president nominates senior executive officials, and judges and justices, as well as negotiates international agreements, but the Senate must confirm appointments and ratify treaties. The president is commander in chief of the military, but Congress provides for its organization and funding and has the power to declare war. Judges and justices adjudicate the laws as passed by Congress and administered by the executive, but Congress largely defines the jurisdiction of the courts and provides "advice and consent" in response to the president's choices of individuals for the bench.

Thus, simply, under the Constitution, with its separation of powers, government authority is widely distributed. Action requires considerable unity of purpose and opinion across the branches of government. "By design . . . national authority . . . should be effective only when these dispersed power centers happen to agree."[18] "The Constitution," suggests William Nelson, "can be understood as a device for placing checks and balances in the path of majoritarian, democratic change even while conceding the ultimate power of the people to govern themselves as they will."[19]

Soon after the Constitution was ratified and the new government was in place, however, the bearing and implications of the separation of powers, and the practical nature of the checks and balances, were transformed by a relatively quick succession of three profound external and internal shocks to the system. First, political parties—not even mentioned in the Constitution— immediately became the basic organizing mechanisms of American politics. Born out of the Federalist and Antifederalist debates surrounding the Constitution itself and giving an institutional face to the competing visions held by the framers of the new Republic, they "gathered up power and redistributed it from Congress to the president. . . . What the Constitution dispersed, political parties collected back up."[20] Although far from completely, noted Richard Neustadt.[21] Second, the Constitution had left unaddressed how, and by whom, conflicts would be resolved between its provisions and the text of new statutes enacted by Congress.[22] In the landmark decision of *Marbury v. Madison* in 1803, the Supreme Court declared that it "had the power to invalidate legislation that it judged to be contrary to the Constitution."[23] Third, almost from the start of the Republic, the franchise broadened rapidly, expanding dramatically the size and engagement of the nation's electorate. Aided by the development of improved methods of mass communication, and accelerated by President Andrew Jackson's muscular approach to office, the presidency established direct and unexpected ties to the people, altering the chief executive's place in the constitutional setting.[24] As argued by Charles Stewart, "within the world view of the framers, the president was strong, but still subordinate to Congress. . . . the executive being primarily necessary only to effectuate legislative intentions and to act decisively in rare instances of imminent national peril."[25] With the electorate as a new political resource for the president, the institutional balance shifted.

Since those early days of the Republic, external challenges, experience, statutory provisions, and evolving interpretation have further altered the nature and meaning of the separation of powers. The effects have perhaps been most pronounced for the presidency. A country that was at its inception small and weak and relatively isolated, with no standing army, a relatively primitive and largely agrarian economy, and a government that played essentially no role in social and domestic affairs, had become by the twenty-first century the world's sole superpower, its defense spending equal to that of the rest of the world combined, with an economy larger than any other, substantial domestic policy commitments, and an elaborate regulatory structure.[26] Increasingly expected to have primary responsibility for both national and economic security, "presidents confront a yawning gap between the duties of their office and the inadequate formal powers at their command."[27]

Building on the Jacksonian revolution and carrying through from Abraham Lincoln claiming emergency powers during the Civil War to Theodore Roosevelt and Woodrow Wilson exploiting public opinion, party leadership, and opportunities for legislative initiative, the stage was set for the "modern presidency." Franklin Roosevelt fused these practices, "bequeathing to his successors both a system and a style of governance that would make both independent action and program activism routine features of the . . . presidency."[28] Although as a result of the veto provision of the Constitution "the president was essentially made a third legislative branch [after the House and Senate]," at first presidential legislative involvement was usually "tacit"; direct engagement was considered "an encroachment that insulted [the] institutional prerogatives" of Congress.[29] After Roosevelt and Truman, the president's legislative program emerged in full flower and was expected, indeed demanded, by Congress.[30] Employing aggressive personnel selection in the executive branch and taking advantage of all available administrative resources, subsequent presidents also "sought out additional tools with which to shape policy unilaterally—that is, without seeking Congress's statutory assent."[31] Because of the role courts can have on policy implementation, modern presidents have in addition been assertive in using the solicitor general and other legal arms of the executive departments to influence federal court dockets.[32] Exploiting their formal authority to nominate judges and justices, they have regularly tried to constitute the federal courts in their own policy image, although historically "very few presidents have managed to mold the federal courts to their liking."[33]

In Article II of the Constitution, the meaning of the executive power conferred to presidents "was left radically underspecified."[34] Proponents of expansive presidential authority have read this imprecision as an invitation to reach as far and wide for constitutional power as possible, beyond past conceptions of checks and balances—often (but certainly not always) with congressional backing. Notwithstanding periodic "dramatic confrontations" with the courts, "only rarely [have the] federal courts ruled that the president has exceeded his constitutional powers."[35] According to Richard Brisbin, "judicial interpretation of the actions of the presidency has often resulted in the approval of unilateral presidential actions that extend executive powers. . . . The judiciary seems only willing to check presidential power when [the incumbent] has lost public and congressional support," as was the case with Richard Nixon after the Watergate scandal.[36] The overall result has been what Scott James characterizes as an "improvisational and opportunistic presidency" that has produced "a profound conceptual reworking of the office."[37] By the twenty-first century, even without amending the text of the Constitution itself, the original meanings of the president's constitutional roles as head of state, chief executive, and commander in chief had been transformed, and to these may now comfortably be added the informal title "chief legislator" as well. In the modern era, with some exceptions, "presidents by-and-large set the overall agenda and tone for most of the policy debate in Washington."[38]

As is reflected in the vesting of congressional powers in Article I, the authors of the Constitution considered the legislative branch, not the president, to be the first among equals and the most obviously and directly connected to the people. "To the framers," writes Charles Stewart, "the legislature was the keystone of republican government."[39] Although certain presidents made inroads, for much of the nineteenth century Congress largely retained that stature. From the beginning of the twentieth century, however—frequently voluntarily and typically in response to particular exigencies—the legislature ceded leadership to the president. For example, in response to the Great Depression of the 1930s, the legislature's acceptance of President Roosevelt's New Deal agenda and policies "formally shifted oversight of the economy from Congress to the president."[40] More routinely, it delegated policy details and decision making to the executive agencies. At other times in the latter twentieth century, especially during periods of divided government, Congress fought back, striving to reinvigorate its role and responsibilities in war making, budgeting, deficit control, oversight of executive agencies, and appointments to the executive agencies and the courts.[41] Whatever the complaints expressed by presidents, "the judiciary has seldom limited congressional power."[42] Indeed, it was through court action on issues of policy implementation that congressional constraints on the executive branch as a whole were enforced—"Hundreds of times each year, lower court judges interpret federal statutes in ways that substantially reduce the discretion of the White House and political executives appointed by the president."[43] Although the place of Congress within the constitutional framework of separation of powers has been redefined over time, it is essential to underscore that "Congress is the only [national legislature in the world] that still plays a powerful, independent role in public policymaking. . . . Only Congress initiates legislation, makes decisions on major provisions, and says 'no' to executive proposals."[44] For example, in his study of twenty-eight major laws enacted from 1947 to 1990, Charles O. Jones found that Congress had "preponderant" influence in 25 percent of the cases (more than was true of presidents, at 21 percent), and 54 percent of the time there was a balance in influence between the executive and legislature.[45]

At the time of the Constitution's ratification debates, Alexander Hamilton, writing in *Federalist* 78, posed the judiciary as the "least dangerous" branch. Unlike the president and Congress, it "has no influence over either the sword or the purse; no direction either of the strength or of the wealth of the society; and can take no active resolution whatever. It may truly be said to have neither FORCE nor WILL, but merely judgment."[46] However, just as Article II left executive power scarcely defined, the third article of the Constitution did "not specify the role of the judiciary in the overall polity, [did] not explicate precisely what it is that courts and judges do, and [did] not untangle the relationship between the countermajoritarian judicial branch of government and the more democratic executive and legislative branches."[47] Precisely because there were no "details of the checks and balances to be exercised by and upon the judiciary, the critics of the Constitution feared the appearance of a judicial aristocracy unresponsive to the people," which was the very concern that Hamilton had sought to nullify.[48] Although the courts had "not often bucked the political branches of the federal government," the latitude in the constitutional text and sufficient wherewithal among judges and justices had permitted the development of a strong, albeit cautious, judicial branch.[49] First, of course, was the assertion, surprisingly not forcefully challenged by presidents and Congresses, that the Supreme Court would determine the constitutionality of statutes and executive action in cases brought before it. Following the reasoning of *Marbury v. Madison,* however, the courts maintained a distinction between law, where they would rectify contradictions between statutes and the Constitution, and politics, where policy decisions would be left to the "democratic" executive and legislative institutions. Until 1954, that is, when the Supreme Court handed down its unanimous decision in *Brown v. Board of Education,* overturning racial segregation of the public schools. The Court's decision in this case "changed everything. . . . *Brown* did not resolve a constitutional ambiguity or defer to the political branches and take constitutional law in some new direction demanded by the people. Instead, it made a policy judgment that Jim Crow [segregation laws endorsed by state legislatures] was so profoundly unjust that it had to be ended, whatever the will of the people."[50] As noted by Kermit Hall and Kevin McGuire, modern "courts . . . do not simply 'announce' the law; as much as any other set of institutions, they make policy."[51]

The judiciary, though, remains in the full mix of the system of checks and balances. On the one hand, the Supreme Court has "bounded some excesses of congressional and presidential power . . . [and] diminished the threat of governmental tyranny," protected by the now ingrained norm of legislative and executive deference to even its most contentious rulings. On the other hand, the courts move warily. As summarized by Brisbin, "only at critical political moments has the judiciary risked its legitimacy and set its own seal on the meaning of separation of powers.... The Supreme Court justices ... have adopted practices of restraint to avoid some politically charged cases in which they might have to make controversial policy choices contrary to the interests of other powerful political forces."[52] Because the judiciary depends on executive branch enforcement and its members are appointed by the president, and Congress may affect the jurisdictions of the courts in general and "defin[es] the [Supreme] Court's authority," the judiciary remains "responsive to the political opposition" and is ordinarily "cautious about running afoul of a clear popular consensus."[53] It cannot afford to be an isolated judicial aristocracy.

The Special Role of War

In the continuous "invitation to struggle" among the branches, with each important political and policymaking player striving to find or claim its appropriate place in the separation-of-powers system, war has always provided the impetus for the most aggressive assertions of presidential prerogative powers. It is also the setting in which Congress and the courts have been the most accommodating to those declarations. Exploiting the ambiguities of Article II and the lack of specifics associated with the term "executive power" and the title "commander in chief," and harking back to sovereign power in foreign affairs long attached to national governments, including the British predecessor to the American Republic, presidents have maintained their constitutional right and obligation to pursue policies to protect the national security and the national interest without interference from others.[54] At the time of World War II, Congress acquiesced to President Roosevelt's leadership in these terms, and often provided formal legislative approval. The Supreme Court typically endorsed these provisions.[55] Edward Corwin suggested that "the principle canons of constitutional interpretation are in wartime set aside so far as concerns both the scope of national power and the capacity of the President to gather unto himself all constitutionally available powers in order the more effectively to focus upon the task of the hour."[56]

Building on the legacies of Roosevelt, Truman, Kennedy, and Nixon, the administrations of Ronald Reagan and George H. W. Bush went even further, despite the lack of a "hot" war creating an immediate threat to the nation's survival. "Members of the executive branch," writes Gordon Silverstein, "began to articulate a new reading of the Constitution, particularly in reference to foreign affairs. This executive prerogative argument held that in foreign affairs the president alone had final authority, and when the national security was imperiled (a judgment left to the executive), the president was legitimately entitled to override constitutional constraints to preserve and protect security."[57]

These claims were fully recognizable in the period following the terrorist attacks of September 11, 2001, when President Bush declared a "war on terror" and launched the armed incursion into Afghanistan to topple the Taliban, and the full invasion of Iraq to overthrow Saddam Hussein. In the process, however, the Bush administration pushed even further beyond the broad reach for presidential power attempted by previous presidencies. As the legal scholar Noah Feldman argued in 2005,

> Not since Watergate has the question of presidential power been as salient as it is today. The recent revelation that President George W. Bush ordered secret wiretaps in the United States without judicial approval has set off the latest ground of arguments over what the president can and cannot do in the name of his office. Over the past few years, the war on terror has led to the use of executive orders to authorize renditions and the detention of enemy combatants without trial. . . . The administration of George W. Bush, emboldened by the Sept. 11 attacks and the backing of a Republican Congress, has sought to further extend presidential power over national security. Most of the expansion has taken place in secret, making Congressional or judicial supervision particularly difficult. Administration lawyers have gone so far as to claim that the president as commander in chief is not bound by laws that ban torture because he is empowered by the Constitution to fight the nation's wars however he sees fit. . . . The administration has also suggested, in other memos, that the president may violate international treaties if necessary to fight the war on terror. When added to the newly declared presidential right to arrest American citizens wherever they might be and detain them without trial as enemy combatants, these claims add up to what is easily the most aggressive formulation of presidential power in our history. . . . The stakes of the debate could hardly be higher: nothing is more basic to the operation of a constitutional government than the way it allocates power. . . . For better or worse, though, this is not the system envisioned by the framers of the Constitution.[58]

Because terrorism is a method of violence and not a specific, explicit enemy, and not likely to have an identifiable end, this new context of war and its implications for the application of checks and balances in the Constitution were potentially profound. Writing in another era, long before the ambiguities associated with modern terrorism, Corwin commented that "today the concept of 'war' as a special type of emergency warranting the relaxation of constitutional limits tends to spread, as it were, in both directions, so that there is not only 'the war before the war,' but the 'war after the war.'"[59]

The war motif of presidential authority can spread in other directions as well, including into the domestic sphere. President Bush, for example, did not use the veto power provided in the Constitution until the sixth year of his administration. Instead he relied on a practice begun in the Reagan administration of using "signing statements" (formal documents that presidents may choose to present when they sign bills into law) to identify provisions of statutes that he considered unconstitutional, whether relevant to foreign or domestic policy. Indeed, he took this approach to unprecedented levels. As of April 30, 2006, "President Bush has quietly claimed the authority to disobey 750 laws enacted since he took office, asserting that he has the power to set aside any statute passed by Congress when it conflicts with his interpretation of the Constitution. . . . Many legal scholars say they believe that Bush's theory about his own power goes too far and that he is seizing for himself some of the law-making role of Congress and the Constitution-interpreting role of the courts."[60] In the view of these scholars, the Constitution provides the veto power for presidents to block legislation they believe to be unconstitutional.

Separation of Powers: Public Perceptions

Although almost all Americans are exposed to the basic constitutional outlines of their government in the course of their primary and secondary educations, as noted in Chapter 1 in this volume, one may perhaps forgive the general public for retaining a less than nuanced understanding of these arrangements of institutions, powers, and checks and balances, especially as they have evolved in the modern era. In addition, given the general increased centrality of the presidency, the concentrated media coverage of the chief executive, and the contemporary expectations of executive leadership on everything ranging from the economy to the environment to international security, one may well assume that "'presidentialism' seems completely normal to most Americans, since it is the only arrangement most of us have ever known," even if President Bush took it to unprecedented heights.[61] It would not be a surprise, then, to find that the public in general fails to appreciate the governing parameters established by the separation of powers and checks and balances in the Constitution, uncritically accepts presidential power as paramount, does not recognize the implications of the government's complexity of institutions and authority, and longs for a more streamlined policymaking process that would bring policy resolution more quickly.

Nonetheless, the 2005 Annenberg Congress and Executive Branch and Courts surveys of the public reveal a people perhaps remarkably (although far from overwhelmingly) in tune with both the constitutional design and its intentional impediments to speedy action. When asked about the intention of the "founding fathers," 57 percent of all respondents (and 62 percent of those who expressed an opinion) recognized that it was "to have the president, Congress, and the Supreme Court have different but equal powers." Only 35 percent agreed with the erroneous proposition that the framers "intended each branch to have a lot of power, but the president to have the final say" (7 percent reported not knowing, and 1 percent did not give an answer). Why do not even more people get this fundamental question of American government correct? Level of education makes an enormous difference. As shown in Figure 1, even though to someone with an eighth-grade education the separation of powers should be familiar territory, those with a high school degree or less schooling—almost half of the population[62]—alarmingly split almost evenly in knowing whether the Constitution created branches of equal power or granted the president "the final say." Among the most educated Americans, those with at least college degrees, the figures are more comforting (80 percent to 17 percent overall for this group). Other than the boldest and most controversial assertions of some presidents, much of the development of the modern presidency has been more about affording the president an influential first say, a sustained say, but not a final one. A majority of citizens, and a supermajority of the most educated individuals, get that core point of American government.

Presidents may find it even more disconcerting that 70 percent of the public (82 percent of college graduates, 76 percent of informed individuals, and 75 percent of regular voters) agreed that "legislative checks are good" and only 20 percent believed that they "cause gridlock and inaction."[63] More generally, the public expressed beliefs about the general policymaking process that are quite consistent with the assumptions guiding the drafters of the Constitution and the fundamental arguments presented in the *Federalist Papers*.

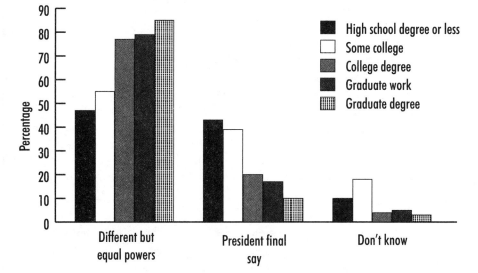

Figure 1 Understanding of Founders' Intentions for Power of Each Branch by Level of Education

Despite considerable media attention given to both partisan and individual squabbling among public officials, which could give a sense of artifice to policy disputes, about two-thirds of the public (in general, among the most educated, the most informed, and the most politically engaged) concluded that "conflict is a natural part of the policymaking process." Only 29 percent gravitated to the view that "policymakers create conflict where there need not be any." And given a choice between thinking that "the country would be better off if policymakers debated less and just took action" and that the nation "would be better off if policymakers discussed issues more thoroughly before acting," the public favored the latter assessment 79 percent to 17 percent. One senses the spirit of Madison smiling in contentment.

Survey research has long shown, however, that the public displays much greater acceptance of core governing concepts in the abstract than in practice. Make these trade-offs concrete, and broad minds can become parochial. People are far more inclined, for example, to support the First Amendment's protection of freedom of speech in principle than they are willing to permit actual speech of particular sorts that they find politically distasteful.[64] Our task now is to probe deeper, including comparing the public's views with those of policymakers (who have the benefit of greater knowledge and direct experience), as we sharpen the focus on more specific features of policymaking involving the separation of powers among the primary institutions of American government.

Shared Powers and the Activities of the Three Branches

Although one conventionally speaks of the separation of powers with checks and balances, the presidential scholar Richard Neustadt countered with the compelling observation in his classic work, *Presidential Power*, that in fact the Constitution "created a government of separated institutions *sharing* powers."[65] The three branches of government not only have the capacity to "check" one another, the very process of governing under the Constitution requires that they intersect and do so frequently, because policymaking is predicated on the concerted action of their shared powers. Their different constituency bases, resources, capabilities, and perspectives, though, promote the tension that can turn the invitation to struggle into actual contention, if not outright institutional warfare. When government action is under consideration and two of the branches each have authority to be involved in the policy decision, which one do the public and the respective policymakers believe has, or should have, the advantage, if any? Here we explore the possible pairings of institutions—the president and Congress, courts and the "political" institutions, and presidential and congressional influence on the courts—in each case presenting how the public and policymakers judge multiple points of their interaction.

The President and Congress

No interbranch relationship is more active or, likely, more important than that of the president and Congress. Most policymaking involves legislating, a government function that constitutionally requires the involvement of both Congress and the president. The emergence of the modern presidency with its presidential legislative program has made the chief executive's engagement with Congress a daily, if not an hourly, affair. Regular appointments made by the president to executive agencies and the courts lead to further continuous engagement.

Modern presidents typically send to Capitol Hill hundreds of initiatives, including numerous major proposals, with the White House and the agencies actively working the seams of politics to secure support for their priority legislative objectives. Because of the constitutional separation of powers, presidents, unlike prime ministers in command of parliamentary majorities, cannot expect the legislature to simply approve of their programs, or even to consider them. But Congress usually does take some kind of action and has enacted in some form roughly six in ten presidential initiatives in the modern era.[66] About half the time, too, these legislative encounters have been resolved in a fairly cooperative manner, either by consensus or by the negotiating of compromises.[67] Some periods have been more contentious, however. At least from the Nixon through the Carter administrations, and after the first year of the Reagan presidency, Congress was more willing to ignore the president's priorities and acted with fewer instances of consensus.[68] After the Republican takeover of Congress as a result of the 1994 election, President Clinton even felt compelled to announce that he was still relevant to the policymaking process.[69] Despite these periods of conflict, and the prominent instances when a presidential choice has prompted real battles in Congress, the relationship has been less contentious and rather more successful for presidents when they have sent treaties to the Senate for ratification or submitted their nominations of appointees to federal agencies and the courts for Senate confirmation.[70]

When it comes to the act of policymaking, which of these mutually dependent institutions—Congress or the presidency—is likely to perform more effectively? As noted earlier, the framers posited the primacy of the legislature and noted its more proximate connection to the people from which sovereignty springs. They also argued, however, via the pen of Alexander Hamilton, that while Congress would be appropriately slow in decision making and deliberative as different opinions competed, the "energy in the Executive is a leading character in the definition of good government," noting that the "unity" of the executive is "conducive to energy."[71] The executive connotes action, coherence, and direction. Moreover, with the more expansive policymaking demands engendered by the country's emergence as a military and economic power, and the rise of the modern social policy and regulatory state, presidents felt the call—which Congress often heeded—to provide a government of dispersed powers with greater responsibility and leadership.[72]

As before, the public seems to respond in ways reasonably consistent with these inherent policymaking trade-offs reflected in the innate strengths and weaknesses of legislature and executive. Even with the "presidency-centered" perspective of much scholarship and media coverage,[73] the public has not lost sight of the unusually significant role of Congress in the U.S. form of government. When asked, "When it comes to important decisions, do you think the decisions should be made by Congress or by the president?" 14 percent of the public said both, while the rest with opinions on this matter split 59 percent to 21 percent in favor of Congress. The survey also posed this question with respect to a series of specific policy areas (taxes and budget, foreign policy, homeland security, environment, and agriculture). Across these issue areas, as shown in Figure 2, Congress was chosen by 57 to 75 percent of the public, and the president by only 11 to 27 percent—with the president being looked to least for agricultural policy and most on foreign policy and homeland security. The public also expressed more confidence—57 percent to 36 percent (with an even slightly greater edge among college graduates)—that Congress, rather than the president, will "respond to the wishes of the public," and 50 percent to 42 percent that it will "act in the best interest of the people." When it comes to providing leadership, however, the tides are logically turned, with 56 percent (slightly more

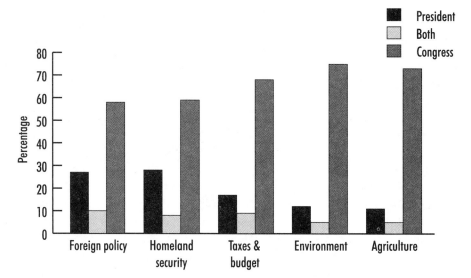

Figure 2   Public's View of Who Should Make Important Policy Decisions

among the educated and informed) favoring the president and just 38 percent giving the nod to Capitol Hill.

Having secured the primary leadership responsibilities in the complex system built around the separation of powers, facing all of the exigencies of modern government, how far can presidents push this broad recognition of their essential leadership role? Here, too, presidents are likely to be disappointed by the responses of the public and other policymakers. Despite the president's leadership advantage in policymaking, especially in foreign affairs, more people expect the legislature (56 percent) than the president (37 percent) "to make good policies." Well within the framework of "separated institutions sharing powers," neither the public nor policymakers in the legislative or executive branches wished to confer upon presidents an entirely free hand. The more expansive the proposed autonomy granted the chief executive, the more antagonism that both the public and elite survey respondents expressed.

On the one hand, modest majorities (in the 53–58 percent range) of the general public, informed citizens, and regular voters agreed that "if the president believes something should be done about an important national issue," then "other policymakers should defer to him." Perhaps surprisingly, only a bare majority of political appointees—the officials in the federal bureaucracy selected by presidents—shared that view. On the other hand, a slender majority of college graduates with an opinion on the issue joined significant majorities (about two-thirds) of congressional staff in opposition. Affirming that Congress is understood to be a separate and distinct branch of government, not a parliament expected to ratify the executive's proposals, the surveys reveal somewhat greater resistance to the notion that "if the president and the party that controls Congress agree on a policy matter, Congress should go along." Although favored by 52 percent of the public in the sample (and 55 percent of those who stated an opinion), disagreement with that proposition is found among 53 percent of college degree recipients, 80 percent of congressional staff, and majorities of career officials and even political appointees in the executive branch. When general deference becomes the particular matter of congressional acquiescence, it appears that a deliberative process is favored by much of the public and by most policymakers—led, of course, by the congressional staff projecting the legislature's institutional interests. Reflecting the nature of the expected give-and-take in American policymaking, required by a system of separation of powers with checks and balances, supermajorities of all kinds of survey respondents—from 80 to 90 percent—agreed that "even though it may result in compromise, the president should accommodate a wide range of interests in policymaking."

What if Congress passes legislation counter to the president's views or that contains provisions that the president believes are inconsistent with the Constitution? The Constitution itself furnishes the president with the veto power—a president can formally block the legislation, spelling out the reasons why in a statement to Congress. Congress may then choose to enact an amended version of the legislation that accommodates the president's objections. The specific threat of a veto by the president may also persuade Congress to adapt to the president's position, avoiding a direct confrontation.[74] As noted earlier, President Bush used the veto power but once in his first six years in office, instead permitting bills to become law but asserting in signing statements that the executive branch will not enforce provisions that contradict his interpretations of presidential authority and the Constitution. The public overwhelmingly rejects this approach to a presidential check on Congress. When there is "legislation the president thinks is good legislation but he thinks there is part of the legislation that is unconstitutional," almost three-quarters of the public (73 percent) agreed with the proposition that the president should "veto the legislation and send it back to Congress," while only 18 percent agreed with the proposition that the president should "sign the legislation but only carry out the part that he thinks is constitutional."[75]

The Annenberg surveys also posed a series of questions that asked about potential actions taken unilaterally by the president in the general area of foreign policy and national security, where modern presidents have enjoyed the greatest latitude from the public, Congress, and the courts; President Bush, in particular, had asserted expansive claims to "unitary" authority.[76] As shown in Figure 3, the suggestion that "the president should have the authority without the consent of Congress to disregard international laws or treaties to which the U.S. is a signatory" was rejected by all types of respondents by at least three to one. Even presidential appointees in the executive branch, the individuals regardless of partisan background who would most likely be sympathetic to the wielding of presidential power, were opposed 68 percent to 18 percent (another 8 percent volunteered that "it depends"). Surprisingly, the most support—33 percent—came from staff members in the Senate, the chamber of Congress that has the sole constitutional authority to ratify or reject treaties. There is somewhat greater endorsement of the president having "the authority without the consent of Congress to take preemptive military action, even if an attack is not imminent," but the public, congressional staff, and career and appointed officials in the executive branch all dissented by at least two to one (with an additional 8 percent of policymakers saying that it depends). The most opposition is expressed in reaction to the question, "Should the president have the authority without the consent of Congress to suspend constitutional protections for certain individuals?" Congressional staff and executive branch officials said no by well over five to one; the public was slightly more supportive (24 percent supported, 70 percent opposed). Even though these queries were posed after 9/11, in the midst of the United States battling the threat of terrorism and engaging the world as the sole superpower, and in the general domain of policymaking where presidential leadership is most recognized and desired, the supermajority responses underscore

Do you believe that the president should have the authority without the consent of Congress to:

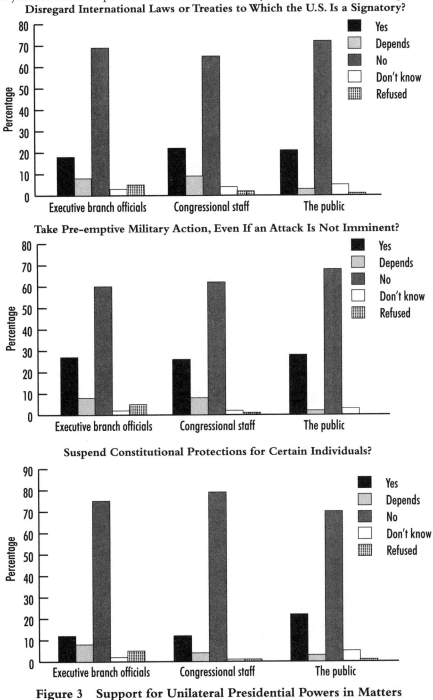

Figure 3   Support for Unilateral Presidential Powers in Matters
of National Security

the continued value of checks and balances in the minds of the public and public officials alike.[77]

One of the most intriguing areas of executive-legislative roles and relationships has to do with the management and oversight of the departments and agencies in the executive branch. A superficial understanding of the president as "chief executive," and the terminology "executive branch," may lead one to assume that the departments and agencies are formally arrayed in a bureaucratic hierarchy below the president. To be sure, the executive power resides in the president. The Constitution grants presidents the authority to nominate "officers of the United States," and they "may require the opinion, in writing, of the principal officer in each of the executive departments." In fact, however, the executive branch per se is not mentioned in the Constitution. Moreover, Article I confers upon Congress the revenue-raising and other legislative powers necessary to establish executive departments and agencies, and authorize and fund the programs that they administer. As Barry Weingast notes, "The federal bureaucracy is embedded in the American separation of powers system. . . . In a real sense, the bureaucracy is 'caught in the middle.'"[78] One could well inquire, however, whether this constitutional subtlety is understood by the public, actively secured by Congress, and willingly accommodated by executive branch officials. For the most part, the answer is yes. Once again the public shows firm recognition of what the separation of powers, with checks and balances, implies. When asked to "consider an agency that is running an established program," 50 percent of the public responded that Congress should have "about the same amount [of influence] as the president"; altogether, 78 percent believed that congressional influence should either match or exceed that of the chief executive (more than the combined total who would endorse either a balance of influence or greater presidential influence). Needless to say, congressional staff shared this predisposition, over half supporting equal balance with the president and another fifth indicating that Congress should have "somewhat more influence than the president" or even "almost all the influence over such an agency." There is less acquiescence from the executive officials themselves, though, even the permanent career officials who historically have the closest ties to the Hill. Fewer than a third favored balanced influence, and fully two-thirds expressed the view that Congress should have less influence than the president (including 6 percent who think Congress should have none)—tilting far more toward the president than the legislative staff leaned toward Congress. For an agency developing rules to implement a new statute enacted by Congress—thus writing the regulations that will fill in the programmatic intent of the legislation—the distribution of responses shifts a bit. Congressional staff are more emphatic about the role of Congress (36 percent said that the legislature should be more influential, on top of 48 percent holding to balanced influence). In this situation, 42 percent of executive officials supported balance, and only 44 percent (49 percent of political appointees) would give the advantage in influence to the president.[79]

The Courts and the "Political" Institutions

Ever since judicial review was asserted by the Supreme Court in *Marbury v. Madison*, federal courts in general, and the Supreme Court in particular, have had the capacity not only to impose limits on the two "political" institutions—the executive and Congress—but also to participate more directly in policymaking and its implementation. In addition to judging the compliance of federal law and administrative action with constitutional dictates, the courts also engage in statutory interpretation, assessing legislative intent and weighing administration actions to enforce the laws and assure, from their own perspectives in the judiciary, that implementing agencies are fulfilling their programmatic obligations. These activities of judges and justices, of course, raise questions about whether federal courts in the current era are remaining true to the judiciary's place in the system of separation of powers or, instead, have reached beyond the interbranch boundaries established by the Constitution and, in the view of critics, end up "legislating from the bench," the common refrain of conservatives.

Neither the public nor the lawyers who interact most frequently with the courts of appeals or Supreme Court express deep concerns about a judicial branch out of control. To start, the public seems to have some sense of the Supreme Court's more expansive role in a constitutional system. Only 31 percent (19 percent of college graduates) supported the narrowest reading of the Court's "primary role," believing it to be to "ensure that the judicial system runs smoothly." Nearly half (two-thirds of those with college degrees) viewed its primary function as "interpret[ing] the Constitution," and 14 percent adopted the most sweeping position, believing the Court's primary role is to "oversee the actions and policies of the federal government."

The public is rather more fuzzy on the details, however, even ones of some moment. Especially in the period from 1960 into the 1990s, but throughout the modern era, the Supreme Court has declared substantial numbers of federal statutes unconstitutional (sometimes dozens per decade) and overturned far more state and local laws (nearly two hundred in the 1970s), often on subjects receiving intense media coverage, such as bans on child pornography, special penalties for violence against women, strategies for gun control, prohibitions of flag burning, limitations on campaign finance, and the outlawing of homosexual sodomy by states.[80] It may be comforting to know that a majority of the general public (55 percent) recognized the long-settled fact that the Supreme Court "can . . . declare an act of Congress unconstitutional," but it should be worrisome that not only did 23 percent not know whether or not the Court has this power, more than a fifth (22 percent) explicitly, and mistakenly, claimed that it does not.

As revealed in Figure 4, level of education once again plays an important role in determining what Americans know about their system of government. Among the small part of the population with graduate degrees, relatively few (11 percent) indicated uncertainty about the Court's powers in this respect, and correct responses dominated incorrect ones seven to one. For the roughly half of the public holding at best a high school degree, 28 percent said they did not know whether the Court could declare laws unconstitutional, and the people who got it right (less than a majority, 45 percent) outnumbered those who did not by only 1.7 to 1. As reported in the introduction to this book, there is also considerable ambiguity among the public about whether presidents should follow Supreme Court rulings with which they disagree—a simple majority said yes, but close to four in ten responded that presidents should instead do what they think is in the nation's best interest. Less-educated Americans, whose knowledge and understanding of the American political system has been shown to be quite limited, are far more willing to leave important matters in the hands of the president alone. Among those with no more than a high school degree, more would grant full discretion to the president (49 percent) than believe he should comply with the Court's decision (43 percent). Individuals with at least a college degree reported a quite different understanding of checks and balances. Three-quarters (74 percent) responded that the president should follow the ruling of the Court, while only 20 percent said that the president should instead be free to do what he thinks is in the nation's best interest.

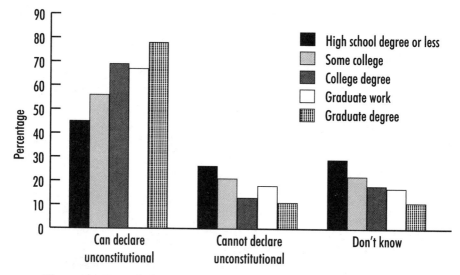

Figure 4   Knowledge That the Supreme Court Can Declare Laws Unconstitutional, by Level of Education

Have the federal courts used their authority to become too intimately involved in the overall political and policymaking process? The public does express a concern about the insinuation of politics into the judiciary, with 71 percent agreeing (37 percent strongly) that "the Supreme Court gets too mixed up in politics." But only a minority—about four in ten—responded that "the courts in general have too much power" or that the Supreme Court is excessively powerful. Just about half of the public, and approaching two-thirds of the most educated citizens, concluded that the courts, in particular the Supreme Court, have "just the right amount of power." The lawyers who practice before the major federal courts were even clearer in their judgment: 85 percent indicated that the courts possess an appropriate level of power, and only 10 percent stated that they have unwarranted power. To be specific, only 17 percent of the lawyers in the Annenberg survey thought that the Supreme Court "makes decisions in too many cases that are not within its mandate," and eight in ten rejected that claim. They offered these conclusions despite 70 percent suggesting that the "current Supreme Court [is] involved in policymaking" to a "great extent" or a "moderate extent" and 28 percent asserting that the Court's policymaking involvement had increased over the last decade (1995 to 2005); 12 percent believed it had declined; 56 percent that it had not changed. The vast majority of the lawyer respondents—87 percent—disagreed with the notion that "the Court is overturning too many federal laws" and 80 percent strongly disagreed (93 percent disagreed overall) with the idea, which has gained prominence among conservatives,[81] that "Congress should take away the right of the Supreme Court to decide certain types of controversial issues."

Presidential and Congressional Influence on the Courts

Short of the extraordinary act of altering the Supreme Court's jurisdiction by statute, the Constitution provides both the president and Congress with other, more routine means to affect the direction and decision making of the federal bench. The question remains, how should they be used and do they have any impact? A good place to start is the appointment of court personnel. The Annenberg surveys asked specifically about appointments to the U.S. Supreme Court and how the president and Congress should approach their constitutionally mandated roles. The public and the lawyers once again were in general concord. Each tended to support the position that both the president and Senate should "only consider [the] person's legal qualifications and background" when the president "chooses a Supreme Court nominee" and the Senate performs its "advise and consent" duties, rather than "also consider[ing] how [the] nominee might vote on controversial issues." To be clear, the public was more split (50 percent favored the sole focus on legal credentials and background—though 56 percent among college graduates—and 46 percent would look at how a nominee might vote), while the lawyers endorsed the sole reliance on qualifications rather than including possible voting positions 54 percent to 43 percent when the president selects a nominee and 63 percent to 34 percent when the Senate is weighing confirmation.

These positions on the appointment process may reflect concerns about protecting the judiciary's autonomy within the separation-of-powers system, harking—in reverse—back to Chief Justice John Marshall's distinction between "law" and "politics." The public and the lawyers at the courts of appeals or Supreme Court bar agreed that both the president and the legislature exert sway over decision making by the Supreme Court. Roughly 80 percent of the public and 75 percent of the lawyers saw some presidential or congressional influence over the Court's decisions (about 60 percent of the public estimated a "moderate" or "great" extent of influence; approximately only a third of the lawyers placed it that high). What is telling is the difference between the influence the lawyers perceived and what they believed, normatively, to be actually appropriate. Three quarters of them said that the Court's decisions should be "not at all" influenced by the president. They granted more leverage to Congress, but even in that case 58 percent suggested that it should not have any weight in the Court's decisions. Of course, attorneys are likely to take a legalistic approach to judicial institutions, even those engaged in policymaking. Other "experts" on the courts and judicial process—and judges and justices themselves—may have rather different perspectives on both the role of the courts and the proper application of checks and balances by elected officials.

Conclusion

The U.S. Constitution established a remarkably complicated governing structure for the nation, made all the more dynamic and complex by the imperative to govern in the modern age using, at the core, the same basic institutional framework set in place in the eighteenth century. The separation of powers among the three branches of government, with the various mechanisms for each branch to check and balance the others, is a paramount feature of American government. It compels deliberation (although not necessarily substantively rich deliberation) and cooperation among policymakers across the two chambers of the legislature and the other branches, if significant and enduring policymaking is to be accomplished.

The results from the Annenberg Institutions of Democracy surveys presented in this chapter suggest that a majority of the American public has a working grasp of the features and consequences of the separation of powers, including how the system has evolved, with the officials in each branch of government pursuing strategies to enhance their leverage within the policymaking process. The survey data also show that a majority of the public is roughly in tune with the realities of politics and policymaking created by American constitutional government, and that the public and insiders as a whole have similar worldviews of government power and the inherent complexities of the policymaking system. Given the intricacy of government, the political traumas of the times, and the media focus on political conflict and competition, often manipulated by politicians,[82] these may be considered remarkably optimistic and welcome assessments. In this most basic sense, the civics education that most Americans have received in their schooling and through exposure to media of politics and government appears to have had some long-standing success.

There are also worrisome signs, however, about how all too many people remain confused about the nation's governmental system and how insufficient primary and secondary education has been for producing a knowledgeable electorate. With respect to some essential features of government—such as the founders' intended division of authority among the three branches of government, and the later acceptance of judicial review of both congressional and presidential actions—substantial minorities or even pluralities of less-educated or informed citizens misunderstand the constitutional arrangements. The presence of simple majorities who seem to comprehend the fundamentals of American government and politics also obscures the potential incapacity of those with high school or less education—again, nearly half of the population—either to hold the nation's leadership accountable or to ensure the practical vitality of the system's means for checks and balances. On many (but not all) of the Annenberg survey questions that in one way or another touch upon presidential discretion or explicit checks on presidential power, these individuals were more likely than their more-educated fellow citizens to favor greater deference to the president.

In addition, two dynamics have been at play in American politics that may render overall a far less hopeful prognosis for the future health of the nation's governing institutions and policymaking process, each of which will be explored in depth in subsequent chapters. The first involves changes in the political party system. In the eighteenth century the rise of political parties immediately altered the character of the constitutional order and the operation of the institutions of government. Emerging late in the twentieth century, another shift associated with political parties transformed (or disrupted) the parameters of politics, intra-institutional procedures and norms, and policymaking. Since the mid-1970s, the parties in government have become increasingly ideological—more, often intensely, unified within their ranks and deeply divided between them.[83] The 2000 presidential and congressional elections and the subsequent elections held during the presidency of George W. Bush offer some evidence of parallel partisan alignments and intensities among the voters who form the electoral base of the political parties. Such intense partisanship has made policymaking in the separation-of-powers system especially conflict ridden, without necessarily enhancing legislative productivity under unified party government.[84]

The effects of partisan polarization may prove particularly problematic during subsequent periods of divided government. In the modern era it has been quite common—well over half the time from 1945 to 2006—for one party to hold a majority in Congress (or at least in one house of the legislature) while a president of the other party resides in the White House. When divided government occurs under such conditions of deep partisan and ideological divisions, as happened as a result of the 2006 congressional midterm election, the setting is primed for severe political combat, increasing dramatically the strain placed on the separation-of-powers system (as a stark illustration, one need only recall the temporary shutdown of much of the federal government in the 1995 struggle between the new Republican Congress and President Clinton).[85]

The second significant trend is the attempt of presidents in the modern era, with George W. Bush being far and away the most aggressive among them, to seek additional means to exercise influence over the scope of governmental authority dispersed by the separation of powers. At the extreme, as summarized in the Institutions of American Democracy series text *The Executive Branch*, "The imperative is to try to govern alone." The previous image of the modern president was one who "cajoles, bargains, and compromises, using the advantages of the office to the best of his or her ability, but always conscious of limits." For the unilateral president, however, "all other actors are effectively subordinate to the president and his team. . . . If they . . . disagree with the president, they are essentially irrelevant." This is an approach to presidential leadership that "is at great variance with the political system designed by the founders."[86]

Taken together, dramatically sharpened partisanship (especially with the prospect of divided government) and the emergence of the unilateral presidency could weaken the nation's representative institutions and transform the understanding and performance of checks and balances within the separation of powers. Instead of worrying about fundamental differences between the public and policymaking insiders writ large, or among insiders according to their institutional roles—neither of which were found to be present in the analysis presented here—the chapters that follow by Paul J. Quirk on Congress and Joel D. Aberbach on the executive branch direct readers' attention to a very different divide. Republicans and Democrats in Congress, in the executive branch, and among the public—capturing a core ideological schism in American society—have distinctly divergent views in the early twenty-first century, not only on matters of public policy, but also about the norms of how policy debate is engaged, the manner in which Congress legislates, the power of the presidency, and the basic organizational structure of government authority.

Notes

1. Lloyd N. Cutler, "To Form a Government," *Foreign Affairs* 59 (Fall 1980), 126–27.

2. Jimmy Carter, interview with Mark A. Peterson, Plains, Georgia, June 20, 1984.

3. Edward S. Corwin, *The President: Office and Powers* (New York: New York University Press, 1940), 200.

4. Mark A. Peterson, *Legislating Together: The White House and Capitol Hill from Eisenhower to Reagan* (Cambridge, Mass.: Harvard University Press, 1990).

5. Sarah A. Binder, *Stalemate: Causes and Consequences of Legislative Gridlock* (Washington, D.C.: Brookings Institution, 2003); Mark A. Peterson, "Stalemate: Opportunities, Gambles, and Miscalculations in Health Policy Innovation," unpublished book manuscript.

6. For this analysis, "educated" individuals are defined as those having at least an undergraduate college degree; "informed" are those who claim to pay a "great deal" or "fair amount" of attention to "policy decisions the federal government makes" *and* who believe that they "understand the issues the federal government deals with" at least "very well" or "somewhat well"; and "engaged" individuals are those who report having voted "regularly" in national elections.

7. Editorial, *New York Times*, December 23, 2005, A26.

8. Quoted in Douglas Jehl, "Spy Briefings Failed to Meet Legal Test, Lawmakers Say," *New York Times*, December 21, 2005, 36.

9. Joel D. Aberbach, "The State of the Contemporary Presidency: Or, Is Bush II Actually Ronald Reagan's Heir?" in *The George W. Bush Presidency: Appraisals and Prospects*, ed. Colin Campbell and Bert A. Rockman (Washington, D.C.: CQ Press, 2004); Joel D. Aberbach and Mark A. Peterson, "Control and Accountability: Dilemmas of the Executive Branch," in *The Executive Branch*, ed. Joel D. Aberbach and Mark A. Peterson, Institutions of American Democracy (New York: Oxford University Press, 2005).

10. Quoted in David E. Sanger and Eric Schmitt, "Cheney's Power No Longer Goes Unquestioned," *New York Times*, September 10, 2006, 22.

11. Quoted in Elizabeth Drew, "Power Grab," *New York Review of Books*, June 22, 2006, 10.

12. Quoted in Sheryl Gay Stolberg, "Republican Lawmakers Fire Back at Judiciary," *New York Times*, July 1, 2005, 10. See also Lawrence Baum, "The Future of the Judicial Branch: Courts and Democracy in the Twenty-First Century," in *The Judicial Branch*, ed. Kermit L. Hall and Kevin T. McGuire, Institutions of American Democracy (New York: Oxford University Press, 2005).

13. Joel D. Aberbach and Mark A. Peterson, "Presidents and Bureaucrats: The Executive Branch and American Democracy," in *The Executive Branch*, ed. Aberbach and Peterson, xxii.

14. James Madison, *Federalist 10*, in *The Federalist: A Commentary on the Constitution of the United States* (New York: Modern Library, 1947), 54.

15. James Madison, *Federalist 51*, in *The Federalist: A Commentary*, 337.

16. Ibid., 336.

17. Ibid., 337.

18. Charles Stewart III, "Congress and the Constitutional System," in *The Legislative Branch*, ed. Paul J. Quirk and Sarah A. Binder, Institutions of American Democracy (New York: Oxford University Press, 2005), 3.

19. William E. Nelson, "The Historical Foundations of the American Judiciary," in *The Judicial Branch*, ed. Hall and McGuire, 20.

20. Stewart, "Congress and the Constitutional System," 3.
21. Richard E. Neustadt, *Presidential Power: The Politics of Leadership* (New York: Wiley, 1960).
22. Richard A. Brisbin Jr., "The Judiciary and the Separation of Powers," in *The Judicial Branch*, ed. Hall and McGuire, 95.
23. Kermit L. Hall and Kevin T. McGuire, introduction to *The Judicial Branch*, xxi.
24. Scott C. James, "The Evolution of the Presidency: Between the Promise and the Fear," in *The Executive Branch*, ed. Aberbach and Peterson.
25. Stewart, "Congress and the Constitutional System," 23–24.
26. Aberbach and Peterson, "Presidents and Bureaucrats."
27. James, "The Evolution of the Presidency," 3.
28. Ibid., 10–21.
29. Stewart, "Congress and the Constitutional System," 24.
30. Andrew Rudalevige, "The Executive Branch and the Legislative Process," in *The Executive Branch*, ed. Aberbach and Peterson, 420–24.
31. James, "The Evolution of the Presidency," 27.
32. Brisbin, "The Judiciary and the Separation of Powers," 109.
33. Ibid. See also R. Shep Melnick, "The Courts, Jurisprudence, and the Executive Branch," in *The Executive Branch*, ed. Aberbach and Peterson, 470.
34. James, "The Evolution of the Presidency," 5.
35. Ibid. See also Melnick, "The Courts, Jurisprudence, and the Executive Branch," 453; and Stewart, "Congress and the Constitutional System," 26.
36. Brisbin, "The Judiciary and the Separation of Powers," 103.
37. James, "The Evolution of the Presidency," 3.
38. Stewart, "Congress and the Constitutional System," 28.
39. Ibid., 3.
40. Ibid., 27.
41. Paul J. Quirk and Sarah A. Binder, "Congress and American Democracy: Institutions and Performance," in *The Legislative Branch*, xx; and Forrest Maltzman, "Advice and Consent: Cooperation and Conflict in the Appointment of Federal Judges," in *The Legislative Branch*, ed. Quirk and Binder.
42. Brisbin, "The Judiciary and the Separation of Powers," 100.
43. Melnick, "The Courts, Jurisprudence, and the Executive Branch," 454.
44. Quirk and Binder, "Congress and American Democracy," xix.
45. Charles O. Jones, *The Presidency in a Separated System* (Washington, D.C.: Brookings Institution, 1994), Chapter 7.
46. Alexander Hamilton, *Federalist 78*, in *The Federalist: A Commentary*, 504. See also Nelson, "The Historical Foundations of the American Judiciary," 8.
47. Nelson, "The Historical Foundations of the American Judiciary," 5.
48. Brisbin, "The Judiciary and the Separation of Powers," 89.
49. Ibid., 98.
50. Nelson, "The Historical Foundations of the American Judiciary," 28; Cass R. Sunstein, "Judges and Democracy: The Changing Role of the United States Supreme Court," in *The Judicial Branch*, ed. Hall and McGuire, 49–50.
51. Hall and McGuire, introduction to *The Judicial Branch*, xxi.

52. Brisbin, "The Judiciary and the Separation of Powers," 90–95.

53. Sunstein, "Judges and Democracy," 33.

54. James, "The Evolution of the Presidency"; Richard M. Pious, *The American Presidency* (New York: Basic Books, 1979), 47; Louis Fisher, *Constitutional Conflicts between Congress and the President*, 3rd ed. (Lawrence: University of Kansas Press, 1991), 245–47.

55. Corwin, *The President*, 236.

56. Ibid., 262.

57. Gordon Silverstein, "Judicial Enhancement of Executive Power," in *The President, the Congress, and the Making of Foreign Policy*, ed. Paul E. Peterson (Norman: Oklahoma University Press, 1994), 44.

58. Noah Feldman, "Who Can Check the President?" *New York Times Magazine*, January 9, 2005, 52.

59. Corwin, *The President,* 262.

60. Charlie Savage, "Bush Challenges Hundreds of Laws, President Cites Powers of His Office," *Boston Globe*, April 30, 2006, A1.

61. Feldman, "Who Can Check the President?" 52.

62. In both of the Annenberg national public surveys used for the analysis in this chapter, 50 percent of the respondents reported having "a high school degree or less." That percentage is consistent with the 2004 census data for educational attainment of the population age fifteen years old and over—50.5 percent had high school degrees or stopped at a lower grade. U.S. Census Bureau, Current Population Survey, Table 4, "Educational Attainment of the Population 15 Years and Over, by Household Relationship, Age, Sex, and Hispanic Origin: 2004," www.census.gov/population/www/socdemo/eduacation/cps2004.html.

63. See Cutler, "To Form a Government."

64. James W. Protho and Charles M. Grigg, "Fundamental Principles of Democracy: Bases of Agreement and Disagreement," *Journal of Politics* 22 (May 1960), 276–94.

65. Neustadt, *Presidential Power*, 33.

66. Peterson, *Legislating Together*, 96; Andrew Rudalevige, *Managing the President's Program: Presidential Leadership and Legislative Policy Formulation* (Princeton, N.J.: Princeton University Press, 2002), 137.

67. Peterson, *Legislating Together*, 189.

68. Ibid.

69. Elizabeth Drew, *Showdown: The Struggle between the Gingrich Congress and the Clinton White House* (New York: Simon and Schuster, 1996).

70. Mark A. Peterson, "The President and Congress," in *The Presidency and the Political System*, ed. Michael Nelson, 6th ed. (Washington, D.C.: CQ Press, 2000), 478–81.

71. Alexander Hamilton, *Federalist 70*, in *The Federalist: A Commentary*, 454, 455, 458.

72. Aberbach and Peterson, "Presidents and Bureaucrats"; James, "The Evolution of the Presidency."

73. Peterson, *Legislating Together*, 3–6.

74. Charles M. Cameron, *Veto Bargaining: Presidents and the Politics of Negative Power* (Cambridge and New York: Cambridge University Press, 2000).

75. These results are from the 2006 Annenberg Judicial Independence survey.

76. John Yoo, *The Powers of War and Peace: The Constitution and Foreign Affairs after 9/11* (Chicago: University of Chicago Press, 2005).

77. There is a less reassuring interpretation to be given to these survey results. Anyone troubled by the aggressive and go-it-alone direction of American government and foreign policy following 9/11 may well be alarmed that as many as a fifth to a third of even the nation's most educated and informed citizens expressed support for unilateral presidential action to contravene treaties, launch unprovoked preemptive military strikes, and suspend constitutional protections for targeted individuals.

78. Barry R. Weingast, "Caught in the Middle: The President, Congress, and the Political-Bureaucratic System," in *The Executive Branch*, ed. Aberbach and Peterson, 313.

79. The public was not asked this question.

80. Harold W. Stanley and Richard G. Niemi, *Vital Statistics on American Politics, 2003–2004* (Washington, D.C.: CQ Press, 2003), 292; *Constitution of the United States, Analysis and Interpretation: 2002 Edition & 2004 Supplement*, including "Act of Congress Held Unconstitutional in Whole or in Part by the Supreme Court of the United States" (Washington, D.C.: Government Printing Office, 2002 and 2004), http://www.gpoaccess.gov/constitution/index.html.

81. Baum, "The Future of the Judicial Branch," 533.

82. Lawrence R. Jacobs and Robert Y. Shapiro, *Politicians Don't Pander: Political Manipulation and the Loss of Democratic Responsiveness* (Chicago: University of Chicago Press, 2000).

83. Barbara Sinclair, "Parties and Leadership in the House," and Steven S. Smith, "Parties and Leadership in the Senate," both in *The Legislative Branch*, ed. Quirk and Binder.

84. See Binder, *Stalemate*.

85. Drew, *Showdown*.

86. Aberbach and Peterson, "Control and Accountability," 529, 530, 548.

5

THE LEGISLATIVE BRANCH:
ASSESSING THE PARTISAN CONGRESS

Paul J. Quirk

The contemporary Congress is prone to nasty conflicts over procedures. In a 2003 meeting of the House Ways and Means Committee on a pension-reform bill, the Republican committee chair Bill Thomas of California brought up a ninety-page substitute bill that committee Republicans had drafted just the night before, and moved to bring it to a vote, even though the Democrats had not yet had a chance to read it. Amid angry words on both sides, Thomas refused the Democrats' demand for more time to study the bill. To delay action, the Democrats insisted on a full reading of the bill, a procedural formality usually dispensed with by unanimous consent. They then walked out of the committee room, with one member, Pete Stark of California, staying behind to monitor the proceedings, and met for further discussion in a nearby House library. Inexplicably, Thomas called upon the Capitol police to expel the Democrats from the library. But the police merely assured them that they were free to stay.

Back at the committee meeting, Stark got into a shouting match with one of the Republicans. When his opponent told Stark to "shut up," the seventy-one-year-old Stark challenged the Republican to "come over here and make me," calling him a "wimp" and a "fruitcake."[1] Thomas asked for unanimous consent to dispense with the reading of the bill, immediately brought down the gavel—ruling Stark's objection "too late"—and declared the consent given. The committee went ahead with the vote and approved the measure with all the other Democrats absent.

Outraged by the Democrats' exclusion from the decision process, the Democratic leadership introduced a formal resolution rebuking Thomas. The Democratic whip, Steny Hoyer of Maryland, blasted the Republicans: "You are trampling on the rights of the minority! You are trampling on the rules of this institution!"[2] The Republicans defeated the resolution, but some of them criticized the committee's conduct. It was "one of the saddest days we've had in the House," said a moderate Republican, Ray LaHood of Illinois. "What has happened to the Democrats is shameful."[3]

Meanwhile, in the Senate, a protracted dispute over the confirmation process for judicial nominees threatened to transform the fundamental character of the upper chamber.[4] During George W. Bush's first term as president, Democrats used the filibuster to block confirmation of ten nominees to the courts of appeals whom they criticized as ideologically extreme, ignoring Republican protests that the nominees were entitled to an up or down vote. To pressure the Democrats, the Senate majority leader, Bill Frist of Tennessee, in 2004 warned that Republicans might resort to a novel and inflammatory strategy to abolish the filibuster on judicial nominations. If the Democrats persisted, a Republican senator would raise a point of order to assert that filibustering a judicial nomination was unconstitutional. Senate precedents failed to support such a claim. But as Frist explained, a Republican presiding officer, possibly Vice President Dick Cheney, would rule in favor of the objection. And the Republican majority, organized in advance, would vote to uphold the ruling and proceed to act on the nominations.

Democrats threatened to retaliate by using every means available to block action on other matters important to the Republicans. They referred to the Republican plan as "the nuclear option," suggesting that it would destroy the Senate. Certainly it would severely compromise the Senate's long-standing consensual procedures for changing its rules.

In 2005 and 2006 a coalition of sixteen moderate Republican and Democratic senators negotiated an agreement to avert this collision. The Democrats agreed not to support a filibuster to block confirmation of a qualified mainstream conservative, and the Republicans agreed not to support cloture for an extreme nominee. The agreement facilitated the confirmation of two Supreme Court justices in 2006. But apart from this vaguely defined ad hoc agreement among a self-selected "Gang of 16," there was no resolution of the procedural dispute, and the Senate's traditional consensual practices remained at risk of collapse.

Although these conflicts surrounding the congressional rules of the game were especially dramatic, they were not isolated. Both the House and the Senate had seen numerous, often heated disputes about institutional rules and practices since the Republican takeover of Congress in 1995 and especially the beginning of the Bush presidency in 2001.[5] But what do such conflicts reveal, if anything, about the health of Congress?

This chapter looks at the changes that have occurred in Congress's structures, procedures, and ways of doing business. The causes of those changes are identified and their implications for performance are assessed. Going beyond anecdotal evidence, the discussion uses the Annenberg Congress survey of congressional staff to discover what insiders think about Congress's condition, and the Annenberg Congress and Executive Branch survey of the general public to consider the views of ordinary citizens.

In brief, this analysis finds grounds for serious concern about the condition and performance of the contemporary Congress in the first decade of the twenty-first century. As a result primarily of extraordinarily severe partisan conflict, Congress appeared to have lost some of its ability to perform important tasks—from resisting pressures from organized interest groups, to controlling budget deficits, to deliberating carefully about policy decisions, among others.[6] Even congressional insiders were quite critical of the institution—with Democrats, in particular, complaining of procedural disorder and unfair treatment by the majority. Complicating matters, the public distrusted Congress but was largely unaware of the main conditions that concerned insiders.

The concluding section of the chapter considers the prospects for reforms designed to strengthen Congress as an effective institution of American democracy. Among the difficulties, reformers must choose between, on the one hand, trying to restore Congress's traditional capabilities for bipartisan deliberation and cooperation and, on the other, working to solidify and improve emerging practices of party government.

People, Party, and Ideology

How an institution operates depends partly on the people who work in it—their qualifications, abilities, and dispositions. Popular lore holds that members of Congress are "political hacks." In fact, they are often impressively qualified. In important respects, so are their staffs. The only difficulty with the people in Congress is the increasingly severe ideological conflict between Republican and Democratic members.

Qualifications

For the most part, members of Congress arrive in Washington with impressive credentials.[7] Most members have had successful careers prior to holding elective office. They come from a wide range of occupations. In the House in the 107th Congress (2001–2), 159 members reported prior occupations in business or banking; 92 in education; and 156 in law. One hundred and twenty-six had worked in public service or politics. In the upper chamber, 24 senators reported occupations in business or banking; 16 in education; 53 in law; and 26 in public service.[8] As more specific examples, consider an arbitrarily selected handful of members—the four senators and seven representatives in 2006 whose last names began with the letter *A*. These members had been a college professor; an editor and publisher of a local newspaper and president of an advertising agency; a municipal judge and assistant legal adviser to a governor; a public school principal, director of a state agency, and gubernatorial assistant; a marketing manager for IBM and executive of a small steel company; a president of a state university; a veterinarian and owner of an animal hospital; an attorney; a Rhodes scholar, graduate of Harvard Law School, congressional staffer, and public policy consultant; and an attorney and adjunct professor at a state university law school.[9] In addition, most members had risen through the ranks of state and local elective office.

The congressional staff, if nothing else, is well educated. In the Annenberg Congressional Staff Component sample of 252 staff, nearly all had completed college degrees.[10] Most had attended prestigious private universities or major state universities, and 62 percent had graduate degrees or had done graduate work.

This formal education, however, comprises most of what the staff had to offer—they did not have much congressional experience. About half of the staff respondents had worked on Capitol Hill for five years or less, and the same proportion had worked for their current member for three years or less. Although a few staffers make a career of working on the Hill—one respondent had worked for the same member for thirty-five years—many just get their tickets punched there, so to speak, on the way to higher-paying jobs in law or lobbying. Less than 20 percent of the staff had worked for the same member for more than eight years.[11] In any case, whatever weaknesses Congress exhibits in its performance are certainly not due to any shortage of energetic, highly qualified people.

Party and Ideology

Those people, especially the members, are a problem in a different way, however. Difficulties arise from the members' partisan and ideological dispositions. Of course, unlike in the executive branch, where many high-level civil servants are political Independents, nearly all members of Congress and their staff are Democrats or Republicans. (A rare staff member and a very rare senator or representative is an Independent.) Over time, the balance of party power varies.[12] Sometimes one of the parties has been dominant within Congress; for example, the Democrats had nearly veto-proof majorities in the post-Watergate Congress of the mid-1970s. Since 1969 at least one chamber of Congress has been controlled by the party opposed to the president's party more often than not—with Democratic Congresses during most of the Republican presidencies of Nixon, Reagan, and George H.W. Bush, and Republican Congresses during most of the Clinton presidency. Republican President George W. Bush had the luxury of a Republican Congress until halfway into his second term, except for Democratic control of the Senate during most of his first two years in office.[13] But the party balance had been nearly even, with the Republicans holding only narrow majorities in both the House and the Senate. After the 2004 elections, Republicans controlled the Senate 55 to 44, with one Independent, and the House, 232 to 201, again with one Independent. After the sweeping Democratic gains of the 2006 election, the Democrats controlled the Senate 51–49 and the House 231–201.[14]

The most problematic feature of the personnel of the contemporary Congress is the sharp ideological conflict between the two parties, or ideological polarization.[15] Scholars have developed measures of the ideological positions of senators and representatives that permit valid comparisons over lengthy periods.[16] By historic standards, the contemporary Congress is extraordinarily polarized—with nearly all Democrats liberal or very liberal, nearly all Republicans conservative or very conservative, and few moderates in either party. As Sarah Binder notes, the two parties have had "virtually no ideological common ground."[17] In the 108th Congress, in fact, there was daylight between them: the most conservative Democrat was more liberal than the most liberal Republican. Figure 1 shows the ideological locations of the House members from each party in that Congress.

Although staff are not likely to alter significantly the policy preferences that Congress acts on, they are, if anything, a moderating influence. Nearly all staff respondents reported party identification consistent with that of the member they represented; only 2 percent reported identifying with the opposite party.[18]

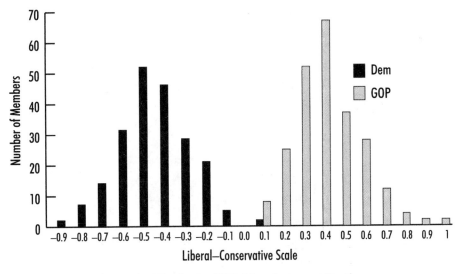

**Figure 1 Ideological Division between Parties:
The House in the 108th Congress**

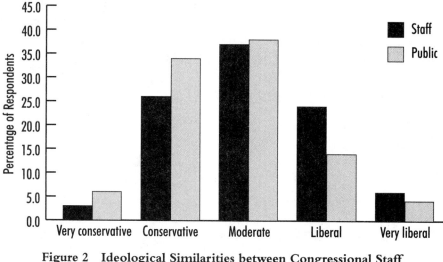

Figure 2   Ideological Similarities between Congressional Staff and General Public

Although the analysis does not include directly comparable measures of staff and member ideology, staff were evidently more moderate than the senators and representatives. Indeed, judging from the Annenberg surveys, staff ideological positions and policy preferences are comparable to those of the general public. Staff respondents were somewhat more liberal than the public, but they were no more prone to the extremes (see Figure 2). Thirty-seven percent of the staffers described themselves as moderate, and only 10 percent as "very liberal" or "very conservative."[19]

As this discussion will show, the sharp ideological differences between the senators and representatives of the two parties lead to significant difficulties in Congress's performance. To understand this performance, however, one must also consider the development of Congress's structures, procedures, and management practices.

Institutional Transformations: From the "Textbook" to the Partisan Congress

Most people probably think of Congress as a well-defined, elaborately organized institution, whose structures and methods of work were initially set by the Constitution and then followed a consistent path of development. Until the late twentieth century, academic literature largely supported that account, describing the main changes in Congress as a process of institutionalization.[20] In truth, Congress is a highly dynamic institution, whose modes of operation depend heavily on the state of party politics, prevailing policy concerns, and other circumstances.[21] In the idiom of a popular television game show of a generation ago, one might be tempted to ask, "Will the real Congress please stand up?" But there is no *real* Congress.

Constitutional Foundations

Article I of the Constitution, which contains provisions establishing the legislative branch, specifies the legal qualifications for the offices of senator and representative, the scheme of representation, some aspects of the electoral system, and the powers of Congress—which are most of the powers of the federal government.[22] But it has virtually nothing to say about how the House or the Senate will operate or their organizational structures. The article gives the vice president a vote in the Senate in the event of a tie vote of the senators. Most important, it states that "each House may determine the rules of its proceedings." In short, the House and Senate were each called upon to invent themselves.

They invented very different legislative bodies. What is most fundamental, the House and Senate differ dramatically in how they make decisions about rules and structures. On the one hand, the House makes such decisions through simple majority votes of the whole body. The majority party sticks together on those votes and, therefore, controls the outcomes. So House rules generally enhance the authority of the majority party. On the other hand, the Senate from an early point adopted rules that require a broad consensus to end debate and thus to act.[23] And those rules subsequently have been modified only in modest ways— most importantly, through the establishment of a cloture motion to end a filibuster. Compared with the House, therefore, Senate rules more often protect the interests of the minority party, and any other concerned minority.

In many other respects, the Senate and House have developed in response to similar forces. In a complex political process that Eric Schickler has described as "disjointed pluralism,"[24] members of each chamber seek to shape the institution to serve various, often competing purposes—to advance their policy interests, to alter the distribution of power among the members, to adjust Congress's relationship with the executive, to facilitate electorally beneficial credit-claiming and constituency service, and to vindicate party goals.[25] To a great extent, congressional institutions reflect the changing politics of the congressional parties— especially the intensity of the ideological and electoral conflicts between them.[26] After a long period of stability through most of the twentieth century, Congress has changed almost continuously from the early 1970s to the present.

The Textbook Congress

From 1909 to 1911, the House revolted against the authoritarian rule of Republican Speaker Joseph "Czar" Cannon, sharply reduced the Speaker's authority over committees and floor activity, and ushered in the period of what came to be known as the textbook Congress.[27] Its features were firmly established by 1930 and remained largely intact until the early 1970s. They also provided some of the virtues sought by the founders in their design of the separation of powers.

The central feature of the textbook Congress was the committee system.[28] Although committees were less important in the Senate than in the House, the main features of the two chambers' committee systems were similar. Members of each chamber sought appointment to standing committees on the basis of their constituency interests, policy concerns, or aspirations for congressional leadership. Variously composed committees on committees, with considerable influence from party leaders, made the appointments, often deferring to the members' preferences.[29] Once appointed, members could count on keeping their committee appointments as long as they continued to be reelected. The committee chair was selected strictly by seniority: the member of the majority party who had served on a committee for the longest time became the chair. With solid Democratic control of the South until the late 1960s, conservative southern Democrats enjoyed long careers and held numerous committee chairmanships.

The chairs, moreover, had a great deal of power over their committees. They created subcommittees, assigned them jurisdiction, appointed their members, selected their chairs, allocated their staff, including staff for the minority party—and decided which bills, if any, to delegate to them. A chair who wished to do so could deal with all of the committee's legislation in the full committee. The chair also largely determined the committee agenda, deciding which subjects to tackle and which bills to use as the starting point for committee action. A strong committee chair could put his or her stamp on committee legislation.

Most important, committee bills were usually approved by the full House or Senate without major amendments. Members observed a norm of reciprocal deference to the committees. And in the House, because most votes on floor amendments were not recorded, members were protected from constituency pressures to support them. The Senate, with fewer members, and with rules protecting the prerogatives of individual senators, permitted more scope for floor-based entrepreneurship. But even in the Senate most policymaking was done in committee.

The respective majority party leaders—the Speaker of the House and the Senate majority leader—played coordinating rather than directive roles.[30] Along with the House Rules Committee, they controlled the scheduling of floor action, and thus had leverage over Congress's agenda. But this agenda control was mostly limited to allocating time for agenda items initiated by others. The party leaders did not define their respective party agendas. The parties operated whip systems to keep leaders abreast of the members' intentions on a bill, to gently lobby them, and occasionally to make deals for their support; but these systems provided very little actual discipline.[31] Partisan conflict, therefore, was subdued.

Indeed, until the mid-1970s a conservative coalition of Republicans and southern Democrats often dominated the legislative process.[32]

These institutional dynamics were reflected in the character of policymaking. Legislation reflected committee preferences, constituency interests, and expertise, and generally had a conservative tilt. Many policies were bipartisan, with major bills often passing by overwhelming majorities.[33] Importantly, Democrats and Republicans sometimes set aside conflicting partisan interests to pursue common interests of the nation.[34]

What was generally overlooked about the textbook Congress was how it depended upon the peculiar and inherently vulnerable alignments of southern politics.[35] A century after Reconstruction, the South, the most conservative region of the country, remained loyal to the generally liberal Democratic Party. There also remained pockets of liberal Republicanism in the Northeast. Both parties were split ideologically and mostly incapable of exerting discipline. They could easily cooperate because they overlapped considerably in their ideological positions.

The Reform Congress

In the early 1970s, a series of dramatic institutional changes, styled "reforms" by their advocates, swept away the textbook Congress.[36] Elections in 1958, 1964, and especially 1974—following the Watergate scandal—greatly expanded the liberal wing of the congressional Democratic Party. The resulting large numbers of junior liberal Democrats, along with many Republicans, were dissatisfied with a Congress dominated by the so-called barons, the committee chairs. Liberals especially disliked the disproportionate influence of the conservative southern Democrats who occupied many of the chairmanships. The reforms commenced a period of structural churning that continued into the twenty-first century.

The most dramatic changes of the reform period occurred in the House.[37] The Legislative Reorganization Act of 1970 provided for the recording of roll call votes on amendments in the Committee of the Whole. The publication of these votes, in many instances, strengthened members' incentives to support amendments to committee bills. It thus encouraged members to propose such amendments, and led to a dramatic increase in floor amending activity and a corresponding decrease in deference to the committees. Solidly under liberal control, the Democratic Caucus imposed a "Subcommittee Bill of Rights" that transformed the operations of the House. It weakened committee chairs and strengthened subcommittees, subcommittee leaders, and rank-and-file committee members. For example, the measure required chairs to assign subcommittees definite jurisdictions and to allow them to control their own agendas.

To bind committee chairs more strongly to party priorities, the caucus also abolished the seniority rule and provided for electing the committee chairs.[38] In 1975 the caucus fired three southern committee chairs—putting all chairs on notice that they needed to cater to the rank-and-file members and refrain from obstructing liberal bills. The caucus also gave the Speaker greater powers over the committees, including more direct authority over the appointment of committee members.

The Senate, which had never accorded as much authority to the committees as the House, took steps in similar directions.[39] Senate Democrats spread attractive committee assignments more broadly among the members. They also relaxed the seniority rule and gave the majority leader and the party caucus more control over the appointment of committee chairs.

Aside from the general measures concerning committees and party leaders, Congress effected an historic reform of the congressional budget process.[40] Charging Congress with fiscal irresponsibility, the Nixon administration simply refused to spend funds that Congress had appropriated. In an effort to restore its credibility, Congress created several new institutions and procedures to overcome the fragmentation and lack of coordination in prior congressional budgeting—including House and Senate Budget Committees, a Congressional Budget Office, and a concurrent budget resolution to define priorities. Budget reform ensured that Congress would make explicit decisions about the broad dimensions of fiscal policy, and would have means for enforcing those decisions.

Policymaking in the reform Congress, as intended by the reformers, was often highly responsive to liberal policy impulses, such as environmentalism and consumer protection. With the propensity toward making policy on the House or Senate floor, it was also chaotic and disorganized. Carefully constructed coalitions unraveled, and policies took unexpected turns, during floor action. During the Jimmy Carter presidency, from 1977 to 1980, the reform Congress was relatively unproductive, despite unified Democratic control of the two branches.

The Partisan Congress

The liberal Democrats' efforts in the 1970s to reduce committee autonomy and strengthen responsiveness to party priorities proved to be just the beginning of a thirty-year movement, promoted by both parties, toward greater party leadership and discipline. The shift reflected an increasing ideological polarization between the two parties from the 1970s into the first decade of the twenty-first century.

There were several causes of this polarization.[41] A geographic realignment of the parties erased regional alignments that had been established during the Civil War and Reconstruction. Southern Democrats, who were generally moderate, were replaced by Republicans, who were mostly very conservative. Northern Republicans, who were generally moderate, were replaced by Democrats, who were mostly very liberal. In addition, however, moderates were being replaced by ideological hard-liners in both parties all over the country, as ideological groups in both parties became more active in primary election campaigns.[42] Moreover, highly partisan redistricting processes in most states multiplied the number of safe districts, those likely to elect hard-liners of the dominant party. As a result of all these developments, both congressional parties moved toward their respective ideological extremes—especially the Republicans.[43]

By the late 1980s, commentators were describing a so-called postreform Congress, an institution pulling back from the excesses of fragmentation and individualism produced in the reform period.[44] After the 1982 election, House Democrats sought to fashion a congressional party organization that could do battle effectively with the aggressively conservative Reagan administration. Since then, both parties have designed party rules and promoted arrangements in Congress that were designed mainly to advance partisan policy and political objectives. They have given secondary priority, at best, to enhancing Congress as an institution, or to distributing opportunities for influence and participation.

Since the late 1990s, moreover, conflict between the parties has intensified because, in addition to the sharp ideological differences between them, control of each chamber of Congress has been closely contested.[45] Since the 1994 election, the majority party in the House has never had more than 234 seats (16 more than a bare majority), and the majority party in the Senate has never had more than 55 seats (4 more than a bare majority)—the most closely contested control of Congress in half a century.[46] Most members have been intensely concerned, therefore, with strengthening their party's prospects in the next election.

After the Republican takeover of Congress in the 1994 election, the movement toward centralized and disciplined party control accelerated. Led by Speaker Newt Gingrich, the House Republicans adopted measures to transform the committees into instruments of the party.[47] Erasing the decentralizing measures of the reform period, they gave committee chairs plenary authority over the subcommittees; the full committee chairs determined the subcommittees' jurisdictions, appointed their chairs, assigned their staff, and decided whether and when to refer bills to them. In a word, subcommittees became creatures of the full committee chair.

In turn, the Republicans gave party entities, especially the Speaker, powerful leverage over the committee chairs. They imposed six-year term limits on committee chairmanships and required reappointment at the beginning of every Congress. The Republican Conference selected chairs largely on grounds of ideological commitment and party loyalty. In a few cases, Gingrich simply named his personal choice for a chairmanship, despite the absence of any authority for him to do so in the party rules. The Senate Republicans took somewhat more restrained steps to discipline the committees. Thus both the committee barons of the textbook era and the entrepreneurial subcommittee chairs of the reform era were eliminated. So too, however, was some of the ability of a hardworking committee chair—like Wilbur Mills of the House Ways and Means Committee or

Sam Nunn of the Senate Armed Services Committee—to bring expertise and institutional memory to bear on committee decisions.

Beyond bringing the committees to heel, Republicans in both chambers greatly expanded the roles of party committees, the party conferences, and especially the leadership in developing legislation. To a considerable extent, the leadership has decided the major provisions of important bills and conveyed instructions to the committees; the committee's task, in such a case, has been to work out the details. The Republican leadership has sometimes bypassed the committees entirely. When committees were bogged down or headed in a direction the leadership did not favor, they have used the extraordinary procedure of drafting their own bills and taking them directly to the House or Senate floor.[48] More often, the leaders have incorporated major policy decisions in omnibus budget measures, where they could be decided without involvement by the substantive committees. Whether the leadership actually bypasses the committees or just gives them specific instructions, they substitute deliberation within party councils, or among themselves, for the public hearings and two-party discussion and amendment processes of conventional committee deliberation.

Finally, both congressional parties, in both chambers, elaborated their whip organizations, enabling the leadership to lobby for members' support on party agenda issues. More than in the past, the whip organizations not only inform and cajole reluctant members; they also apply pressure. Members who withhold their support on party issues realize that the leadership may reciprocate by denying desired committee appointments, chairmanships, or other advantages.

During the George W. Bush administration, the Republican congressional agenda was mainly to enact the president's program. The Republicans followed the administration's lead not only when it fit their own preferences, such as in cutting taxes, but even, for the most part, when administration policies departed from mainstream Republican policies. The Republicans dutifully helped pass Bush's education reform and his expansion of a Medicare program to cover prescription drugs, and only occasionally asserted an independent position. Republicans in Congress allowed Bush's social security proposal, featuring long-term benefit cuts, to languish in 2005 and 2006, and helped kill an administration-approved transfer of port-management operations at several U.S. ports to a corporation based in the United Arab Emirates. Nevertheless, congressional Republicans recognized that their own policy and political success was tightly bound to the president's. The Bush Congress was one of the most deferential to a presidential administration since the founding.

Party leadership in the contemporary Congress is not cast in the authoritarian mold of Czar Cannon. According to Barbara Sinclair, House Republican leaders have had the members' enthusiastic support for an assertive approach. They also recruit members to serve on party committees and task forces that help shape the party agenda.[49]

The Republican leaders, however, have been much less accommodating of the Democratic minority—especially in the House. On party-agenda legislation, the House leadership has often allowed the Democrats to bring up only a single floor amendment—namely, a Democratic substitute for the entire Republican bill. The leaders calculate that few Republicans will defect from the party if the result is to abandon the party bill. The Democrats, therefore, have an opportunity to defend their alternative policies in floor debate, but virtually no chance to affect the outcome. Nor do Republicans who might prefer some aspects of the Democratic proposal have a real opportunity to consider them.

In some instances, the Republican leadership used their control of the agenda and procedures more heavy-handedly to minimize the Democrats' influence. Republican delegations to conference committees sometimes excluded Democrats from meetings in which they negotiated the differences between House and Senate bills—not only outvoting the minority, as a unified majority can always do, but also preventing them from making their case. On some bills, the Republicans used control of a conference committee to do an end run around a Democratic filibuster in the Senate. They made concessions to the Democrats in the Senate to avoid a filibuster, and then simply ignored the Senate bill, with support by Senate Republicans, in the conference committee. In violation of House traditions, the Republican leadership held floor votes open for up to three hours, enabling Republicans to round up enough votes to turn defeat into victory. Democrats complained that such manipulation deprived them of elementary fairness. Then–House minority leader Nancy Pelosi pronounced in one case that "this vote was stolen from us by the Republicans."[50] As described above, Republicans in turn objected violently to Democratic filibustering to block confirmation of several of Bush's judicial nominees. In 2004 Senate minority leader Tom Daschle called the preceding session the "single most partisan session" of Congress in his experience.[51]

By President Bush's second term, it was clear that the partisan Congress of the first decade of the twenty-first century represented a departure from any Congress since well before Daschle's experience—at least the beginning of the twentieth century. On some views, however, the partisan Congress represents only a different, not necessarily a worse, form of representative democracy—in a word, party government.[52] The remaining sections examine the performance of the contemporary Congress more closely.

Assessing Performance

This section examines several dimensions of congressional performance, considering the judgments and perceptions of insiders in Congress's work—the congressional staff—and taking stock of significant episodes in legislative policymaking. The focus here is not only on insider perceptions of Congress and its performance, but on the degree of conflict between Democratic and Republican views. The assumption is that if congressional elites generally are deeply critical of Congress, or if Democratic and Republican elites have fundamentally conflicting perceptions of the institution, this reflects an unhealthy institution.

The survey data in this section derive from the 2004 Annenberg Congress survey of congressional staff. The sample, again, includes 252 staff members, working in legislatively relevant capacities—chief of staff, legislative director, legislative assistant, and other similar positions—in 190 Congress members' offices. These include 70 from Senate offices (39 Republicans, 31 Democrats) and 182 from representatives' offices (76 Republicans, 105 Democrats, and 1 Independent).

The study sought to ensure that responses reflected a wide range of congressional policymaking, not just activity on a few exceptionally salient issues, such as tax cuts or the Iraq war. Thus respondents were asked early in the interview to identify, in their own words, the principal policy area they were responsible for dealing with (or, if they did not specialize, the main area of their member's activity). Then, for many of the subsequent questions, they were asked to report perceptions about policymaking in their own chamber in that same area—using question wording that repeated their description. That is, they were asked to report perceptions about policymaking on environmental policy in the House, tax policy in the Senate, homeland security in the Senate, or the like—as appropriate to the given staff member. The staff identified a wide range of issues and issue areas—from agriculture to defense, and from Medicare to Indian affairs, among many others. For some purposes the identified policy areas were divided into six categories that are likely to reflect different political and institutional conditions. As noted above, staff respondents were relatively moderate ideologically. One can suppose that their perceptions and evaluations of Congress were, if anything, less polarized than those of members.

Influence and Participation

Congressional staff who responded to the survey largely agreed about the broad outlines of the distribution of influence in the contemporary Congress. Majorities in both parties reported that two groups—the White House and Executive Office of the President, and the Republican leadership of the House or Senate—had "a great deal" of influence in the respondent's chamber and area of policy (see Figure 3). More than 55 percent of Republican respondents attributed such influence to each of these groups, as did 68–70 percent of the Democrats. These findings underline the centralization of power and deference to presidential leadership in the contemporary Republican Congress. The strength of these findings is impressive, considering that respondents addressed a wide range of policy areas, not just a few issues at the top of the presidential or

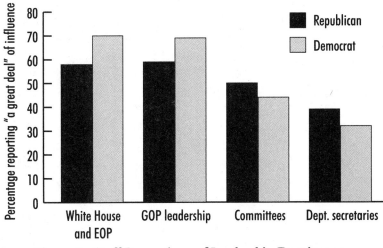

Figure 3   Staff Perceptions of Leadership Dominance

party agenda. Democrats perceived highly centralized power more often than Republicans did; but majorities of both parties held that view.

Democratic and Republican staff respondents also largely agreed about actors who had "not too much" or no influence (see Figure 4). More than 65 percent in both parties said that the Democratic leadership in the House or Senate did not have much influence, and about 70 percent offered this view of the

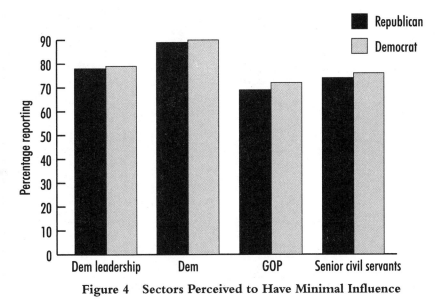

Figure 4   Sectors Perceived to Have Minimal Influence

Democratic rank and file. These perceptions of minimal influence on the part of the minority party—even the minority leadership—suggest a major departure from the consensus-seeking tendency historically associated with American politics. Large majorities (64 percent among Republicans and 66 percent among Democrats) attributed modest influence to senior civil servants. More remarkable, respondents saw modest influence even among the Republican rank and file. Indeed, a majority (59 percent) of the Republican respondents themselves judged that Republican rank-and-file members had little or no influence.

Also noteworthy, the committees—for most of the twentieth century the central actors in the legislative process—were seen as only moderately influential. Only half of the Republicans and 44 percent of the Democrats assigned the committees a great deal of influence. Department secretaries were rated somewhat lower, still in the moderate range, with 39 percent of Republican staff and 32 percent of Democratic staff attributing a great deal of influence to them. That the committees barely beat out department secretaries in perceived influence demonstrates their diminished role in the legislative process.

Relationships and Procedures

While largely agreeing about who has and does not have influence, respondents differed sharply about the character of the central relationships in the legislative process—above all, the relationship between the majority and minority parties. Regardless of their influence, competing actors can interact in different ways. They may seek to identify and promote common interests; or they may focus on conflicting interests. They may listen to each other's concerns and proposals with open minds, or refuse to do so.[53]

Staff respondents expressed generally negative views—and revealed dramatic partisan differences—in characterizing the working relationships in the contemporary Congress. They were asked: "More broadly, how often do Republicans and Democrats, in general, agree on important matters" in the respondent's area of policy, and were given response options of "often," "occasionally," or "rarely." Most staff found agreement between the parties in short supply. Only about one-quarter (27 percent) of the overall sample reported that agreement between the parties occurred often on important matters. Almost as many—23 percent—reported that it occurred rarely, with the largest group, 50 percent, seeing agreement occasionally. Reflecting the more consensual style of the upper chamber, Senate staff were more likely to report frequent agreement (34 percent) than House staff (25 percent). Republicans were somewhat more upbeat on the frequency of agreement (with 36 percent reporting it "often") than Democrats (20 percent). Judging from these responses, the legislative process in Congress largely does not consist of efforts at problem solving, intended to serve widely shared interests. It is mostly a matter of opposing parties seeking to advance partisan goals.

Even if the two parties do not agree, the majority party, especially its leadership, might listen to the minority and make efforts to accommodate its interests. At least in the view of the Democratic staff respondents, however, the Republican majority in place at the time of the survey was not so inclined. Nearly all Democratic staff (90 percent) agreed or agreed strongly with respect to policymaking in their chamber and area of policy that "the majority party leadership make most of the important policy decisions." More striking, the same 90 percent of the Democrats agreed that "the majority party makes policy decisions regardless of the minority's views"—with 47 percent agreeing strongly.

Republican staff had essentially the same views on the dominance of the majority leadership; 75 percent of the Republicans agreed that their leadership made most of the important decisions. Most Republicans did not agree that their party ignored the minority's views; but even among Republicans, 35 percent endorsed that account of the party's methods. Finally, one might think that the majority's tendency toward dictating decisions would not affect areas of policy with considerable agreement between the parties. But in fact even the 20 percent of Democratic staff who said that the parties agree "often," overwhelmingly said that the majority makes decisions without regard for the minority views, with 81 percent endorsing that claim.

Even if the Republican majority generally ignored the Democratic minority's views, it might at least maintain orderly procedures—ensuring careful consideration of bills and affording the minority a fair chance to argue its case. Here again, however, Democratic staff offered a less benign portrayal. Only a third of Democratic staff endorsed the statement that, in their chamber and area of policy, "the decision making process faithfully follows established rules and procedures." Sixty-four percent rejected the statement, in effect lodging a complaint about a lack of procedural regularity. The preponderance of Republicans took the opposite view, with 79 percent agreeing with the statement. But even 16 percent of the Republicans joined the Democrats in rejecting the statement, and another 6 percent refrained from offering an opinion. The concern about procedural regularity was especially strong in the House, where only 29 percent of Democratic staffers reported faithful adherence to established procedures.

To find out how legislative processes and relationships varied with the issues at stake, the survey used the staff respondents' primary areas of responsibility to divide them into five relatively coherent policy areas, plus a residual area.[54] Staff in the areas of taxes, budget, and economic policy; social policy; and energy and environmental policy perceived the least agreement between the parties. Democratic staff in these areas were most likely to report that the majority party made policy decisions without regard for the minority. For example, the fifteen Democratic staff with responsibilities in the area of energy and environmental policy made that report unanimously.

In some respects, staff saw more frequent agreement in the areas of sectoral and economic development policy (where 51 percent reported frequent agreement) and foreign and security policy (43 percent). But even in these areas, most Democrats felt that Republicans made decisions regardless of the minority's views. The contemporary Congress appears to miss opportunities for bipartisan consultation and accommodation even when a foundation of underlying agreement exists.

Policymaking

The staff survey included several items that asked respondents to assess policymaking in their own chamber and self-designated area of policy. As is to be expected, Republican staff took a more favorable view of congressional performance than Democratic staff. Democrats were more critical of the House than the Senate, where the minority party usually has more leverage; Republicans were more critical of the Senate. Aside from these expected differences, the two parties' responses tracked each other fairly well. Evidence is found for some of the difficulties one might expect with extreme partisan conflict, obsessive electoral rivalry, and manipulation and shortcutting of decision processes. The critical assessments are especially significant in that respondents were asked about their own chamber and area of policy; one might expect a bias toward favorable responses.

An overwhelming majority of the staff respondents perceived Congress as excessively influenced by narrow organized groups. Most respondents (54 percent) said that interest group representatives had a great deal or a fair amount of influence in their chamber and area of policy—a result comparable to that for congressional committees. Three-quarters of them agreed that "policies are distorted by pressure from special interests."[55] Moreover, even though allegations of excessive deference to business interest groups were a major theme of Democratic attacks on the Republican Congress, Republican staff mostly echoed the criticism about interest group distortion, rather than rejecting it.

Indeed, the Bush-era Republican Congress enacted several important laws that bestowed large benefits on business and industry groups. A major measure expanding Medicare to provide prescription drug coverage for the elderly, for example, gave the drug and insurance industries control of the program on terms that would result in high profits, limited coverage, and complexity and inconvenience for beneficiaries.[56] Congress enacted an energy program whose central provisions reportedly had been drafted by the industry and conveyed to the White House in secret meetings with Vice President Cheney. Democrats portrayed these bills as rewards for corporate lobbying, campaign contributions, and ties with leading administration figures, including the president and vice president.[57] Republicans defended the measures as curbing governmental interference with the economy. Congress also restored costly and inefficient farm subsidies that had been eliminated in a major reform law in 2002; it developed the most expensive, pork-laden highway bill in the history of the federal highway program; and it dramatically expanded the use of special-interest earmarks directing funds to particular states and districts.[58]

In 2005 and 2006, the role of lobbyists and interest groups in Congress came under unusual scrutiny. Bribery and influence-peddling investigations implicated several Congress members in the largest congressional corruption scandal in a quarter-century. Jack Abramoff, a lobbyist with close ties to many Republicans, including then–House majority leader Tom DeLay, pled guilty to charges of fraud, tax evasion, and conspiracy to bribe public officials. A key DeLay aide pled guilty to influence peddling, and DeLay resigned from the House as he awaited trial on separate charges of campaign finance violations. A Republican House member, Bob Ney, pleaded guilty to accepting bribes. As of fall 2006, several other members were reportedly still under investigation.

The Abramoff investigation turned up unusually explicit evidence of the use of campaign contributions to influence legislation. The popular image of interest groups using contributions to buy legislation is wildly exaggerated; as a general matter, research shows that contributions do not in fact change many votes.[59] But an e-mail message from a deputy in Abramoff's lobbying firm, uncovered in the investigation, demonstrated that the firm expected the Republican leadership to earn their contributions through action benefiting the firm's clients: "We're going to seriously reconsider our priorities in the [political donation] lists . . . if our friends don't weigh in with some juice. If leadership isn't going to cash in a chit for (easily) our most important project, then they are out of luck from here on out."[60]

The scandal prompted a reform effort. In 2006 the Republican leadership in both chambers pushed ethics and lobbying reform bills intended to respond to public concern about the scandal and defuse criticism of the Republican Congress in a midterm-election year.[61] Speaker of the House Dennis Hastert called for prohibiting members from accepting gifts from lobbyists or taking privately sponsored trips. Others introduced measures to reform earmarks, one of the principal devices used by members to deliver benefits to special interests.[62] By the fall of 2006, however, reform ardor had cooled. Republicans were divided on the gift and travel bans, and it was unlikely that Congress would adopt substantial reforms.

Considering that the staff were asked about their own areas of policy, rather than a few issues widely covered in the media, it is significant that many reported that the influence of public opinion was strong. Thirty-two percent said that the general public had a great deal or a fair amount of influence over policymaking in their respective chambers and areas of policy. In principle, such influence is desirable; public opinion should shape policy outcomes in a representative democracy.

But many staff described conditions that suggest a likelihood of problematic consequences. On the one hand, most felt that the public was quite concerned about their area of policy. Thirty-one percent of the staff said that "the general public notices and cares about the policies" in their area "a great deal," and another 43 percent said "a fair amount." On the other hand, they did not perceive a comparable level of understanding. Even of those who said that the public cared a great deal, 39 percent also said that the public understood those policies somewhat poorly or very poorly. (If anything, these responses undoubtedly overestimate actual public understanding of issues facing Congress. As survey research has shown, most citizens know very little about public policy.[63]) This combination of public concern about an issue and lack of understanding of it entails obvious risks—namely, that the public, perhaps owing to manipulative appeals by political leaders, may impose demands for unworkable or counterproductive policies.[64] And in fact a majority of staff respondents in both parties, 55 percent, reported that policymaking in their areas was distorted by pressure from uninformed citizens, with similar findings in the House and Senate. That a majority reported this effect is especially significant considering that many respondents worked in policy areas to which relatively few citizens pay much attention.

Although identifying cases is always somewhat controversial, there have been several very important plausible instances of such distortion of policymaking in recent Congresses. The apparent potential for strong voter responses helped to account for tax and budget policies in Bush's first term that the nonpartisan comptroller general called the most fiscally irresponsible in U.S. history.[65] The impetus for major tax cuts came primarily from conservative activists, Republicans in Congress, and the Bush administration, not from public demand.[66] But many in Congress, including moderate Democrats, went along with them because they feared angering voters by opposing tax cuts. Even the Republicans shrank from cutting middle-class entitlements or other popular spending programs enough to pay for the tax cuts. Bush's 2005 social security reform proposal—designed partly to correct a long-term imbalance between obligations and revenues—died largely because congressional Republicans were afraid to give Democrats a campaign issue by enacting a modest reduction in the growth of benefits.[67] In 2006, deferring to public fear of terrorism, Congress enacted a Bush administration bill that authorized constitutionally dubious military tribunals and sanctioned interrogation methods apparently in violation of the Geneva Convention on Human Rights.[68] Even though interest-group pressures probably affect more issues than public opinion, the pressures that arise from superficial media coverage, manipulative popular rhetoric, and an uninformed public may affect broader, more consequential ones.

The external pressures from interest groups and public opinion, among other things, appear to compromise the quality of deliberation about policy decisions. Many staff respondents to the survey, including a large majority of the Democrats, offered critical assessments of Congress's deliberative performance. On the positive side, most respondents (72 percent) said that Congress often or almost always has the information that it should have about the likely consequences of policies.[69] Most Democrats and some Republicans, however, offered a dim view of what Congress does with such information. Respondents were asked to choose between two views of how the House or Senate uses information in making policy decisions in their area: (1) that "it looks at the relevant information quite objectively," or (2) that "it often overlooks or distorts relevant information." Responses were sharply partisan. Seventy-four percent of Democrats said that their chamber overlooks or distorts, and only 21 percent that it looks at information objectively. Republican responses were just the reverse: 77 percent said Congress looks at information objectively, and only 19 percent that it overlooks or distorts. A close analysis of congressional debate from the mid-1990s to the early 2000s on welfare reform, telecommunications deregulation, and estate-tax repeal indicates a high rate of such distortion.[70]

Similarly, an overwhelming 90 percent of Democrats said that policies in their area are based on ideological beliefs, rather than evidence. On this point 37 percent of Republicans agreed, although the majority rejected the criticism. Put simply, Democratic staff doubted Congress's ability to act upon reliable evidence about problems and policies, and here again, a considerable number of Republicans agreed.

The Bush-era Congress was criticized as ignoring the evidence or distorting reality in several areas. Throughout the first six years of the Bush presidency, Congress acted on rosy estimates of long-term budget balances, with the consequence of accumulating massive long-term deficits. In pursuit of the Christian conservative agenda, it favored education and public-service programs that promote sexual abstinence rather than contraception, despite a lack of evidence that such programs actually reduce sexual activity. In debating the repeal of the inheritance tax, Republican advocates exaggerated by orders of magnitude the tiny percentage of the population actually subject to the tax.[71] Most important, Congress failed to undertake a thorough examination of the Bush administration's case for preemptive war in Iraq. It voted to authorize the war two days after receiving a lengthy intelligence report on Iraq's alleged possession of weapons of mass destruction. As subsequent analysis demonstrated, a rigorous assessment of the evidence would have revealed the weakness of the administration's claims.[72] A more adequate deliberative process might have prevented the war.

Considering that policymaking in the contemporary Congress is largely dominated by the majority party and is prone to superficial deliberation, one might expect it to be, at least, efficient—able to produce important policy changes relatively rapidly. That expectation is not borne out by the staff surveys. About half of the respondents in each party agreed strongly that "significant policy change is extremely difficult." Most of the rest agreed somewhat, with only one in ten rejecting the statement. Notwithstanding the unusual level of coordination and discipline that characterized the majority Republican Party, enduring features of Congress—bicameralism, separation of powers, the Senate filibuster, the committee system, geographic representation, and candidate-centered election campaigns—often frustrate efforts to produce policy change.

In the end, congressional staff provided an ambivalent and highly partisan assessment of Congress's performance. Most said that in general they trusted Congress to operate in the best interests of the American people. Ninety percent of the Republicans expressed such trust, and even a sizable majority of the Democrats (62 percent) did so. Yet far fewer gave positive assessments of policymaking performance in their respective chambers and areas of policy. Only a 66 percent majority of the Republicans pronounced that performance good or very good; a third of the Republicans (34 percent) called it fair or poor. The preponderance of the Democrats, 82 percent, rated policymaking in their areas fair or poor. It seems that most staff who responded to the survey felt that Congress and Congress members seek, in general, to benefit the public. But only two-thirds of the Republicans and one-fifth of the Democrats believed that Congress actually performs satisfactorily in policymaking. In a word, perhaps, the members have good intentions, but the institutions get in the way.

Congressional Elections and Democratic Performance

The most important process for an elected legislature, from the standpoint of democracy, is, of course, the election. Unfortunately, congressional elections in recent years have fallen short of reasonable expectations for a well-functioning democratic electoral system.[73] To varying degrees, Congress itself is implicated in the shortcomings, through its actions and omissions on issues concerning the conduct of elections. In particular, congressional elections have had three problematic aspects.

First, the system of financing congressional election campaigns, based entirely on private contributions, arguably has several adverse effects.[74] It creates a danger, and sometimes the reality, of corrupt or inappropriate influence on the part of contributors.[75] Even in the absence of any actual influence, it leads to the appearances and reasonable suspicions of corrupt influence—compromising the legitimacy of the legislative process and potentially undermining public trust. Regardless of any apparent wrongdoing, the privately based campaign finance system tilts the electoral competition to the advantage of candidates, or the political party, with superior access to private contributions. It even enables extremely wealthy individuals to finance their own, generously funded campaigns. Democratic senator Jon Corzine spent more than $50 million of his own money to narrowly win a Senate seat from New Jersey in 2000—suggesting that a wealthy candidate can buy a seat in Congress.

Since the Bipartisan Campaign Reform Act (BCRA) of 2002, which eliminated unregulated "soft money" contributions to candidates and parties, a large proportion of campaign advertising has been sponsored by independent groups, the so-called 527 committees, such as the liberal Americans Coming Together (ACT), which spent more than $76 million to help Democratic candidates in 2004, and the conservative Progress for America, which spent more than $35 million to help Republicans.[76] These groups sponsor advertisements on behalf of selected candidates, without explicitly coordinating with them. The candidates, therefore, cannot be held responsible for the advertisements, an invitation to reckless and misleading appeals.

Several circumstances have militated against effective regulation of campaign finance. Opponents of such regulation argue that campaign contributions are essentially a form of political speech, and that Congress should not, or cannot constitutionally, interfere with them. The Supreme Court has partly endorsed that view. It ruled in 1976 that Congress can regulate campaign contributions—for example, limiting the amount that an individual can donate to a single candidate—but that it cannot regulate campaign spending—such as by limiting independent expenditures or total spending by a candidate. The two parties often have conflicting interests in campaign finance legislation. Republicans raise more money than Democrats from individuals; Democrats raise more of their funds from political action committees (PACs). Each party wants to protect its best sources of funding.

Since the 1980s, large majorities of the public have supported campaign finance reform; but only rarely has more than a tiny sliver of the public identified campaign finance as one of the most important problems facing the country.[77] The BCRA was adopted only after the Enron scandal boosted public concern about corporate misconduct. In any case, the public has not supported public financing of congressional campaigns—which is probably the only workable means of reducing the role of private contributions.

Second, the rhetoric of election campaigns, for Congress as well as other offices, has become increasingly manipulative, misleading, and scurrilous.[78] Critics and citizens often complain when campaigns are "negative." But negative appeals can be pertinent and useful to voters: "my opponent supported the war in Iraq," "voted to cut social security," "has no experience," or the like.[79] The real problem is that the negative appeals are often disreputable—using unsupported innuendo about personal misconduct, or gross distortion of policy positions. In a 2006 House race in California, for example, a television advertisement sponsored by the National Republican Congressional Committee claimed that the Democratic candidate, as a member of a school board, had "praised a teacher reported to have child porn saying he was always willing to lend a hand." It failed to mention that she had also voted to fire the teacher.[80] Such methods, used by both parties, are more distracting than informative.

No prospect for an end of such campaigning, or even a significant reduction in its prominence, is in sight. Under the First Amendment, Congress cannot prohibit innuendo or distortion in political campaigns. It could create forums or provide resources for campaign debate under conditions that would encourage responsible conduct. But doing so would require a widespread recognition that does not now exist of a national interest in more intelligent, responsible campaign discourse.

Third, largely as a result of redistricting decisions within each state since the late twentieth century, the number of competitive seats in the House has declined almost to the vanishing point.[81] Partisan influence in the redrawing of district lines after each decennial census has led to the proliferation of seats that are safe for one party or the other. If Republicans control the redistricting process in a state—as they have in states with a majority of House seats during the post-2000 redistricting—they create as many safe Republican seats as possible. They crowd Democratic voters into as few districts as possible—making the Democratic seats even safer than the Republican ones. In the 2004 House elections, 97 percent of incumbents won reelection by more than a 10 percent margin, and only five were defeated. Considering that many states are safe for one party or the other in Senate elections, and that only one-third of the Senate seats are up for election every two years, Congress has become virtually immune to substantial short-term change in its partisan composition. In 2006, even with pre-election polls for several months pointing toward a banner Democratic year in the total national vote for the House, it was not until a week or two before the election that analysts expected a Democratic takeover of the House.[82]

Congressional elections, therefore, have lost most of their ability to transmit changing preferences in the electorate into the halls of government—a central function of democratic elections.[83] In this area, Congress has potential leverage. It could enact standards or procedures for congressional redistricting that would reduce partisan influence and favor or even require creation of competitive districts. But there has been no public demand for such reform. One reason may be that the redistricting process, by maximizing the number of safe seats, also maximizes the number of voters whose preferred candidate wins election. Although national outcomes are unresponsive to changes in national opinion, therefore, most voters are satisfied with the local result.

In short, contemporary congressional elections are severely flawed exercises in democracy. Through various kinds of legislation, Congress has means to mitigate, if not to overcome, each of the problematic features of these elections. But with the exception of highly conflicted efforts to reform campaign finance, it has shown little interest in addressing them. One lesson is that elected officials, especially those of the majority party, have little incentive to challenge the arrangements that put them in office.

The Public and Congress

What does the American public think of Congress? The question is pertinent from several perspectives.[84] In the first place, the public is the ultimate sovereign in a democracy, and has a right to be satisfied with Congress's structures and performance, or if it is not satisfied, to demand change. From another perspective, however, Congress is part of a constitutional system, and the public should understand and help to maintain that system. Finally, the public may play a role in advancing the prospects for reforms to improve congressional performance, or may fail to do so. Regardless of the perspective, however, a central fact (also noted in previous chapters) is that few citizens pay enough attention to Congress to make informed judgments.

The 2004–5 Annenberg Congress and Executive Branch survey of the general public asked a number of questions about Congress. Some were designed to find out how much ordinary citizens know about the institution. As with other studies of citizen attitudes toward Congress, the results reveal a public that pays very little attention to events in the national legislature.[85]

To begin with, respondents were asked whether they knew which party controlled the Senate. Most respondents (74 percent) correctly identified the Republican Party, indicating that most had some awareness of current political events. They were also asked whether they could identify the jobs of two political figures, Bill Frist (then the Senate majority leader), and Nancy Pelosi (then House minority leader). Correct answers were defined liberally—to include, in Pelosi's case, for example, House Democratic leader or Democratic congressional leader.[86] Only 8 percent were able to identify both leaders. Of respondents who had at least a college degree, 19 percent were able to do so.

In addition, respondents were given a series of names, with the explanation that some of them were prominent in Washington and some were not, and were asked which ones they recognized. Nearly all (95 percent) said they recognized Edward Kennedy, and more than half (56 percent) Orrin Hatch, two of the most recognizable senators. But only about 28 percent, on average, recognized four Congress members from a second tier of prominence (Barney Frank, David Dreier, Chuck Hagel, and Dick Durbin). Moreover, considering that an average of 21 percent said that they recognized each of two fictitious characters, a large fraction of the 28 percent was probably guessing.[87] Probably about one in ten citizens pay enough attention to Congress to reliably distinguish names of relatively prominent members from those of fictitious characters.

Most respondents, accordingly, were unaware of the sharply increased partisan conflict that has been the most dramatic and important institutional development in Congress in recent years. In one of a series of questions about Congress, respondents were asked, "Do you think the Democrats and the Republicans agree with each other more now than they did in the past, less now than in the past, or about the same amount?" A third of the respondents (33 percent) said the parties agree less than in the past, by all accounts the correct answer. Forty-seven percent said they agree about the same amount as in the past, and 17 percent said they agree more. College-educated respondents did somewhat better, with 42 percent correctly reporting less agreement. Considering the frequency of wrong answers (64 percent), most respondents probably guessed the answer to this question. And probably no more than 15–20 percent had actually been aware of the increased conflict.[88] While having such information about Congress is not essential for competent citizenship, the findings suggest that few citizens make informed judgments about the condition of the institution.

In the absence of much information, many citizens seem to base their judgments about Congress on their impressions about the moral character of politicians.[89] Most have an unfavorable view of it: Although a sizable minority of the general-public respondents (36 percent) said that Congress and the president do what they think is best for the country, a 52 percent majority said that Congress and the president do what they think is popular with the voters. These negative views probably reflect, among other things, citizens' responses to the unedifying features of contemporary elections—the frequently misleading, manipulative appeals and especially the prominence of private money. In May 2006, amid several congressional ethics scandals, nearly half of the public (47 percent) agreed with the extraordinary statement that "most members of Congress are corrupt," up from 38 percent five months earlier, according to a Gallup Poll.[90]

Motivation, in the view of citizens, goes a long way in determining performance. Of those respondents who saw members of Congress as trying to please voters, only 17 percent rated Congress's performance in policymaking good or very good. Of those who saw them as trying to serve the country's interests, a substantial 42 percent assigned those favorable ratings. The results were similar on trusting Congress to operate in the best interests of the American people: those who perceived members of Congress trying to do what is best for the country also trusted Congress as a whole to succeed in doing so. These responses show the lack of any awareness of institutional constraints. If citizens believe that members of Congress have their hearts in the right place, they believe that Congress does a good job of serving the country.

At the same time, most citizens make few distinctions between institutions. A narrow majority of the public (56 percent) expressed trust in Congress. But essentially identical majorities trusted the federal government, federal agencies, and the president—with only the Supreme Court scoring several percentage points higher, at 63 percent. Along with the respondents' lack of specific information about Congress, this pattern suggests that public trust in Congress mainly reflects attitudes toward politics and government in general. No one should embark on a campaign to reform Congress, or for that matter, to block reforms, on the basis of the public's attitudes toward the institution.

Even so, the public is to some degree a potential resource for protecting or enhancing Congress. At least in the abstract, it wants Congress to play a major role in the political system. A strong 59 percent majority said that important policy decisions should be made by Congress. Only about one-third as many (21 percent) preferred the president for such decisions. And the findings were not significantly different for respondents who were asked about decisions in areas that have generally been dominated by the president, such as foreign policy and national security. In effect, the public allocates power between Congress and the president much as the framers might have allocated it, if they had answered the question in 1789. Put less charitably, the public responded as if it were oblivious to the broad, sustained, and widely accepted expansion of presidential power that was a signal development of twentieth-century American politics.

On the other hand, the public is sometimes inconsistent in making judgments about presidential and congressional roles. Despite the general preference for congressional responsibility, two-thirds (66 percent) endorsed the statement that "if the president believes something should be done about an important national issue, other policymakers should defer to him." In fact, the public proved to be tolerant of Bush administration practices that arrogated new powers to the president, such as the use of signing statements to negate provisions of legislation.

The public is a potential force for certain kinds of reforms. On the one hand, its chronic suspicion about corruption and self-interested behavior in Congress provides an automatic base of support for reform of campaign finance, ethics, and lobbying. The public is energized and attentive to these issues, however, only during episodes of scandal. On the other hand, the public's lack of awareness of the polarized conflict of the contemporary Congress suggests that any effort to moderate such conflict would have to be driven entirely by elites. With respect to redistricting reform, for example, most respondents (69 percent) had not heard of redistricting plans in their state; had not heard that the plans often reduce competition (66 percent); and had not heard that they give a large advantage to one party or the other (55 percent). Only one-quarter (25 percent) responded that redistricting reform is very important.

Conclusion

Is Congress a healthy institution of representative democracy? What are the implications of current and foreseeable developments?

On the evidence presented here, there are grounds for serious concern. Some of the features of the legislative process that historically defined Congress's contribution to the American political system have been significantly compromised in the contemporary partisan Congress. Individual senators and representatives have lost a good deal of their ability to represent the distinct interests and preferences of their states or districts. With the increased party discipline of recent years, they instead represent primarily the core constituencies of the national Democratic or Republican Party.

The House and Senate floor, and especially the standing committees, have lost much of their role of deliberating about public policy. Policy increasingly has been determined by party committees, the leadership, or, during the Bush administration, the White House; the committees have had the task of filling in the details. As a result, the legislative process no longer routinely subjects major legislative proposals to thorough discussion, with participation by both parties, exposure to public observation, and opportunity for amendment by freely forming majorities in the committee or on the chamber floor. Indeed, the majority party manipulates legislative procedures precisely to avoid such discussion.

Finally, the two parties have lost much of their ability to cooperate on behalf of important national interests. Partisan conflict on legislative issues has become more intense in the first decade of the twenty-first century because electoral competition for control of each chamber of Congress, as well as the presidency, has been almost evenly balanced. With both parties in contention to run the government after the next election, each party has focused primarily on the electoral implications of legislative issues.

There have been two kinds of adverse consequences. First, Congress has lost legitimacy in the eyes of one important group, the minority party. In the Annenberg survey, Democratic staff leveled severe criticisms at the Republican-controlled Congress. Large majorities of Democrats said that it distorted and overlooked information and that the majority acted without regard for the views of the minority. Most important, they charged Republicans with failing even to follow established rules and procedures in their management of the legislative process. A minimal requirement for a healthy legislature is that the legislators, including those of the minority party, believe that it follows reasonably fair and orderly procedures, such that all members can discharge their constitutional roles. In the absence of this belief, procedural opportunism is likely to become more extreme. At some point, the abandonment of procedural regularity threatens the basis for consent in a democratic political system.

Second, Congress has demonstrated significant weaknesses in policymaking. Although any assessment is subject to challenge, the Congresses of the first six years of the Bush presidency were widely criticized for enacting ideologically extreme measures, such as tax cuts targeted toward wealthy taxpayers; for deferring to organized interest groups, mostly representing business, in areas such as energy, the environment, and prescription drugs; for catering to uninformed popular demands on Medicare, social security, and budget policy; for dramatically expanding appropriations earmarks and other district- and state-targeted spending, including by far the most expensive highway bill ever enacted; for failing to constrain constitutionally dubious administration policies on homeland security and surveillance; and, above all, for uncritically accepting a vague, unsubstantiated administration case for preemptive war in Iraq. In a word, there was considerable evidence of impaired performance in legislative policymaking.

The partisan Congress has defenders, and they make a cogent point.[91] The dominance of the majority party in the contemporary Congress is hardly an aberration from the standpoint of democracy. Party government is a defensible conception of representative democracy, and indeed the one that underlies parliamentary government, the world's most prevalent democratic constitutional system.[92] And it does not rely upon the capabilities that have been compromised in the contemporary Congress. The opposing parties in a parliamentary system do not deliberate together. Rather, each party develops its own program, and the electorate chooses one of them to govern. Some critics of American government have long argued the superiority of a strong party system over the loosely organized, deadlock-prone traditional American parties. To a great extent, the trends in the contemporary Congress are giving these reformers their wish.

Yet the partisan Congress and its institutional setting differ, in crucial respects, from the arrangements of parliamentary government. For one thing, the government in a parliamentary system—that is, the ruling party or coalition—relies heavily on advice from a respected, nonpartisan higher civil service to ensure the substantive soundness of its policy initiatives.[93] By contrast, the American executive branch is deeply politicized, with the higher levels of the administrative hierarchy occupied by several hundred political appointees.[94] Its advice to Congress is heavily implicated with party ideology and the president's agenda. The partisan Congress thus has no institutional support for legislative deliberation, comparable to the higher civil service in a parliamentary democracy, to make up for the reduced role of the committees and floor debate.

In addition, unlike in a parliamentary system, the partisan Congress is likely to encounter periods of divided party control—either between the presidency and Congress, or between the House and Senate. From the late 1960s to the early 1990s, there were frequent periods of divided party control of the presidency and Congress. In a seminal study, David Mayhew produced empirical evidence that divided government had essentially no effect on legislative productivity, congressional investigations, the size of the budget deficit, or other dimensions of legislative performance.[95] Subsequent, more refined analyses demonstrated some effects on legislative productivity.[96] Nevertheless, it remains clear that divided government had indeed functioned reasonably effectively during those decades.

To project such performance into the future, however, would be exceedingly optimistic. As ideological conflict between the parties in Congress becomes more sharply drawn and intense, and cooperation between them more difficult and rare, division of party control between the president and Congress will also have more drastic consequences. A Congress that does not readily form bipartisan coalitions will have trouble cooperating with a president of the opposite party.

The prospects for the performance of the partisan Congress are not attractive. As elections produce, in turn, unified and then divided party control, it may lurch from acting with minimal deliberation on an extreme ideological agenda in one Congress, to being mired in partisan warfare in the next.

Notes

1. Juliet Eilperin and Albert B. Crenshaw, "The House That Roared: In Ways and Means Brawl, Names, Police, and Sergeant at Arms Are Called," *Washington Post*, July 19, 2003, A1. The quotation attributed to Representative Stark has been edited for brevity and to remove apparent minor errors of transcription.
2. Quoted in Sheryl Gay Stolberg, "Sound, Fury, Pension Rules: Nasty Party Clash in House," *New York Times*, July 19, 2003, A1.
3. Quoted in Eilperin and Crenshaw, "The House That Roared," A1.
4. Forrest Maltzmann, "Advice and Consent: Cooperation and Conflict in Appointment of Federal Judges," in *The Legislative Branch*, ed. Paul J. Quirk and Sarah A. Binder, Institutions of American Democracy (New York: Oxford University Press, 2005), 407–31.
5. Thomas E. Mann and Norman J. Ornstein, *The Broken Branch: How Congress Is Failing America and How to Get It Back on Track* (New York: Oxford University Press, 2006).
6. As can be seen in Chapter 6 in this volume, the contemporary Republican Congress also surrendered many of its constitutional prerogatives to an institutionally aggressive president of the same party.
7. Roger H. Davidson and Walter J. Oleszek, *Congress and Its Members* (Washington, D.C.: CQ Press, 2002).
8. Norman J. Ornstein, Thomas E. Mann, and Michael J. Malbin, *Vital Statistics on Congress*, 2001–2 (Washington, D.C.: American Enterprise Institute for Public Policy Research, 2002), Tables 1-8, 1-11.
9. Michael Barone and Richard E. Cohen, *The Almanac of American Politics 2006* (Washington, D.C.: National Journal, 2006).
10. Reflecting the relative sizes of the two chambers, the sample has a roughly 2.5 to 1 ratio of House to Senate staffers. Where chamber differences are significant, the findings are reported separately.
11. Susan Webb Hammond, *Congressional Caucuses in National Policy Making* (Baltimore, Md.: John Hopkins University Press, 1998). The Senate, whose members have more prestige and individual influence than House members, had somewhat better-qualified staff—with 70 percent having done graduate work (compared with 59 percent in the House), and 60 percent having six or more years of Hill experience (compared with 50 percent in the House). There were also some party differences—with Democratic staff respondents about twice as likely as Republicans to have attended

a prestigious private university (28 percent to 13 percent), and twice as likely to be female (36 percent to 18 percent).

12. Sarah A. Binder, "Elections, Parties, and Governance," in *The Legislative Branch*, ed. Quirk and Binder, 148–70; Gary Jacobson, *The Politics of Congressional Elections*, 6th ed. (New York: Longman, 2004); David W. Brady, *Critical Elections and Congressional Policy Making* (Stanford, Calif.: Stanford University Press, 1998).

13. After the 2000 election, the Senate was evenly split, with fifty Republicans and fifty Democrats (including one Independent who voted with the Democrats on organizational matters), giving the Republican vice president, Dick Cheney, the tie-breaking vote. But Republican senator Jim Jeffords of Vermont switched to the Democrats in the spring of 2001, giving majority control to the Democrats until 2003.

14. At the time of this writing in early December 2006, three House races were not yet decided.

15. Jon R. Bond and Richard Fleisher, eds., *Polarized Politics: Congress and the President in a Partisan Era* (Washington, D.C.: CQ Press, 2000).

16. Keith T. Poole and Howard Rosenthal, *Congress: A Political-Economic History of Roll Call Voting* (New York: Oxford University Press, 1997). These measures take advantage of the substantial continuity of House and Senate membership to compare the ideological positions of bills considered in different Congresses. The ratings of the bills make it possible, in turn, to compare members who served in different Congresses. Although the changing congressional agenda makes the measures somewhat suspect for comparisons of members over long periods (was Newt Gingrich more conservative than Henry Clay?), they permit one to describe the degree of party polarization in a precise and meaningful way over the whole span of American history.

17. Binder, "Elections, Parties, and Governance," 153.

18. In analyzing the survey data, the party affiliation of the senator or representative was used to characterize the staff member.

19. The moderation was apparent on ideologically charged issues. Only about half (49 percent) of the Republican staff said that keeping taxes low was a "very important" responsibility of the federal government; only about one-third (32 percent) said that of protecting the unborn. By the same token, only about half of the Democratic staff (52 percent) said that promoting racial equality was very important, and 60 percent said that of reducing poverty.

20. Nelson W. Polsby, "The Institutionalization of the U.S. House of Representatives," *American Political Science Review* 26 (March 1968), 144–68.

21. Nelson W. Polsby, *How Congress Evolves: Social Bases of Institutional Change* (New York: Oxford University Press, 2004).

22. Charles Stewart III, "Congress and the Constitutional System," in *The Legislative Branch*, ed. Quirk and Binder, 3–34.

23. With no apparent awareness of the significance of the change, the Senate early in the nineteenth century abolished the motion to call the previous question. It thus enabled any senator to insist on the right to speak or to offer amendments, on any measure, without limit. Steven S. Smith, "Parties and Leadership in the Senate," in *The Legislative Branch*, ed. Quirk and Binder, 255–78.

24. Eric Schickler, "Institutional Development of Congress," in *The Legislative Branch*, ed. Quirk and Binder, 35–62; Eric Schickler, *Disjointed Pluralism: Institutional Innovation and the Development of the U.S. Congress* (Princeton, N.J.: Princeton University Press, 2001).

25. In many ways, as Nelson Polsby demonstrates, congressional change responds to social, economic, and cultural developments in the society. Polsby, *How Congress Evolves*.

26. John Aldrich, *Why Parties?: The Origin and Transformation of Political Parties in America* (Chicago: University of Chicago Press, 1995); David W. Rohde, *Parties and Leaders in the Postreform House* (Chicago: University of Chicago, 1991).

27. Kenneth A. Shepsle, "The Changing Textbook Congress," in *Can the Government Govern?* ed. John E. Chubb and Paul E. Peterson (Washington, D.C.: Brookings Institution, 1989).

28. David W. Rohde, "Committees and Policy Formulation," in *The Legislative Branch*, ed. Quirk and Binder, 201–23; Christopher J. Deering and Steven S. Smith, *Committees in Congress*, 3rd ed. (Washington, D.C.: CQ Press, 1997).

29. Kenneth A. Shepsle, *The Giant Jigsaw Puzzle: Democratic Committee Assignments in the Modern House* (Chicago: University of Chicago, 1978).

30. Barbara Sinclair, "Parties and Leadership in the House," in *The Legislative Branch*, ed. Quirk and Binder, 224–54; Smith, "Parties and Leadership in the Senate."

31. Scholars debated whether the congressional parties actually influenced their members' votes. Keith Krehbiel, "Where's the Party?" *British Journal of Political Science* 23 (April 1993), 235–66; James M. Snyder Jr. and Tim Groseclose, "Estimating Party Influence in Congressional Roll-Call Voting," *American Journal of Political Science* 44 (April 2000), 193–211.

32. James L. Sundquist, *Politics and Policy: The Eisenhower, Kennedy, and Johnson Years* (Washington, D.C.: Brookings Institution, 1968).

33. David R. Mayhew, *Divided We Govern: Party Control, Lawmaking, and Investigations, 1946–1990* (New Haven, Conn.: Yale University Press, 1991).

34. I. M. Destler, *American Trade Politics: System under Stress* (New York: Twentieth Century Fund, 1986); Robert A. Pastor, *Congress and the Politics of U.S. Foreign Economic Policy, 1929–1976* (Berkeley: University of California Press, 1980).

35. Earl Black and Merle Black, *Politics and Society in the South* (Cambridge, Mass.: Harvard University Press, 1987).

36. Roger H. Davidson and Walter J. Oleszek, *Congress against Itself* (Bloomington: Indiana University Press, 1977); Schickler, "Institutional Development of Congress"; Sinclair, "Parties and Leadership in the House"; Smith, "Parties and Leadership in the Senate."

37. Barbara Sinclair, *Legislators, Leaders, and Lawmaking: The U.S. House of Representatives in the Postreform Era* (Baltimore, Md.: Johns Hopkins University, 1995); Sinclair, "Parties and Leadership in the House."

38. Rohde, "Committees and Policy Formulation."

39. Smith, "Parties and Leadership in the Senate."

40. Eric Patashnik, "Budgets and Fiscal Policy," in *The Legislative Branch*, ed. Quirk and Binder, 382–406.

41. Gary C. Jacobson, "Modern Campaigns and Representation," in *The Legislative Branch*, ed. Quirk and Binder, 109–47; Gary C. Jacobson, *A Divider, Not a Uniter: George W. Bush and the American People* (New York: Longman, 2006).

42. Smith, "Parties and Leadership in the Senate."

43. From the 93rd Congress (1973–74) to the 108th Congress (2003–4), the Republican shift to the right was almost twice as large as the Democratic shift to the left. Calculated by the author from the House ideological means data provided by political scientists Keith Poole and Howard Rosenthal at http://voteview.com. See also Jacob S. Hacker and Paul Pierson, *Off Center: The Republican Revolution and the Erosion of American Democracy* (New Haven, Conn.: Yale University Press, 2005).

44. Roger H. Davidson, ed., *Postreform Congress* (New York: St. Martin's, 1992).

45. Steven S. Smith, "Congressional Trends," in *Principles and Practice of American Politics*, ed. Samuel Kernell and Steven S. Smith, 2nd ed. (Washington, D.C.: CQ Press, 2003), 256–73.

46. For a brief period in 2001, the Senate was split fifty-fifty. The Senate figures count Independents with the party that they support in organizing the Senate.

47. Rohde, "Committees and Policy Formulation."

48. Barbara Sinclair, *Unorthodox Lawmaking: New Legislative Processes in the U.S. Congress* (Washington, D.C.: CQ Press, 1997).

49. Sinclair, "Parties and Leadership in the House."

50. See Richard E. Cohen, Kirk Victor, and David Bauman, "The State of Congress," *National Journal*, January 10, 2004. Quoted in Binder, "Elections, Parties, and Governance," 165.

51. See Binder, "Elections, Parties, and Governance," 165.

52. Rohde, "Committees and Policy Formulation"; Gary W. Cox and Mathew D. McCubbins, *Setting the Agenda: Responsible Party Government in the U.S. House of Representatives* (New York: Cambridge University Press, 2005).

53. Marco Steenbergen et al., "Measuring Political Deliberation: A Discourse Quality Index," *Comparative European Politics* 1 (2003), 21–48.

54. The areas were taxes, budget, and the economy; social policies; foreign and security policy (including defense, intelligence, and homeland security); sectoral and economic development policy (such as agriculture and transportation); energy and environmental policy (including natural resources); and miscellaneous. The numbers interviewed averaged about forty in each of these areas.

55. Evidently, many staff found interest group influence distorting even though they attributed greater influence to the committees.

56. Marilyn Werber Serafini, "A Prescription for More Rancor," *National Journal*, January 1, 2006.

57. Darren Goode, "A Waste of Energy?" *National Journal*, November 19, 2005; Bruce Barcott, "Changing All the Rules," *New York Times Magazine*, April 4, 2004.

58. David Baumann, "Finding It Hard to Say 'No,'" *National Journal*, July 13, 2002; Brian Friel, "Don Young's Way, or Another?" *National Journal*, August 6, 2005; Jonathan Weisman, "Proposals Call for Disclosure of Ties to Lobbyists; Lawmakers May Be Forced to Detail Contacts, Cash Received," *Washington Post*, March 27, 2006, A4.

59. John R. Wright, *Interest Groups and Congress: Lobbying, Contributions and Influence* (New York: Longman, 1995). See also Stephen Ansolabehere, John de Figueiredo, and James M. Snyder Jr., "Why Is There So Little Money in U.S. Politics?" *Journal of Economic Perspectives* 17 (Winter 2003), 105–130.

60. John Solomon and Sharon Theimer, "E-Mails Show Abramoff's Donation Leverage," Associated Press Online, April 12, 2006.

61. Jeffrey H. Birnbaum, "Congress to Adopt Scaled-Down Rules on Lobbying," *Washington Post*, July 28, 2006, A8.

62. David Baumann, "Tempest in a Barrel," *National Journal*, February 11, 2006.

63. Michael X. Delli Carpini and Scott Keeter, *What Americans Know about Politics and Why It Matters* (New Haven, Conn.: Yale University Press, 1996); James A. Kuklinski and Paul J. Quirk, "Reconsidering the Rational Public: Cognition, Heuristics, and Mass Opinion," in *Elements of Reason*, ed. Arthur Lupia, Mathew McCubbins, and Samuel Popkin (New York: Cambridge University Press, 2000), 153–82. Among other reasons for the poor understanding, the media generally provide only sketchy coverage of policy debates; and those debates are often dominated by emotional appeals and misleading claims. See Lawrence R. Jacobs and Robert Y. Shapiro, *Politicians Don't Pander: Political Manipulation and the Loss of Democratic Responsiveness* (Chicago: University of Chicago Press, 2000).

64. Paul J. Quirk and Joseph Hinchliffe, "The Rising Hegemony of Mass Opinion," *Journal of Policy History* 10 (1998), 19–50; Smith, "Congressional Trends"; Anthony Stephen King, *Running Scared: Why America's Politicians Campaign Too Much and Govern Too Little* (New York: Martin Kessler, 1997).

65. Comptroller General David M. Walker called 2004 the most fiscally irresponsible year.

66. Gary Mucciaroni and Paul J. Quirk, *Deliberative Choices: Debating Public Policy in Congress* (Chicago: University of Chicago Press, 2006); Hacker and Pierson, *Off Center*.

67. Richard E. Cohen, "No Toes Crossing Party Lines," *National Journal*, July 16, 2005.

68. Carl Hulse and Kate Zernike, "House Passes Detainee Bill as It Clears Senate Hurdle," *New York Times*, September 28, 2006, A1.

69. Compare Walter Williams, *Honest Numbers and Democracy: Social Policy Analysis in the White House, Congress, and the Federal Agencies* (Washington, D.C.: Georgetown University Press, 1998), and Andrew Rich, *Think Tanks, Public Policy, and the Politics of Expertise* (New York: Cambridge University Press, 2004). In fact, support for serious policy research largely disappeared in the federal government under the Bush administration, and it declined dramatically in think tanks.

70. Mucciaroni and Quirk, *Deliberative Choices*.

71. Ibid. In some cases, Congress was led to overlook evidence by the Bush administration, which was widely criticized as doing so. See Michiko Kakutani, "All the President's Books," *New York Times*, May 11, 2006, E1.

72. Commission on the Intelligence Capabilities of the United States Regarding Weapons of Mass Destruction, Final Report, March 31, 2005.

73. Robert A. Dahl, *Toward Democracy—A Journey: Reflections, 1940–1997* (Berkeley: University of California, 1997).

74. Michael Malbin, *The Election after Reform: Money, Politics, and the Bipartisan Campaign Reform Act* (New York: Rowman & Littlefield, 2006).

75. See Wright, *Interest Groups and Congress*, and Ansolabehere, Figueriedo, and Snyder, "Why Is There So Little Money in U.S. Politics?"

76. Malbin, *The Election after Reform*.

77. Grant J. Tobin and Thomas J. Rudolph, *Expression vs. Equality: The Politics of Campaign Finance Reform* (Columbus: Ohio State University Press, 2004).

78. Kathleen Hall Jamieson, *Dirty Politics: Deception, Distraction and Democracy* (New York: Oxford University Press, 1992).

79. John G. Geer, *In Defense of Negativity: Attack Advertising in Presidential Campaigns* (Chicago: University of Chicago Press, 2006).

80. "Another Misleading Republican Attack Ad in California," FactCheck.org, May 1, 2006, www.factcheck.org/article389.html.

81. Ralph Blumenthal and Kate Zernike, "Day of Joy Dawns for Republicans, Proud Owners of Texas Districting Map," *New York Times*, June 29, 2006, A22; George F. Will, "An Election Breakwater? In 2002 and 2004, only 98 percent of incumbents were re-elected. Appalled, incumbents are working to eliminate that awful 2 percent," *Newsweek*, February 27, 2006, 68; David Broder, "No Vote Necessary," *Washington Post*, November 11, 2004, A37.

82. Adam Nagourney and Janet Elder, "Only 25% in Poll Voice Approval of the Congress," *New York Times*, September 21, 2006, A1.

83. Robert S. Erikson, Michael B. MacKuen, and James A. Stimson, *The Macro Polity* (New York: Cambridge University Press, 2002).

84. John R. Hibbing, "Images of Congress," in *The Legislative Branch*, ed. Quirk and Binder, 461–89.

85. John R. Hibbing and Elizabeth Theiss-Morse, *Congress as Public Enemy: Public Attitudes toward American Political Institutions* (New York: Cambridge University Press, 1995); Hibbing, "Images of Congress."

86. "Congressional leader" was not accepted. To qualify as correct, a response had to mention either the correct party, the correct chamber, or the correct (majority or minority) status.

87. The two fictitious names were Paul Burke and Joel Katzenbach.

88. It is likely that a great deal of guessing occurred, because few respondents declined to answer and many answered incorrectly. It can be assumed that a substantial fraction of the 33 percent who answered correctly did so by guessing. The percentage of correct answers that resulted from guessing cannot be estimated with any precision, however, because it cannot be assumed that guesses were evenly distributed across the possible responses. If it is understood that respondents who guessed were equally likely to choose the more-agreement and less-agreement options, then 17 percent of correct responses were guesses and 16 percent reflected knowing the right answer. But estimating such a high percentage of knowing correct responses would imply a much smaller advantage for those with a college education than was found for the name-recognition items reported earlier.

89. Compare Hibbing, "Images of Congress."

90. "Gallup Finds Sudden Upsurge in Number of Americans Who Think Congress is Corrupt," *Editor & Publisher*, May 17, 2006.
91. Rohde, "Committees and Policy Formulation"; Sinclair, "Parties and Leadership in the Senate."
92. Arend Lijphart, *Patterns of Democracy: Government Forms & Performance in Thirty-six Countries* (New Haven, Conn.: Yale University Press, 1999).
93. Colin Campbell, *Managing the Presidency: Carter, Reagan, and the Search for Executive Harmony* (Pittsburgh: University of Pittsburgh Press, 1986).
94. Hugh Heclo, *A Government of Strangers: Executive Politics in Washington* (Washington, D.C.: Brookings Institution, 1977); Joel D. Aberbach, Chapter 6 in this volume.
95. Mayhew, *Divided We Govern*.
96. Binder, "Elections, Parties, and Governance"; see also John J. Coleman, "Unified Government, Divided Government, and Party Responsiveness," *American Political Science Review* 93 (December 1999), 821–35.

6

THE EXECUTIVE BRANCH
IN RED AND BLUE

Joel D. Aberbach

The political appointees and senior civil servants of the executive branch live in an often uneasy marriage of convenience and necessity. They need one another, but they do not always see eye to eye. A certain amount of this is healthy—bringing different viewpoints and skills to the process of making and administering policy—but it can also be a problem. This chapter utilizes the Annenberg Institutions of Democracy Executive Branch survey data to look at the people involved (political appointees and career civil servants), their perceptions, and the nature of their often complex relationships. Data from the Annenberg Congress and Executive Branch surveys of the general public are also employed, both to compare the views of executive branch elites to those of the public and to emphasize a main theme of the analysis: that there is a marked partisan split (a polarization, in popular terms) permeating the views of respondents to the surveys. This division goes beyond differences on the public policy questions of the day to deeper issues such as those concerning the nature and proper exercise of presidential power, and the extent to which the executive branch operates in the best interests of the American people.

A long-festering tension continues between Republican presidents and the Democratic segment of the career bureaucracy, with the two often taking demonstrably different positions, not only on standard policy issues but on fundamental issues of governance. This mirrors a similar divide in the public and reinforces the import of questions about how Republican presidents relate to the government's permanent employees (career civil servants) and whether the expertise and experience these career employees bring to the policy process will be productively utilized. The split also brings to the fore fundamental questions about the role of the president and presidential appointees within the executive branch, questions that have intermittently roiled American politics since the ill-fated Nixon administration. It spotlights as well related questions about increased centralization of decision making within the executive branch and about the degree of legitimacy accorded to many of the decisions and actions taken by the political leadership of the contemporary executive branch, both by the public and within much of the government itself.

After an introduction to the people at the top of the executive branch, this chapter provides a brief sketch of the tensions that have marked it—though at different levels of intensity depending on the party and the approach of the administration in power—over the years since the late 1960s.[1] The discussion then turns to analysis of the often wide gulf in opinions within the executive branch. Topics covered include the party affiliations and political ideologies of top-level officials—both those appointed by the president and those who have made their careers in the executive branch and are currently members of the Senior Executive Service of the United States government. The chapter next examines other views of these same officials: the public policies they endorse; their views on the powers of the presidency; their levels of trust in the executive branch to do the right thing when it makes decisions; and their understanding of how decisions are actually made. It then turns to more day-to-day elements of the operation of the executive branch in an effort to look in greater detail at patterns of influence, examining perceptions of the level of responsiveness of civil servants to the policy decisions of the president and his appointees, assessments of who has influence over departmental policy decisions, and data on how frequently political appointees and senior civil servants have contact with other actors in the policy process. The final section considers the implications of the findings for American democracy, with emphasis on the wide partisan splits that mark the opinions of both top executive-branch officials and the general public.

The chapter, in short, uses the Annenberg Institutions of Democracy survey data to demonstrate that political perspectives in the United States are clearly, and often quite deeply, split based on partisan affinities. The split goes beyond the usual, well-known, and increasingly strong relationship between party identification and views on ordinary policy issues that separate liberals from conservatives, and extends to positions on the nature and uses of executive power, issues that are at the core of how the American political system should operate. It is present among those who have served in the governmental elite, including among those at the top of the career civil service, as well as in the population at large.[2] It goes beyond normal tensions between career civil servants and presidential administrations and it is more basic than the controversial theme of red and blue states[3]—after all, there are many reds in the blue states and vice versa—illuminating and amplifying a major concern for the country, namely, the presence and implications of markedly different ideas about how Americans should be governed, held by the executive branch's policy elites and mirrored among partisans in the public at large.

The Annenberg Executive Branch and Congress and Executive Branch surveys were conducted from August 2004 to January 2005. Respondents were members of the United States government's Senior Executive Service (SES), career officials working in the Executive Office of the President (EOP), political appointees of the George W. Bush and Bill Clinton administrations, and the general public. Full information on these surveys is found in the appendix. For the purposes of this chapter, only data from career members of the SES or career executives in the EOP were included; political appointees in the SES and the EOP were excluded to keep the presentations as simple as possible.[4]

The People at the Top of the Executive Branch

Concern about the quality of the people at the top of the executive branch is a persistent theme of contemporary reform commissions. The first National Commission on the Public Service (known as the Volcker Commission after its chairman, Paul A. Volcker), in its 1989 report, expressed grave concern about a "quiet crisis" in the public service where "too many of the best of the nation's senior executives are ready to leave government, and not enough of its most talented young people are willing to join."[5] An erosion of the quality of the public service, it was argued, would undermine the ability of the government "to respond effectively to the needs and aspirations of the American people," ultimately damaging "the democratic process itself."[6] In 2003 the second Volcker Commission expressed renewed dismay about "vanishing talent" in the public service, fearing that by the end of the decade "the federal government will have experienced one of the greatest drains of experienced, [talented, and highly motivated] personnel in its history."[7]

The commissions had numerous other concerns, including the growing number of political appointees and various flaws in the appointments and congressional-approval processes, the need to improve accountability for performance in the federal service, problems in both the levels of compensation and method of determining compensation for federal executives, the need to reorganize the federal government into "a limited number of mission-related executive departments,"[8] and the demand for more flexible personnel-management systems. Major efforts in many of these areas were under way in 2006. They are not a focus of this chapter, but they are vitally important for those who wish to understand contemporary debates about reforming the executive branch.[9] The focus in this section is on a limited element of the debate about personnel—the nature and quality of high-level federal executives—and in the balance of the chapter, on questions about the nature and significance of different views of executive power and about differences in views of political appointees and career executives and the possible consequences of these differences.

Based on the Annenberg survey data (and data reported elsewhere, including a set of studies done in the 1970s, 1980s, and 1990s),[10] it is clear that the current generation of high-level federal executives is remarkably well qualified in educational terms. Over 80 percent of Bush administration appointees, Clinton administration appointees, and SES career executives interviewed for the Annenberg project surveys had done at least some graduate work, and more than 60 percent in each category had a graduate degree of some sort. This contrasts to 12 percent of the general population surveyed who had done some graduate work and 7 percent who had a graduate degree. Of those executives who had a degree, one-third of the career SES members surveyed were PhDs (compared to 21 and 25 percent of Bush and Clinton appointees, respectively), while the modal, or most frequent, category among political appointees was a law degree (44 percent of Bush appointees and 42 percent of Clinton appointees). Further, federal executives in each sample were often graduates of prestigious private colleges or universities (26 percent of Bush appointees and career SES executives and more than 40 percent—44 percent, to be exact—of Clinton appointees).[11] Those who went to graduate school were similarly likely to have gone to highly prestigious private institutions, though in this case the Bush appointees match the Clinton appointees, with over 40 percent having degrees from such institutions.[12]

Top federal executives are also highly specialized, particularly career personnel. Of the career members of SES sampled who went to graduate school, for example, almost 20 percent studied science (including applied science) or mathematics and another 10 percent studied engineering. Additionally, and not surprisingly, the career SES people sampled had a great deal of experience working for the federal government (90 percent had worked for the federal government for more than fifteen years, and just over 70 percent had worked in their current department or agency for fifteen or more years). In brief, the top of the federal executive branch is populated by people with impressive educational credentials who, especially among the career executives, have the experience and, presumably, the technical skills and knowledge needed to operate an intricate government that plays a role in many aspects of American life.

These credentials, along with the slowly increasing diversity of the personnel at the top of the executive branch, give promise of a corps of public executives, especially career executives, who can serve the country well. Their educational backgrounds and the institutional experience of career executives, however, do not assure that they have the leadership skills, motivation, or flexible personalities that enable them to operate in a fast-changing environment. Critics and reformers have expressed great concerns about these general areas, and have put stress on reforms that provide a variety of mechanisms and incentives to make management nimble and responsive to new circumstances.[13] It is outside the scope of this chapter to evaluate the need for such changes, but the reader is cautioned that an emphasis on such things as performance-related pay (linking pay to a measure of individual, group, or organizational performance) can easily backfire in an environment where material rewards will surely remain less attractive than those in the private sector. In the end, a dedication to public service and a sense that what the government does is important to the betterment of American life (particularly in the specific agencies the executives serve) is the key to recruiting and retaining the sorts of people most Americans would want in the public service. And it is also important to remember that good leadership from political appointees, something not always present, is essential to effective use of whatever talents career public servants have.

Moreover, in addition to expertise and organizational skills, executives at the top of the government service need the skills and values necessary to operate in a complex, often highly charged political environment. And beyond that, it helps for their leaders, both the president and the president's top aides and cabinet officials and their aides, to have sufficient respect for other federal executives and confidence in their ability to carry out their missions effectively so that all can work in relative harmony. Unfortunately, that has often not been the case.

Some Historical Background

A degree of tension between the political leaders of the administration (especially in the White House) and the bureaucracy is almost inevitable. Bureaucrats have as a major duty the implementation of existing policies. In most cases, this leads them to establish ties to the interests served by those policies, both psychologically and organizationally, and to try to maintain those ties. They need the organized interests for information and political support, and they either have or soon develop an identification with the underlying purposes of the policies they are administering, be they building the country's defenses, protecting its environment, or assisting its citizens in need. Administrations, particularly those that desire to make significant changes in policy, are therefore often wary of the willingness or ability of the established organizations and their personnel to make the changes they deem necessary.

The tensions have been especially acute in the period since the New Deal when Republican presidents have been in office. That is not surprising, since many of the most prominent programs of the modern American administrative state (particularly welfare state programs and programs to shape the economy) were the products of Democratic presidents, with agencies to implement them built and staffed by Democratic administrations. Republicans not only have feared that many of the agencies might be sluggish in embracing or implementing changes, a fear shared with Democratic administrations (though the direction of change desired has usually been different—Democrats aiming to modify or expand programs in ways that sometimes break routines or perhaps disrupt established bureaucratic relationships, and Republicans often aiming to cut back or drastically transform programs identified with Democrats), but suspected that the civil servants in many of the domestic agencies were downright hostile to what they wished to accomplish.[14]

Indeed, since the late 1960s much of the administrative side of presidential politics has been dominated by fears of this sort and by actions taken to assure bureaucratic responsiveness. By fits and starts, presidents, particularly three of the Republican presidents in this era (Nixon, Reagan, and George W. Bush), developed a strategy and set of tactics to dominate both the Congress and the bureaucracy and to govern from the White House by centralizing control of policymaking and key elements of administration. They largely rejected traditional notions of bargaining with other actors in favor of presidential command.[15] A short history of the presidency, starting with Richard Nixon, should make this clear.

Nixon began his presidency in a conventional manner, appointing cabinet officers to represent a wide variety of interests in his own party and in the nation, and allowing cabinet members to select their subordinates (the political appointees who are found at the top of executive branch agencies). Nixon also forged a full legislative program and worked with Congress in an attempt to bring it to fruition. However, he was soon frustrated by the complex loyalties of the personnel of the executive branch and by his limited control of the process, a level of control that was consonant with the system of "separated institutions *sharing* powers" designed by the writers of the U.S. Constitution, but extraordinarily exasperating to a man who craved extreme deference from all in his environment.[16] Nixon then set about designing what came to be known as the "administrative presidency."[17] Its aim was to "take over" the government by ignoring Congress when it stood in the way of what the president wished to do, using regulation writing to change the meaning of statutes and placing Nixon loyalists in all key posts. Civil servants, especially those in the domestic agencies suspected of Democratic loyalties, were to be harassed and, wherever possible, isolated from any significant role in agency decision-making.[18] The goal was to centralize power in the White House through a system of command that relied on loyal subordinates in key roles throughout the executive branch, with other interests and institutional actors (including Congress) rendered relatively powerless. This was almost precisely the opposite of what served as the reigning analysis of the presidency as well as the conventional wisdom of the time—that the design of the American constitutional system, with its separation of powers and checks and balances, meant that no one actor or institution could command and that presidential influence was fundamentally and necessarily based on the "power to persuade."[19]

Nixon made clear in his autobiography what he regarded as his initial failures in getting control of the executive branch, and even looked to some data that he felt backed him up:

> I regretted that during the first term we had . . . failed to fill all the key posts in the departments and agencies with people who were loyal to the President and his programs. Without this kind of leadership in the appointive positions, there is no way for a President to make any major impact on the bureaucracy. That this was especially true of a Republican President was confirmed a few years later by a study reported in the *American Political Science Review*. Researchers Joel Aberbach and Bert Rockman found that in 1970 only 17 percent of top career bureaucrats in the executive branch were Republicans; 47 percent were Democrats and 36 percent were independents, who "more frequently resemble Democrats than Republicans."[20]

Nixon's former aide and speechwriter, Patrick Buchanan, used more colorful images in a 1976 column that reacted to the same data Nixon had cited:

> When Richard M. Nixon looked upon his executive bureaucracy as a barricade manned by political enemies to frustrate the expressed will of the American people, he was right on the mark. And when he sought to seed that bureaucracy with political loyalists, his instincts were unerring. . . .
>
> One puts down the Aberbach-Rockman analysis with the thought that conservative Republicans must rethink their traditional opposition to the concept of the Powerful President. . . . If Nixon made a mistake dealing with the departmental roadblocks to conservative reform, it was in not posting enough recalcitrant bureaucrats to Butte, Mont., or Adak, Alaska.
>
> For a new Republican President to expect his handful of appointees to impose upon this savvy leftist bureaucracy a program of reduction, reorganization or reform is to send missionaries into the Central Highlands and Mekong Delta to convert the Viet Cong.[21]

Nixon's administration collapsed in the rubble created by the Watergate scandal, and his immediate successors (Ford and then Carter) were much more cautious in their actions and in their assertions of executive power. The Reagan administration, however, staffed by many who had worked for the Nixon administration or studied its experiences, brought back the basic administrative-presidency strategy. It was greatly advantaged in doing so by its relatively well-developed ideological thrust (loyalty was to be to a set of ideas as well as to the man) and advantaged as well by a clear-cut electoral victory, a Republican Senate, and a civil-service reform bill that increased a president's ability to manipulate who would be in what positions at the top of the civil service. Data

163

on top federal officials that were collected during the Reagan administration demonstrated the efficacy both of the administration's appointment strategy and of its use of available devices to manipulate the civil service system, especially in targeted social service agencies, in order to place Republican career executives in key positions in these agencies. These data also indicated great success in limiting (though certainly not in eliminating) the contacts of top career civil servants with Congress, interest group representatives, and the public at large.[22]

The George W. Bush administration, in office for more than three years when the Annenberg project surveys were conducted, was, if anything, even more determined than the Reagan administration to build presidential power. Vice President Cheney was outspoken in his contention that there had been "erosion" in executive power since the 1960s that must be restored.[23] And the Bush administration embarked on a series of assertive actions and policies designed to enhance presidential prerogatives. For example, the administration asserted sweeping rights for the president, in his capacity as commander in chief of the armed forces, to ignore treaty commitments and existing federal law concerning torture and domestic surveillance; it claimed (successfully as of 2006 as a result of a narrowly decided court decision) the right, without invoking executive privilege, to keep information about attendees at meetings secret from an arm of Congress; it used its rule-making powers and its power to issue executive orders to make major changes in policy; and there is suggestive evidence of aggressive efforts to control the behavior of civil servants in once-sacrosanct areas such as science and actuarial estimates.[24]

It is this background of turmoil and change that gives meaning and historical significance to the Annenberg project survey data on the attitudes and behavior of senior-level officials and the views of the public they are supposed to serve.

Party Identification and Ideology

As President Nixon noted in his autobiography, his deep suspicions while he was in office that career civil servants were much more likely to be Democrats than Republicans were borne out by the results of systematic research done during his administration. Follow-up research that I did with Bert Rockman, however, indicated an increase over time to parity in the percentage of Republican voters in the top ranks of the civil service,[25] though even parity is probably not enough to satisfy zealous partisans or those who have a need for total control.

The Aberbach-Rockman research was focused on civil servants on the general list of the SES, while the Annenberg survey respondents were drawn from the total list of SES executives.[26] And the Annenberg survey included foreign policy and Defense Department executives, while the Aberbach-Rockman study did not. Therefore, results of the two studies can only be compared in a rough manner and with great caution. In addition, the earlier research was based on reports of voting in presidential elections, while the Annenberg survey used a question asking about party identification—that is, whether the survey respondent considered him- or herself a Republican, a Democrat, or an Independent—so there may be differences in the findings due to differences in the questions asked.

What we can say with confidence is that the Annenberg survey results (see Figure 1a) show that Democrats outnumbered Republicans in 2004–5 by a margin of about two to one (32 percent to 16 percent) among a sample drawn from a wide range of career members of the SES. Independents who responded to a question about which party they lean toward were also slightly more inclined to the Democrats than the Republicans—29 percent to 23 percent. So the overall conclusion is that Democrats were clearly a plurality, and, extrapolating from these data on the leanings of Independents, Democratic identifiers plus Democratic sympathizers were about 47 percent among career members of the SES (compared to 28 percent Republicans when one combines identifiers with those who said they lean toward supporting the Republican Party).[27] Similar findings hold among career civil servants in the EOP, although with a greater edge in Democratic identifiers.

These findings stand in stark contrast to the results for the sets of political-appointee samples. There, in keeping with modern trends away from conciliating the other party with appointments, President Bush's appointees are overwhelmingly Republican and President Clinton's appointees are overwhelmingly Democratic. While, as Figure 1a shows, career executives were definitely not as likely as the general public to be Republicans, they (and the career EOP executives) are by far the group most representative of the public among the executive branch samples in their party affiliations simply because they are not totally biased in one direction or the other.

Party affiliation is important because of the assumption that it tells us much about the political and policy leanings of an individual. I will examine policy views in the next section, but a good indicator of what is to come can be found in whether respondents label themselves conservative, liberal, or moderate.

A look at Figure 1b shows similar patterns to the party-affiliation data. Bush appointees identified as conservatives or, to a lesser extent, moderates, with just about none calling themselves liberals. Clinton's appointees, by contrast, were almost equally loath to call themselves conservatives, though more identified themselves as moderates than did Bush appointees. The general public was split, although here, unlike in the party-affiliation data where the two parties are about even, the conservative side of the ideological spectrum clearly gets the greatest percentage of endorsers. While liberals outnumbered conservatives among the career SES (and the career EOP) respondents, the modal respondent self-identified as a moderate. So, once again, as in the case of party identification, while there are definite differences in the distributions of the career executives and the

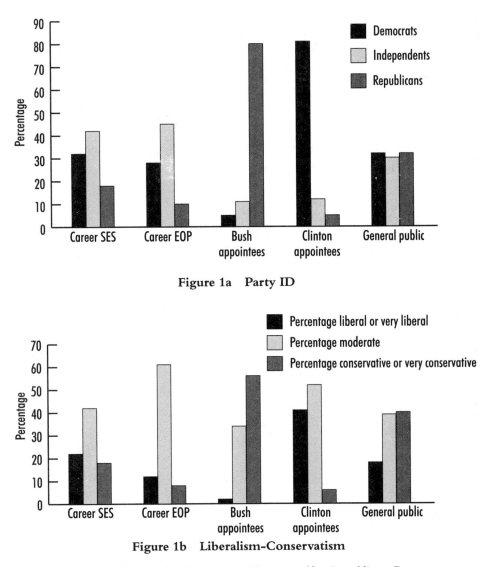

Figure 1a   Party ID

Figure 1b   Liberalism-Conservatism

Question 1a: In politics today, do you consider yourself a Republican, Democrat, or Independent?

Question 1b: In general, would you describe your political views as very conservative, conservative, moderate, liberal, or very liberal?

Source: 2004–2005 surveys by Princeton Survey Research Associates for the Annenberg Foundation Trust at Sunnylands.

Note: In Figure 1 above, as in Figures 2 through 12, entries are percentages of total responses (including Don't Know and Refused).

Figure 1   Party ID and Political Views of the General Public and Top Executive-Branch Officials

general public, neither is anywhere near as skewed (left or right) as the political appointees.

Seen through the eyes of someone who is not part of the executive branch, the data presented in this section seem rather reassuring. Civil servants are not as Republican as the appointees of Republican administrations or as Democratic as the appointees of Democratic administrations. In this they are more broadly representative of the general public. And while top career civil servants are less likely to call themselves conservatives than the members of the general public, they are both less conservative than Republican political appointees and less liberal than Democratic political appointees. However, given the political history of the last century in the United States, particularly of the period since the 1960s, Republican suspicion of the civil service, especially on the part of Republican administrations with ambitious plans to change governmental policies, is likely to be reinforced by the findings so far. Democrats might be uneasy, too, but to a lesser extent because the overall bias at the top of the civil service is clearly in their direction.

In the balance of this chapter, the party-identification measure will be used as a base (independent variable) to explore the views of top federal executives and the public on a variety of conventional (though often contentious) policy issues as well as on some highly controversial notions about presidential/executive power. The impact of party affiliation on respondents' reports on decision-making processes and other behavior inside the executive branch will also be addressed. Beyond the portrait of the politics of the executive branch that the analysis will paint, the larger goal is to understand the implications of the findings for the democratic process in the United States, with emphasis on issues raised by controversies about executive power. The data will give clear evidence of partisan divisions, usually stronger for the elites but also present within the general public, with differences of opinion that go well beyond divisions on conventional political issues.

The relatively small number of EOP respondents will now be dropped from the discussion to keep the analysis as simple as possible. The EOP respondents resemble the career SES people enough to warrant exclusion from this point on in the chapter, though their special role clearly justifies more detailed analysis in the future. Party, as noted above, will be used as a key explanatory variable, but one should be fully cognizant of the fact that it is not the only important factor in understanding the complex politics of the executive branch.

Policy Differences within the Executive Branch

At first glance, it appears from Figures 2 to 5 that on many public policy issues top career civil servants in the SES and political appointees differ significantly in their views. And indeed they often do. But equally important is the fact that party explains most of the differences; that is, Democratic career executives' views are quite consonant with the views of Democratic political appointees, and Republican executives' views are in line with those of Republican appointees, with Independent career executives more or less in the middle.[28]

The impact of party and the gap in beliefs between members of the SES as a group and political appointees is quite apparent in the answers respondents gave to a question about the role of the government in the nation's economic affairs. As the data in Figure 2 show, Bush and Clinton appointees differed greatly in their views on the role government should play in the nation's economy, with almost 70 percent of Clinton's appointees endorsing the notion that government should play a greater role in the nation's economic affairs and only 15 percent of the Bush nominees agreeing with this proposition. Career SES executives were in the middle, though closer to the views of the Clinton appointees. Once one controls for party, Democratic career executives look exactly like the Clinton appointees, while Republican career executives, though more moderate than Bush appointees, are much closer to them in their beliefs.[29]

And this general pattern holds when respondents were asked about other responsibilities of the federal government. For example, as Figure 3 demonstrates, when it comes to views on the federal government's responsibility to conserve the country's natural resources, top civil servants were closer to the view of Clinton appointees (almost all Democrats, recall) than to Bush appointees (almost all Republicans). And, controlling for party, Democratic and Republican top civil servants had almost exactly the same views as Clinton administration and Bush administration appointees respectively. The Annenberg surveys of the general public also included the natural resources policy item, and here the public most resembles the career SES in the percentage that see it as a very important responsibility of the federal government to conserve the country's natural resources. Once one controls for party affiliation, the views of the general public are right in line with the partisans among the elites; that is, Democrats in the public share the positions of the appointees of Democratic administrations, and their views are close to those of Democrats in the career SES, while Republicans in the general public resemble Republican political appointees and Republicans in the career SES in their views.[30]

Figure 4, which breaks out the data in terms of the responsibility of the federal government to reduce poverty, shows the same general pattern of party differences as the data in Figure 3, only here civil servants as a whole are closer to Bush appointees, because career civil servants who identify as Republicans are even more conservative than Bush administration political appointees. Civil servants who identify themselves as Independents are also closer to Republicans than to Democrats in their views on the issue, while Democratic civil servants are no more liberal on this issue than Clinton appointees. The general public as a whole is quite sympathetic to government programs to reduce poverty, particu-

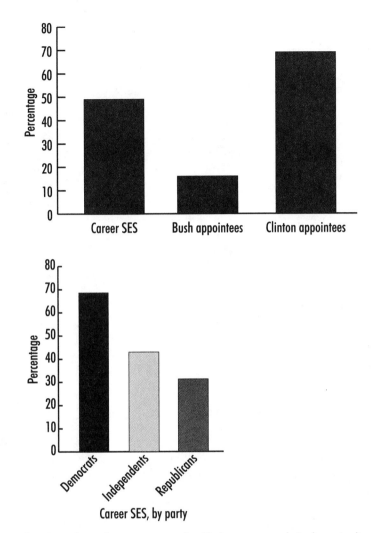

Career SES

Bush appointees

Clinton appointees

Career SES, by party

Statement: Some people say that government should play a greater role in the nation's economic affairs. Others say that decisions in this area should be left to the private sector. On the whole, which of those positions comes closest to yours?

Source: 2004–2005 surveys by Princeton Survey Research Associates for the Annenberg Foundation Trust at Sunnylands.

Figure 2   Government Should Play a Greater Role in the Nation's Economic Affairs (Percentage Saying Government Should Play a Greater Role)

larly Democratic identifiers and Independents. (Republicans in the general public resemble Bush's appointees.)

I will not belabor the point with too many examples, but the data in Figure 5, where the Republican position has been that the federal government has a responsibility to protect the unborn, again shows both the import of party and

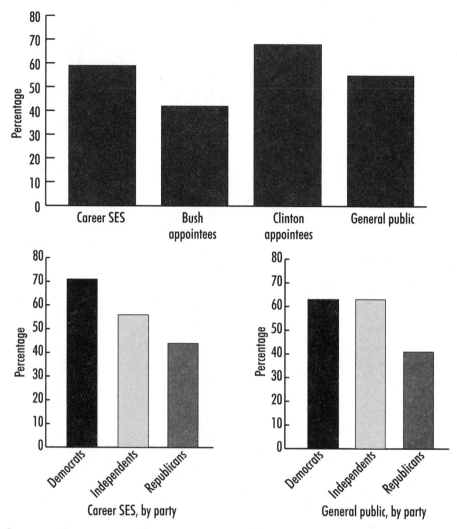

Statement: I now want to ask you some questions about how much responsibility the federal government should have for doing certain things. In your opinion, how important is it for the federal government to do each of the following: Is conserving the country's natural resources a very important responsibility of the federal government, important, not so important, or not important at all?

Source: 2004–2005 surveys by Princeon Survey Research Associates for the Annenberg Foundation Trust at Sunnylands.

Figure 3   Conserving Country's Natural Resources Is a Very Important Responsibility of the Federal Government (Percentage Answering "Very Important")

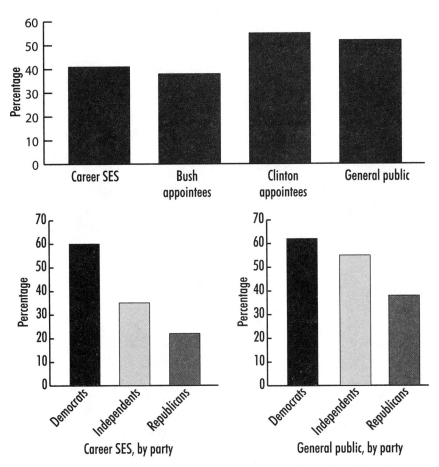

Statement: Same introductory statement as in Figure 3, followed by: What about reducing poverty?

Source: 2004–2005 surveys by Princeton Survey Research Associates for the Annenberg Foundation Trust at Sunnylands.

Figure 4   Reducing Poverty Is a Very Important Responsibility of the Federal Government (Percentage Answering "Very Important")

that the overall position of the career SES is between that of the appointees of Republican and Democratic administrations. Only here Democrats in the general public are much more conservative than Democrats in the elite; in fact, Democrats in the general public are on a par with Bush appointees, while Republicans in the general public endorse this proposition even more than Bush appointees. Note that on this issue, those who felt protecting the unborn to be an "important" responsibility of the federal government were added to those who felt it a "very important" responsibility because, with the exception of

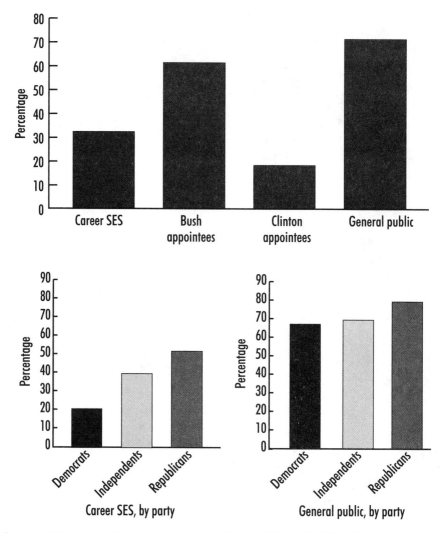

Statement: Same introductory statement as in Figure 1, followed by: What about protecting the unborn?

Source: 2004–2005 surveys by Princeton Survey Research Associates for the Annenberg Foundation Trust at Sunnylands.

Figure 5   Protecting the Unborn Is a Very Important or Important Responsibility of the Federal Government (Percentage Answering "Very Important" or "Important")

Republicans in the general public, "important" represented a larger proportion of the responses than "very important."[31] This is an issue where the general public, particularly a significant part of the Republican base, is more intense in its views than Republican elites, helping to account for the issue's large role in the public debate and its embrace by many Republican political leaders who might otherwise demur.[32]

One key point is simply the import of party for the views of top civil servants and the fact that, with the exception of moral issues like protecting the unborn, career members of the SES are quite similar to the public in their views overall, especially after controlling for party. A second is that because of the diversity in party identification within the career SES, the career SES as a whole holds more liberal views than Bush appointees and more conservative views than those held by appointees chosen by Bill Clinton, reinforcing the results of previous studies and showing why Republicans continue to feel leery about the bureaucracy in many areas and why Democrats have their own, if less passionately held, doubts also. Finally, the views of the administrative elites on these issues are noticeably more polarized than those of the mass public. On the three issues in Figures 3–5, for example, the absolute value of the average differences between Democratic and Republican identifiers is 33 percent for career SES respondents and 19 percent for respondents from the general public.[33]

Views about Presidential Power and the Administrative Presidency

Whatever one makes of the divisions on policy issues, divisions about fundamental questions such as the appropriate extent of presidential power are potentially more serious. And the Annenberg data indicate that views on the powers of the presidency are very strongly split according to party affiliation; they are, in fact, even more pronounced than those on policy issues.

Given the history of the last few decades and the very assertive Republican president who occupied the White House in the early years of the twenty-first century, it is perhaps not surprising—though the consequences for the American political system may be great—that in the 2004-05 Annenberg survey data party affinities have a big impact on views about presidential power. Republicans basically accept the aggrandizement of presidential power that is particularly identified with the presidencies of Nixon, Reagan, and George W. Bush, and Democrats in large part reject it.

The profound nature of the split is evident in Figures 6, 7, and 8. Democratic respondents, both those in the career SES and the appointees of the Clinton administration, were clear in their view that the president should not have the authority to take preemptive military action without the consent of Congress (Figure 6). They also believed that the president should not have the authority to contravene international laws or treaties that the United States has signed (Figure 7). And they rejected the notion that others should simply defer to the president should the occupant of that office believe that something should be done about an important national issue (Figure 8).[34]

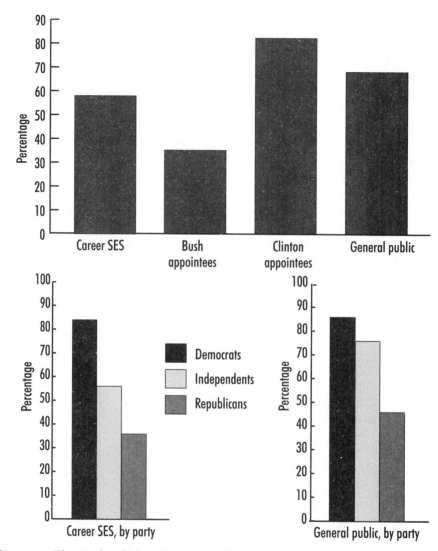

Statement: There is a lot of debate about the president's authority to take action without the consent of Congress to deal with possible threats to the United States. Do you believe that the president should have the authority without the consent of Congress to take military action, even if an attack is not imminent?

Source: 2004–2005 surveys by Princeton Survey Research Associates for the Annenberg Foundation Trust at Sunnylands.

Figure 6   Should the President Have the Authority to Take Preemptive Military Action without the Consent of Congress? (Percentage Answering "No")

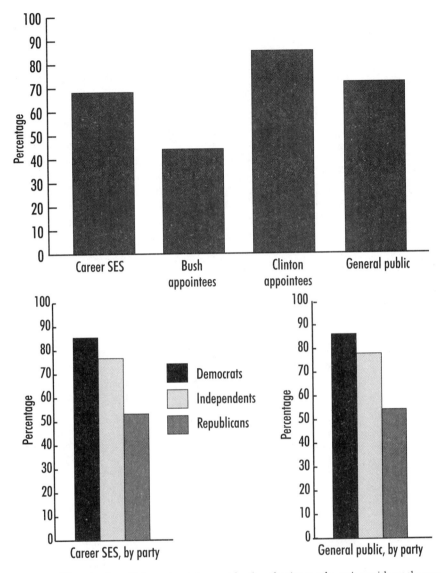

Statement: There is a lot of debate about the president's authority to take action without the consent of Congress to deal with possible threats to the United States. Do you believe that the president should have the authority without the consent of Congress to contravene ("disregard" used for the general public sample) international laws or treaties to which the U.S. is a signatory?

Source: 2004–2005 surveys by Princeton Survey Research Associates for the Annenberg Foundation Trust at Sunnylands.

**Figure 7   Should the President Have the Authority to Contravene International Laws or Treaties Signed by the U.S.?
(Percentage Answering "No")**

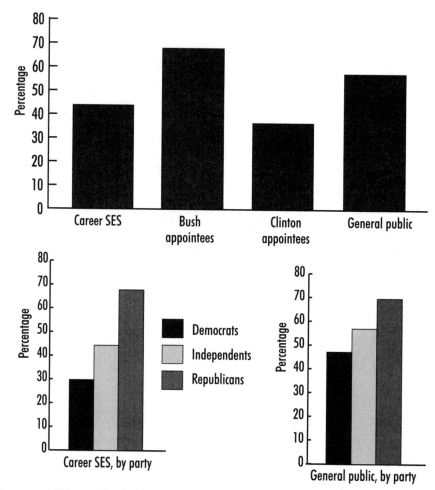

Statement: If the president believes something should be done about an important national issue, other policymakers should defer to him.

Source: 2004–2005 surveys by Princeton Survey Research Associates for the Annenberg Foundation Trust at Sunnylands.

**Figure 8   Others Should Defer to the President
(Percentage Answering "Strongly Agree" or "Agree")**

The same is true of the general public. Democratic identifiers in the public look almost shockingly like the Clinton appointees as do Democrats among the career SES. The one place, it should be noted, where the career SES Democrats differed slightly is that they were the *least likely* of any of the groups in Figure 8 to agree that others should defer if the president believes something should be done about an important issue. In that regard, Democrats in the SES were the least in favor of deference to the president's views on national issues of any subgroup.

Republicans in these surveys are, to a large extent, in a different space. Their answers to the questions detailed in Figures 6–8 differ by an average (absolute value) of about forty points from those of Democrats (forty-one points for Bush appointees and forty points for the Republicans in the career SES). The differences between Republicans and Democrats in the general public are not quite so stark, but still average a very robust 32 percent. (Parenthetically, Independents fall in between but are more likely to fall closer to the viewpoints of Democrats on these issues.)

Based on the foregoing data, it does not seem much of an exaggeration to say that perspectives on presidential power in the United States differ quite a bit and that one view—certainly when the Annenberg data were collected, with Bush in office—tends to characterize Republicans from the base to the elite and the other view Democrats from the base to the elite. The Republican perspective allows the president tremendous leeway to act, arguing that on important national issues others should defer to presidents and that presidents should be able to do such things as take preemptive military action without the consent of Congress. And, though there is more internal party controversy on this issue, many Republican partisans, certainly many more than Democratic partisans, do not even object to the notion that the president should be able, unilaterally, to contravene international laws or treaties signed by the United States.[35] It is easy to see, though not necessarily to justify, why the Bush administration felt so comfortable in actions such as withholding information about its meetings on energy policy and authorizing domestic wiretaps by the National Security Agency without going through the legally prescribed procedures.

Trust in the Executive Branch to Operate in the Public Interest

Democrats interviewed in the Annenberg project surveys not only were likely to reject the approach to the presidency that many Republicans embraced, they were skeptical that the executive branch could be trusted to operate in the public interest.[36] Figure 9 demonstrates the gap in trust that existed in 2005-06 at the time the survey was administered. While 62 percent of Bush appointees said they have a "great deal" of trust in the executive branch—then under the administration of President George W. Bush—to operate in the best interests of the American people, that sentiment was shared by only 15 percent of those who served as appointed officials in the Clinton administration and by only 21 percent of the SES career civil servants who identified as Democrats. It is not that the Democrats surveyed can be described as totally distrustful (their modal category in answer to the question is that they have a "fair amount" of trust), nor is it surprising that they are more distrustful than Republicans, but the figures for career civil servants (both Democrats and Independents) do give one pause because they represent the views of a majority of the personnel of the executive

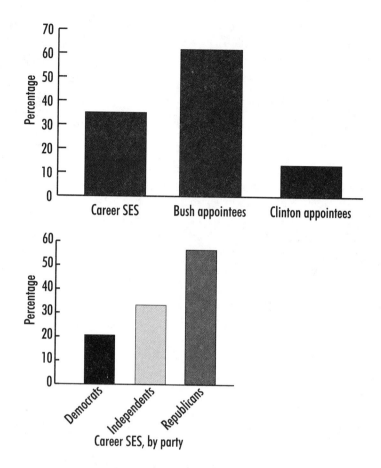

Source: 2004–2005 surveys by Princeton Survey Research Associates for the Annenberg Foundation Trust at Sunnylands.

Statement: Generally speaking, how much do you trust the Executive Branch to operate in the best interests of the American people—a great deal, a fair amount, not too much, or not at all?

Figure 9   Level of Trust that the Executive Branch Will Operate in the Best Interests of the American People (Percentage Answering "Great Deal")

branch who were actually carrying out public policy, and they apparently lacked a "great deal" of trust that the branch of the federal government in which they served operates in the best interests of the American people.

Perspectives on Presidential Decision Making

The relative lack of confidence by Democrats (and to a lesser extent, Independents) that the federal government could be counted on to operate in the best interests of the American people is reflected in their views on how decisions were made by the Bush administration.

Members of the career SES who served both the Bill Clinton and George W. Bush administrations were requested to make a comparative assessment of how each made decisions. They were given a set of items that asked which administration was more likely to base decisions on a variety of factors such as "a comprehensive review of relevant information" or the views of "particular constituencies in the President's re-election coalition." Respondents could choose either the Clinton or Bush administration (see the text of the items reproduced in Figures 10–12); a "both" response was recorded if the respondent volunteered it. Overall, their views are not too surprising. By a ratio of 3.7 to 1, career SES respondents believed that Clinton was more likely to have based decisions on a comprehensive review of relevant information, and they saw him as more likely to have heard competing perspectives from within the executive branch (5.4 to 1), and also to have used public opinion polling in making decisions (4.8 to 1). The Bush administration, on the other hand, was seen as much more likely to make decisions based on ideological principles (10.5 to 1) and to make decisions based on particular constituencies in the Bush reelection coalition (3.2 to 1). The two administrations were about even when it came to making decisions based on immediate political considerations, on doing the right thing even if not politically beneficial, and on management criteria (improving executive-branch management).

As in so many other areas, there are often huge gulfs by party identification in these perceptions—a notable exception is the uniformly high perception by both Democrats and Republicans that the Bush administration makes decisions based on its ideology. Other than this perception of the prominent role of ideology in decision making in the Bush administration, however, it is as if the SES executives were observing different worlds. For example, Figure 10 shows that 78 percent of the Democratic identifiers among career SES respondents who served in both the Clinton and Bush administrations thought that the Clinton administration was more likely to have made its decisions based on a comprehensive review of relevant information, but only 21 percent of Republicans in the SES who served in both administrations perceived this to be the case.[37] As Figure 11 shows, 62 percent of Democrats saw the Bush administration as more likely to make its decisions based on particular constituencies in its reelection coalition; a view shared by only 29 percent of Republicans. Or look at Figure 12: Here 83 percent of Democrats who served in both administrations believed that the Clinton administration was more likely to have made its decisions based on a hearing of competing perspectives from throughout the executive branch. Only 39 percent of comparable Republican members of the SES saw things this way.

I could go on, but the point should be clear. These executives, all of whom served over approximately the same time period in the same government, have

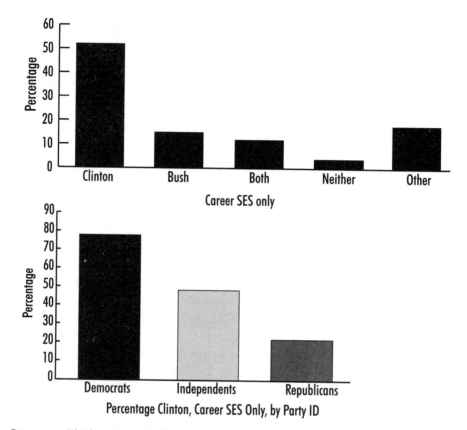

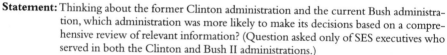

Statement: Thinking about the former Clinton administration and the current Bush administration, which administration was more likely to make its decisions based on a comprehensive review of relevant information? (Question asked only of SES executives who served in both the Clinton and Bush II administrations.)

Source: 2004–2005 surveys by Princeton Survey Research Associates for the Annenberg Foundation Trust at Sunnylands.

Figure 10   Which Administration, That of Clinton or George W. Bush, Was More Likely to Make Its Decisions Based on a Comprehensive Review of Relevant Information?

very different ideas about how decisions were made. To a remarkable extent, they see the process through the lenses of their party identifications. Some of the differences might be explained by the way things looked from the departments or agencies they worked for over this period. Democrats, in this sample as in others, for example, were found disproportionately in the social service agencies.[38] However, they were actually, on average, somewhat less likely than those who worked for other domestic agencies or for the foreign pol-

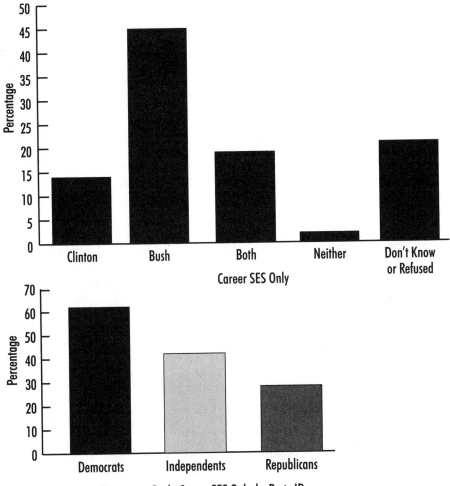

Career SES Only

Percentage Bush, Career SES Only, by Party ID

Statement: Thinking about the former Clinton administration and the current Bush administration, which administration was more likely to make its decisions based on particular constituencies in the President's re-election coalition? (Question asked only of SES executives who served in both the Clinton and Bush II administrations.)

Source: 2004–2005 surveys by Princeton Survey Research Associates for the Annenberg Foundation Trust at Sunnylands.

Figure 11 Which Administration, That of Clinton or George W. Bush, Was More Likely to Make Its Decisions Based on Particular Constituencies in the President's Re-election Coalition?

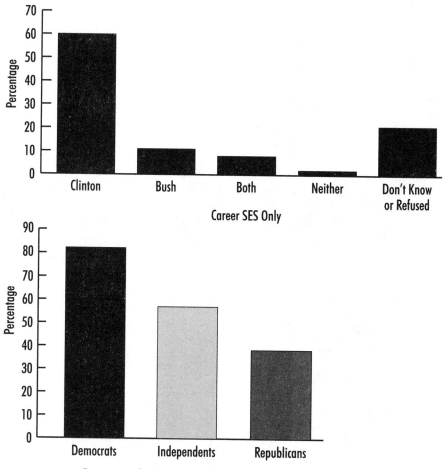

Career SES Only

Percentage Clinton, Career SES Only, by Party ID

Statement: Thinking about the former Clinton administration and the current Bush administration, which administration was more likely to make its decisions based on a hearing of competing perspectives from throughout the executive branch? (Question asked only of SES executives who served in both the Clinton and Bush II administrations.)

Source: 2004–2005 surveys by Princeton Survey Research Associates for the Annenberg Foundation Trust at Sunnylands.

Figure 12   Which Administration, That of Clinton or George W. Bush, Was More Likely to Make Its Decisions Based on a Hearing of Competing Perspectives from Throughout the Executive Branch?

icy or defense-related agencies to see the process through partisan lenses. In other words, party and not agency is key in the perceptions these SES career executives have of the ways in which the Clinton and Bush administrations made decisions.

Responsiveness to the President and Presidential Appointees

There are also differences in the ways SES career civil servants and Clinton administration appointees as compared with Bush administration appointees perceived the responsiveness of civil servants to the policy decisions of the president and his political appointees. About 47 percent of Bush political appointees surveyed said that career civil servants were "very responsive" to the president and his appointees (the location of these appointees—whether in the White House or the agencies, or both—was not specified in the question), while the comparable figure for Clinton appointees was 65 percent, almost twenty percentage points higher, and 68 percent for career members of the SES.[39] At the same time, when asked about their own experiences with top civil servants, there was agreement among Clinton and Bush appointees that civil servants were "very responsive" to them, that is, to the decisions and initiatives of the individual political appointees themselves—about 75 percent of both the Clinton and Bush appointee samples said that senior career civil servants saw senior career civil servants as "very responsive" to their own decisions and initiatives.

The overall picture is one of perceived responsiveness, especially in the one-on-one relationships of SES members and their political appointee bosses. But, as one might have expected from the recent history of politics inside the executive branch, especially when assertive Republican administrations have been in control, there is more than a hint of doubt in responses by many Republican (Bush) appointees to the more general question about responsiveness of career officials to the president, and his appointees where "somewhat" responsive is the modal answer (48 percent).

Influence and Contacts

When it comes to influence over departmental policy decisions in the respondent's area (the area he or she works in), it is not too surprising that the career executives interviewed for the Annenberg project saw themselves as less influential than their department secretaries, the White House, or political appointees. These perceptions did not vary much by party for the career SES, with about 34 percent seeing themselves as having "a great deal of influence" in their areas of interest. About a fourth of the civil servants, moreover, felt that political appointees make decisions in their areas regardless of the views of civil servants.[40]

To get some perspective on the significance of the 34 percent figure for career SES members in the 2004–5 Annenberg survey data who felt they had a "great deal of influence" in the areas they work in most, that is, their work areas of interest, data from an earlier study proves useful. Of the SES executives surveyed for a study done of higher-level executives in 1991–92, during the George H. W. Bush administration, almost 60 percent of the SES executives in those years attributed a great deal of influence to themselves "in their areas of interest." (This contrasts to the 10 percent—8 percent of the very top SES executives and 12 percent of those just a bit below them in the 1991–92 study—who attributed a great deal of influence to civil servants in answering a more general question, that is, a question without reference to their own policy areas, asking for a general assessment of the influence of career civil servants over policymaking).[41] Differences in the samples and response rates and of the studies and slight differences in the question wording make precise comparisons risky, but the 2004–5 data do at least suggest a drop in perceived influence.

The contacts people report may be a more objective measure of their influence than their inevitably subjective perceptions of how much influence they have. Civil servants surveyed reported quite low levels of contacts with central actors in the policy process who are not in the departments and agencies. As Table 1 shows, in fact, they said that they had relatively infrequent contacts with the White House, congressional personnel, and interest group representatives. While it should once again be stressed that comparisons to the data in the Aberbach-Rockman study of top-level administrators must be regarded with great caution, the levels reported here suggest a continuation of the low level of contacts by career SES with the White House, Congress, and interest group representatives—all of them, of course, key players in the policy process—in evidence since Ronald Reagan's administration's successful efforts to control the influence of civil servants it distrusted.[42]

While low levels of regular contact with the White House might be expected of a sample of career civil servants in the agencies, relatively low levels of contact with interest group representatives and with key congressional personnel is an important aspect of the "administrative presidency" approach to governing. The idea is to insulate career civil servants sufficiently from the process, as both sources and recipients of information, roles that they traditionally have played as parts of their jobs, so as to maintain a high level of control by appointees loyal to the administration. The data on contacts suggest that this has been achieved.

When broken down by party identification, the data on contacts also reveal a fascinating pattern that reinforces what has been seen before. With the exception of civil servants' contacts with other senior civil servants and with political appointees (which are uniformly high), there is a distinct party effect in contacts. Republican senior civil servants reported consistently more frequent contacts than Democratic identifiers with all of the other listed actors. The average ratio is

TABLE 1

Frequency of Contacts with Others in the Policy Arena, Career and Political Executives

Percent reporting weekly or more contact*			
		Name of Executive Appointment	
Contacts with	**Career SES**	**Bush Appointees**	**Clinton Appointees**
White House	11	47	57
Members or staff of congressional committees	11	50	59
Republicans in Congress	7	35	49
Democrats in Congress	7	25	52
Interest group representatives	29	39	47
Political appointees in the departments and agencies	82	93	93
Senior civil servants in the departments and agencies	96	97	97

Statement: We're interested in how often you [have][had] contact with certain groups or individuals. For each, please tell me how often you [have][had] contact with them: daily, weekly, monthly, rarely, never.

Source: 2004–2005 surveys by Princeton Survey Research Associates for the Annenberg Foundation Trust at Sunnylands.

*Percent of total responses, including Don't Know and Refused.

2.3 to 1, meaning that Republican senior civil servants were, on average, 2.3 times as likely as Democratic senior civil servants to report weekly or more contacts with actors in the White House, the Congress, or in interest groups.[43] This might be explained by the fact that others recognized who among the career civil servants was likely to have reliable information or to be most "plugged in" (presumably the Republicans among the career executives), or perhaps that these individuals were the ones given the greatest leeway by their political superiors to communicate with others, or, most likely, a combination of the two.

Conclusion

The Annenberg survey data provide strong evidence that the debate about presidential power that has roiled executive politics for many years is, in the first decade of the twenty-first century, reflected in a highly partisan split about governance.

The long-simmering (and sometimes boiling) suspicion that several Republican administrations have had of many of their top civil servants is reflected in a reality marked by clear partisan divisions about the role of the president, about the nature of presidential power, and even about the way the decision-making process has worked. Partisan divisions on policy have, of course, long existed (though research suggests that they have grown stronger in the general public),[44] but the disagreements about governance, about the extent of presidential power, and about the overall trustworthiness of the executive branch to operate in the best interests of the American people are matters that reach beyond concerns about desirable public policies, important though these matters might be.

The bureaucracy as an institution and the career civil servants who staff it have been easy targets for politicians and often derided in the popular culture, but the fact is that the United States has been blessed with a well-educated, skilled, and highly dedicated career civil service. The Annenberg samples demonstrate that the corps of executives at the top of federal government agencies are as highly educated and experienced as their immediate predecessors. There is concern about a big gap in well-qualified people in the next generation of career civil servants caused, in part, by downsizing during the 1990s, and there are always worries about structuring the government and designing systems to get the best leadership possible, but studies (including this one) consistently show that once political appointees in the agencies gain experience in government and work with its employees, they come to appreciate the dedication, effort, and skills of public sector executives.[45] A major problem, however, is that political appointees rarely stay long in their positions (generally averaging less than two years),[46] thus setting the stage for continuously unsettled relationships.

Differing opinions about public policy between civil servants who do not share the party affiliations of the administration in power and the administration are inevitable when one has a career public service chosen on merit rather than political criteria. They will not all be of the same party as the administration—instead actually being more representative of the general public's views politically, especially in the current era of highly partisan criteria for political appointments—or agree with what it wants to do. And suspicions about the loyalty of civil servants, especially when an administration wants to make major policy changes, are also inevitable. Active sabotage, certainly beyond occasional well-placed leaks, is apparently quite rare (as the reports from political executives on their own experiences with top civil servants suggest), but it is known that bureaucrats can subtly undermine an administration's efforts by withholding information about pitfalls (including political pitfalls) in proposals.[47] It is also known that American bureaucrats are, to a surprising extent, willing to endorse the proposition that they should speak out within the councils of government if they feel that policy proposals are "very undesirable or ill-considered."[48] As Aberbach and Rockman note: "Indeed, 'speaking truth to power' (as the civil servant sees truth) is one of the roles of a top civil servant, so long as the conversation does not become too loud."[49] Hearing different views and drawing on the long experience of top civil servants is one of the great advantages of having a career service. It can be disquieting at times for those who wish to push ahead boldly, but it can also save the government from grave errors and, based on the data presented in this chapter on policy issues, might even at times (fully recognizing that there are often agency biases on major issues) help to make its actions more representative of public views.[50] In short, differing views within the varied elements of the executive branch on ordinary policy issues should not, in and of themselves, be a problem for effective governance. Properly utilized, they will often, in fact, be an advantage.

A 2005 book argues strongly that there is a "myth of a polarized America." It uses polling data to demonstrate that the red state–blue state divide masks a lot of similarity in preference patterns across the states, and argues that while partisan polarization has increased, much of this is a reflection of the realignment of the South and a general sorting of the population into the "correct" party.[51] Purist activists, the expansion of the government into spheres of life previously considered private, and the rise of participatory democracy have led to a "hijacking of American democracy,"[52] turning it into a tense, high-stakes game dominated by those who have more extreme views on the issues than mainstream citizens, who mostly go about their business in the world at some distance from the screeching chatter of the political class. "Elites," the authors argue, "have polarized, but . . . public opinion data . . . provide little reason to believe that elites are following voters. Rather, they are imposing their own agendas on the electorate."[53]

Clearly there is measurably greater partisan polarization of administrative elites than of the general public on the conventional policy issues represented by the items in Figures 3 to 5 in this chapter. The items in Figures 6 to 8 on presidential power and authority also show a gap between elite partisans and partisans in the public, but the gap between elites and the general public is noticeably narrower on these measures; that is, the two appear to be closer together in their levels of partisan polarization. This suggests that whomever or whatever has "hijacked" American democracy has done a pretty good job of it, with the split over ordinary/conventional policy issues now extending to more fundamental issues of presidential power, indeed magnified on these more fundamental issues where the differences between Republicans and Democrats are clear, large, and consistent. That could change (with a change in party control of the presidency, for example), and should be carefully monitored in future research, but the record of the years since 2000, which saw the tendency to link party and conceptions of the nature of executive power and how it should be exercised, make it a matter of great concern.

What is particularly troubling about the situation in the executive branch (and apparently the country at large, as well) in the early years of the twenty-first century is not the existence of disagreements, but the fundamental nature of many of the disagreements. They go beyond policy to the heart of how the system should operate—for example: when, and under what limits, the president can take preemptive military action; when, and under what limits, the president can contravene international treaties to which the United States is a signatory; when, and under what limits, the president can decide that domestic wiretapping is permissible; when, and under what limits, government deliberations can be kept secret; when, and under what limits, the president can act without the consent of Congress (or in defiance of the laws it has passed); and even, it turns out, whether or not individuals the government holds as prisoners can be subject to torture.[54] These are weighty issues that can individually and cumulatively rip institutions apart, especially when they are tied to partisan perspectives that are likely both to intensify the disputes and lead to increased suspicion and hostility toward those with whom one disagrees.

One vision of a well-ordered state sees the policy expertise of experienced civil servants within government as a key component in ensuring viable policy-making and implementation. Top career civil servants, while obviously having their own opinions and values, are supposed to provide policymakers of all persuasions with a wide variety of perspectives and the best possible professional judgments. The Annenberg survey results make evident that—while convincing their immediate superiors of their responsiveness—Bush administration senior civil servants (especially the Democrats) were cut off from central actors in the policy process who are not in the departments or agencies and were often perceived, at least by many Bush appointees, as only "somewhat" responsive to the president and his associates. That can have significant implications for the quality of policy and administration, as cases in the Bush presidency involving matters such as estimating the cost of the administration's Medicare prescription drug benefit program and addressing the likely dangers of global warming demonstrate. And, at a more fundamental level, one does not have to be an alarmist to fear that the partisan splits within both the executive branch and the country about the nature of executive power reflect an underlying disagreement about how Americans should be governed that has serious potential for undermining the system's legitimacy and ultimately its effectiveness.

Notes

1. For more complete, though still brief, discussions of recent executive branch history, see Joel D. Aberbach and Mark A. Peterson, "Control and Accountability: Dilemmas of the Executive Branch," and Scott C. James, "The Evolution of the Presidency: Between the Promise and the Fear," both in *The Executive Branch*, ed. Joel D. Aberbach and Mark A. Peterson, Institutions of American Democracy (New York: Oxford University Press, 2005).

2. A good treatment of the theme that "parties in the electorate have experienced a noteworthy resurgence over the last two decades," arguing that "greater partisan polarization in Congress has clarified the parties' ideological positions for ordinary Americans," can be found in Marc J. Hetherington, "Resurgent Mass Partisanship: The Role of Elite Polarization," *American Political Science Review* 95 (September 2001): 619–31. The quotes here are from the abstract on p. 619.

3. For a recent critical analysis of the red state–blue state phenomenon, see Morris P. Fiorina, with Samuel J. Adams and Jeremy C. Pope, *Culture War? The Myth of a Polarized America* (New York: Pearson Longman, 2005), as well as the works cited therein that argue the opposite view.

4. Ns for this chapter are: SES career = 421 (the 23 SES noncareer respondents were excluded); Executive Office of the President career = 31 (the 2 SES noncareer were excluded); Bush political appointees = 113; Clinton political appointees = 152; and the general public sample = 1,500. (Bush's SES appointees generally resemble other Bush appointees on the items used in this chapter.)

5. National Commission on the Public Service, *Leadership for America: Rebuilding the Public Service* (Lexington, Mass.: Lexington Books, 1990), xiii.

6. Ibid.

7. National Commission on the Public Service, *Urgent Business for America: Revitalizing the Federal Government for the 21st Century*, http://www.brookings.edu/gs/cps/volcker/reportfinal.pdf, January 2003, 8.

8. Ibid., 14.

9. See Donald Kettl, "Reforming the Executive Branch of the U.S. Government," in *The Executive Branch*, ed. Aberbach and Peterson, for a succinct and well-informed essay on executive branch reform by a leading public-administration scholar.

10. Joel D. Aberbach and Bert A. Rockman, *In the Web of Politics: Three Decades of the U.S. Federal Executive* (Washington, D.C.: Brookings Institution Press, 2000).

11. Prestige private undergraduate institutions are defined as those in the Ivy League, those rated "highly selective" or above in their admissions criteria, or those private institutions with at least three graduate programs rated among the top ten in the nation. See Aberbach and Rockman, *In the Web of Politics*, notes to Table 4-4, p. 67, for a full explanation.

12. Ibid. The data for graduate institutions was updated with rankings from the National Research Council's 1993 report on graduate programs.

13. See Kettl, "Reforming the Executive Branch," and National Commission on the Public Service, *Leadership for America* and *Urgent Business for America*.

14. See Francis E. Rourke, "Responsiveness and Neutral Competence in American Bureaucracy," *Public Administration Review* 52 (1992): 539–46.

15. There is a large literature on this subject. For a brief summary, see Aberbach and Peterson, "Control and Accountability," especially 527–31.

16. The quotation is from Richard Neustadt, *Presidential Power: The Politics of Leadership* (New York: Signet, 1964), 42, emphasis in original.

17. Richard P. Nathan, *The Plot That Failed: Nixon and the Administrative Presidency* (New York: John Wiley, 1975).

18. Senate Select Committee on Presidential Campaign Activities, Executive Session Hearings on *Watergate and Related Activities, Federal "Political" Personnel Manual,* 93rd Cong., 2d sess., 1974, exhibit 35 in book 19.

19. Neustadt, *Presidential Power,* Chapter 3.

20. Richard M. Nixon, *RN: The Memoirs of Richard Nixon* (New York: Grosset & Dunlap, 1978), 768.

21. Patrick Buchanan, "Nixon's Paranoia Justified," *Chicago Tribune,* August 17, 1976.

22. Aberbach and Rockman, *In the Web of Politics,* 102–8, 114–17.

23. Dana Milbank, "Cheney Refuses Records' Release," *Washington Post,* January 28, 2002, A1.

24. See, for example, Joel D. Aberbach, "The Political Significance of the George W. Bush Administration," *Social Policy and Administration* 39, no. 2 (April 2005), especially 139–44, and Andrew C. Revkin, "Call to Openness at NASA Adds to Reports of Pressure," *New York Times,* February 16, 2006.

25. Aberbach and Rockman, *In the Web of Politics,* 104.

26. According to the 2004 "Plum Book" (the designation commonly used in Washington for the report issued every four years listing top governmental positions), "SES positions are designated Career Reserved when the need to ensure impartiality, or the public's confidence in the impartiality of the Government, requires that they be filled only by career employees (e.g. law enforcement and audit positions). The remaining SES positions are designated General and may be filled by career, noncareer, or limited appointment." Committee on Government Reform, U.S. House of Representatives, *United States Government Policy and Supporting Positions,* 108th Cong., 2d ses., November 24, 2004, 216. In addition to differences in the sampling frames, the response rates and interview methods for the two studies were quite different. Aberbach and Rockman had response rates of 90 percent (utilizing in-person interviews), while the Annenberg Executive Branch survey response rate, calculated in a manner similar to that used by Aberbach and Rockman, was 51 percent (with interviews conducted by telephone).

27. With the foreign policy and Defense Department officials excluded, the sample is 37 percent Democratic, 14 percent Republican, and 39 percent Independent. The foreign policy and defense executives are about evenly split (21 percent Democratic and 19 percent Republicans, with 54 percent saying they are Independents).

28. When asked about party leanings, recall that 29 percent of the career SES Independents expressed a preference for the Democratic Party and 23 percent for the Republican Party. The rest either refused to express a preference (32 percent) or were coded as "other" or "don't know." A general review of the data for the Independents shows, not surprisingly, that the Democratic-leaning Independents resemble Democrats, though usually less liberal, and the Republican-leaning Independents express views that are quite similar to those of Republican identifiers. The remainder of the respondents, those who would not express a preference for either of the major parties, falls in the middle. Therefore, the data in the figures would not look too different if the SES "leaners" had been assigned to a party. (See note 29, for example.)

29. On this particular question, Independents who lean toward the Democrats lean liberal on the issue, with slightly more than half favoring a greater government role,

while Independents who lean toward the Republicans look much like Republicans, with only 33 percent favoring a greater government role. Those who do not express a preference for either party are in the middle, with 45 percent believing that government should play a greater role in the nation's economic affairs.

30. It is not possible, using these data, to examine the views in any detail of Independents among the general public because the survey instrument did not ask them whether they leaned more to the Republicans or to the Democrats. Only the relatively small number who had volunteered that they had "no preference" were asked this question. Parenthetically, among the SES, party "leaners" broke out as expected in their views on the federal government's responsibility to conserve the country's natural resources—the policy issue that is the focus of Figure 3.

31. The relevant figures for "important" on the "protecting the unborn" item are 28 percent for career civil servants in the SES, 37 percent for Bush appointees, and 16 percent for Clinton appointees. (Among Republicans in the general public, 29 percent thought it an "important" responsibility of the federal government and 50 percent thought it a "very important" responsibility.)

32. It should be added that while there are significant partisan differences on most of these issues, it is important to recognize that there are still large numbers of people, including in the policy elite, whose preferences are not intense. For example, on an issue not presented in Figures 3–5, when asked, "Is keeping taxes low a very important responsibility of the federal government, important, not so important, or not important at all?" 35 percent of Bush appointees thought it a "very important" responsibility compared to only about 5 percent of Clinton appointees, but nearly 40 percent of Clinton appointees did agree that it was "important."

33. Taking out the "protect the unborn item," the absolute value of the average differences between party identifiers is 33 percent for the career SES respondents and 23 percent for the general public respondents. The average differences were calculated using absolute values, because the differences are positive for two of the items and negative in one.

34. In data not shown here, Democrats also disagreed with the notion that the president has a broad right to keep his communications with others private, whether or not he invokes executive privilege, and Democrats were much more likely than Republicans to believe that the president should have authority, without the consent of Congress, to suspend constitutional protections for certain individuals.

35. The party differences in Figures 6 through 8 are also found in the study of congressional staff done for the Annenberg project. On whether the president should have the authority to take preemptive military action without the consent of Congress, 89 percent of Democratic congressional staffers say no, but only 32 percent of Republican congressional staffers say no. On whether the president should have the authority to contravene international laws or treaties to which the United States is a signatory, 57 percent of Republican staffers say no, compared to 94 percent of Democratic staffers who say no. And on the notion that other policymakers should defer to the president if he believes something should be done about an important national issue, 49 percent of Republican staffers strongly agree or agree, compared to 15 percent of Democratic staffers. The relationship between party and answers to the

latter question is strong but also reflects greater reluctance in Congress than in the administration or the general public to grant deference to the president.

36. This question (with the executive branch as a focus; exact wording in Figure 9) was not asked in the survey of the general public.

37. It would belabor the point to present comparable statistics for each figure in this series, but on the "comprehensive review of relevant information item" (Figure 10), 48 percent of the Republican SES civil servants thought that the Bush administration was more likely to make its decisions this way, compared to 12 percent of Independents and only 3 percent of Democrats.

38. See Aberbach and Rockman, *In the Web of Politics*, 107–8. In the Annenberg 2004–5 survey of career SES executives, 49 percent of executives in the social service agencies said they were Democrats compared to 32 percent for the entire SES sample.

39. The view that civil servants are "very responsive" to the president is shared by civil servants of both parties.

40. SES executives join political appointees, however, in believing that decisions in their areas were the result of careful analysis and deliberation (abut 87 percent strongly agree or agree with this proposition), though this is true to a greater extent for Republicans and than for Democrats.

41. See Aberbach and Rockman, *In the Web of Politics*, 118. The findings on SES executives' assessments of their own (individual) influence (in their areas of interest) are from the 1991–92 Aberbach and Rockman executive branch survey. These data were not reported there; rather, data on general assessments of the influence of those in various roles (senior civil servants, department secretaries, members of Congress, and the like) were reported and compared.

42. Aberbach and Rockman, *In the Web of Politics*, 116.

43. The figures are 2.7 to 1 for Republicans in Congress, 2.3 to 1 for Democrats in Congress, 2.7 to 1 for members or staff of congressional committees, 2.8 to 1 for the White House, and 1.5 to 1 for interest group representatives.

44. See, for example, Hetherington, "Resurgent Mass Partisanship."

45. See, for example, U.S. Merit System Protection Board, *The Senior Executive Service: Views of Former Federal Executives* (Government Printing Office, 1989), and Aberbach and Rockman, *In the Web of Politics*, 122–25.

46. Aberbach and Rockman, *In the Web of Politics*, 74. About 36 percent of the Annenberg sample of Bush political appointees reported that they had served two years or less in their current jobs.

47. Hugh Heclo, *A Government of Strangers: Executive Politics in Washington* (Washington, D.C.: Brookings Institution, 1977), 175–77, 224–25.

48. Aberbach and Rockman, *In the Web of Politics*, 126.

49. Ibid.

50. A *Newsweek* story discussing the George W. Bush administration's problems with ill-conceived and controversial (and, in the view of many, unconstitutional) decisions on the rules for electronic surveillance of U.S. citizens and prisoner-interrogation techniques included this somewhat patronizing statement about the protests of career government lawyers: "Though 'bureaucrat' can be a bad name, government careerists are sometimes the only ones who will uphold standards of fairness and

decency." It added: "They know, too, that they can be left holding the bag if later congressional hearings look into dubious secret operations." Evan Thomas and Daniel Klaidman, "Full Speed Ahead," *Newsweek*, January 9, 2006, 29.

51. Fiorina, with Adams and Pope, *Culture War?* 25.
52. Ibid., 99.
53. Ibid., 88.
54. The Annenberg data cover many, but not all, of these issues. Aside from those discussed in the text, the survey asked respondents about suspending constitutional protections for individuals and about whether the president has a "broad right" to keep his communications with others on policy matters secret. Party identification was strongly related to answers to these questions, both at the elite level and among the general public.

An Annenberg survey on public attitudes toward the judicial branch done in August of 2006 found that Republicans were also significantly more likely than Democrats (58 percent to 31 percent) to endorse the proposition that "it is okay for the president to ignore a Supreme Court ruling if the president believes it will prevent him from protecting the country against terrorist attacks." Independents were close to Democrats in their answers to this question, with 34 percent endorsing the proposition. Partisans of the two parties, however, were not far apart, at least at this point in time, in their views on whether presidents should generally follow Supreme Court rulings that they might disagree with (54 percent of Republicans and 58 percent of Democrats felt that they should), and over 75 percent of each party's identifiers felt that presidents should veto legislation they think unconstitutional rather than signing it and then only carrying out the parts they think are constitutional.

7

THE JUDICIAL BRANCH:
JUDGING AMERICA'S JUDGES

Kevin T. McGuire

On the evening of December 12, 2000, the justices of the U.S. Supreme Court brought a tumultuous and contested presidential election to a halt. Scarcely twenty-four hours earlier, lawyers on behalf of George W. Bush had presented a novel legal argument to the Court—that having different mechanisms for casting and counting votes across counties in the crucial state of Florida meant that some votes were more likely to be counted than others and that this, in turn, violated the Constitution's guarantee of equal protection of the laws. Such a theory had not been contemplated in previous cases, and indeed even Bush's lawyers did not regard it as their strongest argument. Nevertheless, this became the principal basis for the Court's decision to halt the ongoing recount of ballots in Florida, where officials were trying to verify an outcome in which the candidates were separated by only a handful of votes.[1]

This decision, which clinched Bush's election, was met with varying degrees of skepticism. To many, it reflected little more than rank partisanship on the part of a majority of justices who were determined to derail any efforts that might call the Florida election outcome into question. Judges, academics, and other members of the legal community declared it to be a major blow to the Court's legitimacy, an injury akin to the *Dred Scott* case (1857), the antebellum ruling denounced in the North as motivated by little more than the justices' personal desire to insulate slavery from federal regulation.

These observers declared that the justices had expended a great deal of the institution's legitimacy and that its subsequent rulings would be undercut by a general cynicism toward the Court and its members. At first, public opinion polls confirmed that many had lost faith in the Court. Not surprisingly, supporters of the Democratic candidate, Al Gore, revealed especially low levels of support for the Court.

On closer examination, however, a more complex picture began to emerge. Rather than the decision damaging the Court's prestige, the level of prestige that the Court enjoyed actually determined how the public received the decision. So, quite apart from the impact of partisanship, the public's support for the Court actually governed the reaction to the decision. Those who held the Court in high esteem prior to the decision were significantly more likely to see *Bush v. Gore* as derived from principles of law. Those who were less supportive of the Court's mission, by contrast, greeted its decision with disdain.[2] Ironically, what was seen by the legal community—a sophisticated constituency of the Court— as a major blow to the Court's long-term legitimacy was, in fact, cushioned by the mass public's esteem for the Court prior to the 2000 election.

The story of the reaction of both elites and the mass public to the Supreme Court's decision in *Bush v. Gore* highlights some interesting facets of how different groups understand and evaluate the judicial branch. Among other things, it demonstrates that those who are closest to the judiciary can have substantially different reactions to its policies than the general public; elites, it seems, can be more protective of the Court's institutional interests and thus react more negatively than the public as a whole. The American public, by contrast, uses that institutional legitimacy to evaluate the Court's specific performance. Stated differently, elites see policy as affecting the Court's mission, while the public uses its understanding of that mission to evaluate the Court's policy.

In the broader context, the response to *Bush v. Gore* underscores the importance of having a clear understanding of the connections between public opinion and the judiciary and how those connections work across different groups within the population. To be sure, members of the U.S. Supreme Court and other federal judges are not elected, but the framers of the Constitution nevertheless allocated power such that the Court would be required to enlist the support of other policymakers to put its decisions into practice. As a result, the effectiveness of the Supreme Court is heavily dependent upon the esteem in which it is held not by legal observers only but by the American public. At the state level, where the vast majority of judges are elected, the connection between the judiciary and public opinion is even clearer. Exploring these linkages is critical for mapping the judiciary's role within the democratic system.

This chapter considers public opinion toward the Supreme Court and the judicial system among both lawyers and lay people, utilizing data from the Annenberg Institutions of Democracy Judicial Branch survey (see appendix for survey details). As explained by Gregory A. Caldeira and Kevin T. McGuire, a good deal of scholarly research already exists on the connections between public opinion on the American judiciary, and this research paints a fairly complex picture of how the public understands courts and judges, and their policies.[3]

The data examined here offer an opportunity to revisit some of the findings from that research as well as explore important differences that may exist between the mass public and the lawyers who constitute the community of elites who are the judiciary's principal constituency. Data on the mass public are drawn from a national sample of the U.S. population, while the respondents in the survey of lawyers were drawn from a list of lawyers admitted to practice in either the U.S. Supreme Court or a U.S. court of appeals. In this sense, it is not a random sample of lawyers but rather a reasonably select group of lawyers who are likely to have paid the most attention to the workings of the federal appellate courts. Using data from both of these surveys, we examine such issues as the level of knowledge of the judiciary, perceptions about the factors that shape judicial decision making, and what these publics think about the role and efficacy of judicial policy.

Knowledge of the Supreme Court

In the summer of 2006, the Annenberg Public Policy Center conducted the Annenberg Judicial Independence survey on the relationship between the Supreme Court and the president. It occurred at a time when questions of executive power were much debated by scholars, public officials, and the press; President George Bush's program of trying suspected terrorists held at Guantánamo Bay, Cuba, by military commission had just been invalidated by the Supreme Court, a majority of which concluded that the president's actions had not been explicitly authorized by Congress. For his part, President Bush set about working with the Congress to develop legislation that would authorize specific forms of interrogation and prosecution for these suspects. To be sure, the president was critical of the Court's decision, but he was resigned to abide by its ruling.[4]

The president's grudging capitulation made plain his acceptance of the Supreme Court's authority. Ironically, the Annenberg survey revealed widespread ignorance on the part of the American public about the Supreme Court's role as the final arbiter of federal law. Nearly 40 percent of respondents indicated that the president was not obligated to abide by such a ruling if he believed that the Court's ruling would undermine efforts to prevent terrorist attacks. Scarcely 50 percent believed—correctly—that the president was obligated to adhere to a Supreme Court ruling regardless of the circumstances.[5]

The public's lack of understanding of the basic relationship between the Court and the president reinforces what scholars of public opinion have long professed and what has been emphasized throughout this volume: that Americans do not possess a deep reservoir of political knowledge. Surveys have consistently demonstrated that most members of the electorate are not especially aware of the individuals, interests, and issues that form the basis for public policymaking.[6] As the Annenberg survey showed, this is no less true in the case of the courts. Indeed, the evidence consistently underscores how little Americans seem to know about judges, their authority, and their decisions.

The Justices

In 1986 William Rehnquist became the sixteenth chief justice of the United States. After he had served three years as the nation's leading judicial officer, however, a *Washington Post* survey famously found that more Americans could name Judge Joseph Wapner as the judge on the television program *The People's Court* than could name the chief justice.[7] Of course, Rehnquist had been serving as chief justice for a relatively short time when the survey was conducted, and this might have explained why fewer than one out of ten Americans knew who he was. In the intervening years, he became somewhat more recognizable; at the time of his death in office in 2005, better than a quarter of the population could identify him. (The Annenberg survey asking respondents to name the chief justices was conducted while Rehnquist was serving on the Court.)

In other respects, however, little has changed in the intervening years. In 1989 Justice Sandra Day O'Connor was the Court's best-known member, and she remained so in 2005; shortly before Justice O'Connor left the Court, a third of Americans, according to the Annenberg survey data, were able to identify her as one of the Court's two female justices. Beyond Justice O'Connor and Chief Justice Rehnquist, however, there is only scant knowledge of the justices among the general public. About 70 percent of Americans surveyed, for example, were unable to identify the chief justice, and nearly the same percentage could name neither O'Connor nor Ruth Bader Ginsburg when asked to identify the two women then serving on the Court.

As one might expect, this knowledge differs substantially across education levels. Forty-four percent of college graduates could name the chief justice, for instance, compared to roughly 10 percent of those who did not attend college. Taken by itself, though, education does not account for the public's knowledge of the Supreme Court. After all, a majority of college graduates could not name the chief justice, and 75 percent of that same group could not come up with the name of Ruth Bader Ginsburg as one of the Court's two women members.

Of course, expecting the public to be able to name the members of the Court is somewhat unrealistic. Americans often possess more-general levels of knowledge that can be tapped through alternative measures. When asked to name the Court's most conservative member from a list of the justices, for instance, many respondents made sensible choices, nominating Chief Justice Rehnquist, Justice Antonin Scalia, or Justice Clarence Thomas more often than any other (see Figure 1). At the other end of the political spectrum, Justice Ginsburg was seen as the most liberal member. These results are encouraging, because they suggest that the public is capable of internalizing the ideological

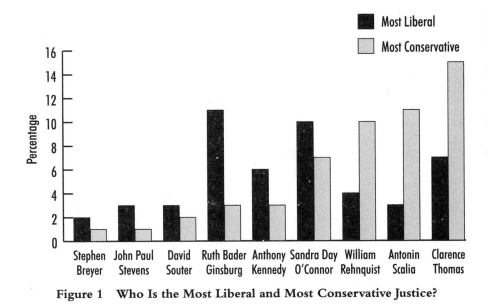

Figure 1   Who Is the Most Liberal and Most Conservative Justice?

orientations of national policymakers, even those who deal with complex and abstract principles of law. At the same time, however, these judgments are made by a relatively sophisticated (and therefore small) segment of the population. Roughly half of Americans were unable to venture a guess as to which justices anchor the ideological spectrum. Not only that, many made some fairly implausible estimates: even though Justice John Paul Stevens was arguably the most liberal member of the Court at the time, respondents were more likely to place Clarence Thomas at the left of the ideological continuum. Justice O'Connor, the moderate conservative at the Court's center, was named as the most liberal justice only slightly less often than Ginsburg. Given the pivotal role that O'Connor played in upholding liberal precedents in areas such as abortion rights and affirmative action, this choice is perhaps more understandable.

In the main, however, citizens have only a rough sense of who serves on the Court. Their notions of left and right on the Court are equally unsophisticated. Of course, such perceptions are not unique to the Court. They are, in fact, representative—perhaps in a more magnified way—of the public's overall political knowledge. Apart from knowing who is president of the United States, Americans are not terribly aware of the identities of their public officials.

The Judicial Process

Despite their lifetime tenure, the individual personalities on the Court are transitory. Justices come and go. The functions of the Court, by contrast, are constant, and therefore one might expect the mass public to have a firmer grasp of the basic responsibilities of the judiciary than of the makeup of the Court. The survey data, however, clearly suggest that the Court is not as well understood as it might be. On the one hand, a substantial majority of Americans claimed to understand the decisions of the Court either moderately or very well. On the other hand, 40 percent either did not know or did not believe that the Court has the power to strike down legislative acts as inconsistent with the Constitution. What is especially noteworthy is that fully 20 percent of those who claimed to understand the Court's rulings very well nevertheless did not have a basic comprehension of the power of judicial review.

Similar confusion seems to exist about the most basic mechanics of the Court's decision making. The outcomes of cases, for example, are governed by simple majority rule, and yet survey results indicate that half of all Americans seem not to know this, with substantial numbers believing that 5–4 decisions are too close to carry legal force and require subsequent review by either the lower courts or the Congress. Scholars have long suggested that, for their part, the members of the Court try to establish large voting majorities (especially in salient cases) as a means of giving greater legal and political emphasis to their decisions.[8] Given that many Americans seem to perceive closely divided decisions as legally dubious, such a strategy seems quite rational.

Not surprisingly, the public's lack of understanding can be explained largely by educational background. Those who have attended college have a much clearer sense of the structure and operation of the Supreme Court than those with less schooling. Education alone, however, does not sustain an understanding of the business of the Court. Indeed, nearly a third of college graduates surveyed believe that 5–4 rulings are "too close" to be final.

Given that the Court is not electorally accountable and makes its decisions removed from the public eye, it is tempting to interpret these findings as unique to a relatively isolated institution. Again, the public's knowledge of the Court is indicative of the larger picture. Americans seem to know as much about the Supreme Court as they do about the popularly elected branches.

There is at least one issue that Americans seem to intuit quite accurately; two out of three believe that their fellow citizens have a poor understanding of the Supreme Court. This is scarcely encouraging as an indicator of the health of a democratic system, which presupposes that the electorate has at least some general awareness of the principals and processes of policymaking.

Perceptions of the Judicial System

Americans regard the Supreme Court as a leading policymaker at the national level. Based on survey data, fully 75 percent believe that the justices' decisions have a direct bearing on citizens' lives. No doubt one reason for this perception is the considerable controversy that swirls around the nomination and confirmation of the Court's members. There is no mystery as to why this controversy exists: the political stakes have been regarded as especially high since the mid-twentieth century, as the Supreme Court has assumed a much greater role in crafting national policy. The Warren Court (1953–69), so named for Chief Justice Earl Warren, for example, pioneered much of the law involving reproductive rights, criminal law, legislative districting, and freedom of religion, to name just a few, and the various constituencies that stand to lose or gain through Court decisions in such areas have come to take a much greater interest in who is selected to serve on the bench.[9]

The resignation of Justice O'Connor and the death of Chief Justice Rehnquist in 2005 highlighted how interests on both the left and right readily mobilized to support or attack even potential nominees. Even before these events began to unfold, fully half of the respondents from the national survey strongly believed that the process of selecting justices had become increasingly political. These and other perceptions held by lawyers and the general public were probed in Chapter 4. The discussion here considers what kinds of forces are responsible for the public's understanding of the judiciary.

Sources of Perceptions

How citizens comprehend the Supreme Court is naturally conditioned by the level and quality of the information they receive about the institution. A good way to illustrate this is to compare the perceptions of the Court based on individuals' different media habits. Because of their capacity to devote greater analytical depth to issues, newspapers are probably a better source of information about the Court than television. Not surprisingly, survey results indicate that Americans whose primary news source is newspapers not only follow the Court more closely but are also more confident about their understanding of the Court than are those who rely on television. Those who turn first to printed news also see the Court's main mission as constitutional interpretation, in greater numbers (65 percent) than those who get their news from television (41 percent). In terms of the impact of the Court's policies, newspaper readers are also marginally more likely to see a link between the justices' decisions and their daily lives.

Educational background also guides the perceptions of the Supreme Court among the general public. Among other things, education provides a basis for making sense of politics, a skill that is certainly requisite to interpreting the often cryptic policies of the justices. Education, consequently, clearly contributes to how the public understands the Court. Some 40 percent of college graduates surveyed, for example, regarded the decisions of the Supreme Court as fair and objective. For those with less education, less than 30 percent shared this view. Instead, they were significantly more likely to see the Court's decisions as motivated by politics. Furthermore, the tendency for educated citizens to see the Court as an evenhanded institution held regardless of political partisanship.

Factors such as media exposure and education surely provide a basis for comprehending the Court. It should be emphasized, though, that the Court has long jealously guarded its secrecy and therefore has made itself considerably less accessible than other government institutions to the media and, thereby, the public. The decision by the Court in 2000 to release audiotapes of the oral arguments in *Bush v. Gore* immediately after they concluded was widely viewed as a major concession by the justices, who obviously sensed the enormous significance of the case. Seen in this way, the justices themselves must bear some of the responsibility for the mass public's perceptions (and misperceptions) of the institution.

As part of the legal culture, lawyers may be safely assumed to be more sophisticated consumers of Court information, but that information is no doubt filtered through their preexisting beliefs. Whether elites perceive the Court to be engaged in policymaking, for example, is determined to some degree by their own views about the proper method of constitutional interpretation. Lawyers who regard themselves as strict constructionists are apt to believe that the Court should limit, not expand, its role; a good many of this group of elites surveyed (33 percent) see the Court as heavily involved in policymaking. By contrast, those who believe the Constitution's meaning ought to be interpreted in light of changing circumstances are typically less troubled by an active policy role by the Court and thus are more prone to perceive the major policies of the Court as merely the kind of dispute resolution in which the justices ought to engage. Only 20 percent of these lawyers saw the Court as an active agent of policy change. To the extent that lawyers view the Court as an agent of policy change, their perceptions of its usefulness are just as revealing. By and large, strict constructionists regard the policy role of the Court as undesirable—66 percent raised this objection—whereas 70 percent of lawyers who take a more flexible view of constitutional interpretation believed that judicial policymaking is a plus to the democratic system.

Understandings of Judicial Motivation

Probably the central research question for scholars who study the judicial process is, "Why do judges make the decisions that they do?" Although most political scientists who analyze the Supreme Court agree that the personal preferences of the justices are an important determinant, there is no clear agreement about just how important such preferences may be and what (or indeed whether) other factors guide the justices' decision making.

As one of the Court's principal constituencies, lawyers have their own views about what motivates the justices. These views are no doubt informed by their training as well as their day-to-day occupations, in which they may deal with judge-made law as a matter of course. The mass public does not have such expertise (or baggage, depending upon one's point of view). As a result, they may trace the root of the Court's policies to systematically different causes.

In making decisions, the members of the Supreme Court may have a number of different motivations, ranging from a desire to make sound legal policy to the need to satisfy their own ideological preferences.[10] From their perspective, most lawyers concede that the justices are sometimes motivated by their personal attitudes, but as a rule lawyers believe that the Court follows the canons of legal interpretation. Some 80 percent of these elites surveyed agree with the statement that, "Most of the time the Supreme Court justices closely follow the Constitution, the law, and the precedents in deciding cases," and nearly one-quarter strongly subscribed to this proposition. There is substantial empirical evidence suggesting that other factors besides constitutional imperatives influence how cases are decided, evidence that is supported by the sometimes intense engagement during the confirmation process of groups ideologically opposed to a Supreme Court nominee. Moreover, it is no secret that some justices who regularly vote together, such as Antonin Scalia and Clarence Thomas, rarely vote with other common voting partners, such as Ruth Bader Ginsburg and John Paul Stevens. This is good circumstantial evidence that personal ideologies may be at work in the Court's decision making.

There seems little doubt that, under the leadership of Chief Justice Rehnquist, the Supreme Court promulgated a good deal of conservative policy. During Rehnquist's tenure, the justices adopted ideas that the chief justice had long advocated. Among other things, it placed the first limits on Congress's power under the commerce clause since before the New Deal, striking down laws regulating handgun possession near schools and restricting the rights of victims of gender-related violence. The Rehnquist Court also limited the power of the federal government to enlist the states in enforcing national laws. Moreover, it insulated states from various lawsuits under the protection of the previously dormant Eleventh Amendment.[11]

Such policy changes notwithstanding, only 50 percent of lawyers surveyed believe that the decisions of the Supreme Court can be labeled as conservative (see Figure 2). Instead, a sizable proportion of these elites—some 42 percent—expressed the belief that the Court's jurisprudence simply reflects "making decisions on a case-by-case basis." Evidently, a great many lawyers see no ideological tenor to the Court's outcomes, regarding them as the product of the justices' applying the law to the individual circumstances that arise in cases. Given their background and training, the views of lawyers may be somewhat surprising. After all, they reach their conclusions with an assuredly better grasp of the Court's policymaking than that of Americans as a whole.

Roughly half of Americans surveyed judged the Supreme Court to be making decisions on a case-by-case basis. A good many saw an ideological orientation to the justices' policies, and they were more likely to characterize it as conservative (23 percent) than liberal (18 percent).

Of course, terms like "liberal" and "conservative" do not always carry a common valence across the public. Indeed, surveys have long documented that the

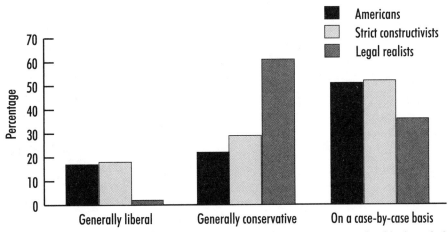

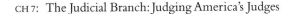

Note: The survey defined "legal realist" as "someone who believes the Court should take today's circumstances into account in decisions"; the item posed the question for the lawyer respondents as a dichotomy: "Do you think of yourself as a strict constructivist or a legal realist?"

Figure 2   How Americans and Lawyers See the Recent Decisions of the Supreme Court

mass public does not organize its political thinking in ideological terms. When asked similar questions without these labels, the public does express a concern that there is a bias in the Court's outputs. An overwhelming 70 percent of the citizens agreed that the decisions of the Supreme Court favor some groups more than others, an opinion held especially strongly by a third of the public.

Not surprisingly, the data reveal that those who see the strongest bias are the least likely to regard the Court as making decisions on a case-by-case basis. Overall, though, the perceived direction of that bias is uncertain; they are just as likely to see a liberal as a conservative bent to the Court. Among the most highly educated of this group, however, the bias perceived is conservative.

Applying this test—that is, examining the perception of the Court's ideological bias among those who believe that the Court favors some groups over others—to the elite sample tells much the same story. Like other highly educated members of the mass public, lawyers who see a bias by the Court toward some groups regarded that bias as conservative.

These data reveal some intriguing complexities. Among those who know the Supreme Court best, a sizable number expressed the belief—perhaps ironically, perhaps not—that the Court makes decisions based upon legal considerations. At the same time, there are those lawyers who believe that there is a bias in the Court, and those who are most convinced of that bias saw it as conservative. Americans as a whole shared the conviction that the Court makes decisions devoid of ideological considerations, but among the highly educated, those who were most skeptical were prone to see a right-leaning Court, too.

Relationship with Congress and the President

Alexander Hamilton in *Federalist* 78 argued that, lacking any tangible political authority, the judiciary was the weakest of the three branches. Indeed, having only the power to announce its interpretation of the law, it was wholly dependent upon the other two branches to act in accordance with its interpretations and to give them legal force. For that reason, the system of separated powers creates incentives for the Supreme Court to take the preferences of the elected branches into account. So rather than simply pursuing their own ambitions, the justices should act strategically and consider the likely reaction of those political actors upon whom the Court's legitimacy depends. To what extent does the public regard these interdependencies as genuinely important to the Supreme Court?

From the perspective of most Americans, the Court pays a good deal of attention to the elected branches. Sizable majorities of the public believe that the Supreme Court is influenced, at least to a moderate extent, by the Congress and the president when making decisions (60 percent and 57 percent, respectively). Furthermore, the public estimates this impact to be considerable; two out of three Americans regarded each branch as a major influence on the Court. In this sense, the mass public seems to subscribe to the Hamiltonian rationale.

Ironically, lawyers—who surely appreciate that the White House and Capitol Hill can check the Court by readily reversing its statutory interpretations—are loath to believe that the justices extend the elected branches much consideration. Only 31 percent of elites believed that the Court is influenced by the Congress in its decision making, half the percentage of the mass public that holds the same opinion. Likewise, only 36 percent considered the president to have at least some modest affect on the justices, fully twenty percentage points lower than in the national sample. As was explained in Chapter 4, lawyers naturally tend to take a more formalized and legalistic view of the Court's decisions, which they are trained to see as driven largely by legal, not political or strategic, considerations.

Still, these views stand in sharp contrast to instances of major opposition that Congress and the president have mounted against the Court. One noteworthy illustration is the effort by lawmakers to overcome some of the Supreme Court's conservative doctrine regarding religious liberty, by enacting the Religious Freedom Restoration Act (1993) and the Religious Land Use and Institutionalized Persons Act (2000). The belief in judicial indifference to elected officials is incongruous with the passage of such significant legislation aimed at undoing the Court. Elites, it would seem, do not believe that the justices are strategic in making decisions. From their perspective, the Court makes its decisions based upon relevant legal considerations, without regard to how lawmakers might react.

Relationship with Interest Groups and the Public

The Supreme Court might also anticipate the reactions of different segments of society as well as the public as a whole. Organized interests constitute a core set of participants in litigation before the high court. Today, the Court hears from interest groups in most cases that it decides. Organized interests make their views known by filing amicus curiae (or "friend of the court") briefs, and groups also provide direct legal support for a fair number of litigants each term.

As institutionalized players in the judicial process, interest groups are regarded by lawyers as legitimate influences on the Court. Thus, even among a group that regards the Court as immune from political considerations, the prevailing view is that the justices are affected by their input. Conservative groups are clearly seen as more relevant than liberal groups. Nearly 40 percent of elites said that the Court is either moderately or significantly affected by conservative groups, while the same percentage believed that liberal interest groups have no influence whatsoever on the Court's policies.

The mass public also believes that the Court responds to interest groups, but unlike the legal profession, the public sees liberal and conservative interests as having equal say before the Court. Regardless of the level of influence—a great extent, a moderate extent, a small extent, or not at all—the mass public believes that ideologically opposed groups carry more or less equal weight. Most Americans believe that these groups are at least of moderate importance (55 percent for conservative groups and just under 50 percent for liberal groups), and approximately 20 percent regard them as a major factor in the Court's calculus. The widespread perception that the justices are solicitous to the views of organized groups perhaps reflects Americans' more general cynicism that government is in the hands of "special interests."

The Court is not democratically accountable, but scholars have often asserted that the justices are attentive to the public's preferences. The evidence on this issue, though, is divided. In the abstract, the justices have at least some reason to care about how the pubic will receive its policies, since the Court's influence depends so heavily upon the perceived legitimacy of its rulings. If those rulings are at odds with popular opinion, it raises the likelihood that they will be taken less seriously by the public and, in turn, their representatives. The justices may well make the strategic calculation to consider public opinion, but as Keith E. Whittington explains in his historical survey of judicial review, the Supreme Court has always been willing to make its share of unpopular policies.[12]

If lawyers were merely skeptical about the political motivations of the Court, they are quite convinced that public opinion does not figure into the justices' decisions. Fully 50 percent said that public opinion matters only to a small extent, and 20 percent believed that it matters not at all. As far as these elites are concerned, remaining impervious to mass opinion promotes the health of the polity. Indeed, nearly 90 percent said that the extent to which the Supreme Court ignores public opinion actually strengthens the democratic system.

The mass public, by contrast, seems to see the Court as simply one of several components of government that is responsible to its citizens. A third of the public, for example, believed that the justices are moderately attentive to public preferences, and another 10 percent asserted that the Court is highly responsive to public opinion. Divided scholarly opinion notwithstanding, the citizens seem generally convinced that their views are on the minds of the justices when they set about deciding cases.

Support for the Court System

Perhaps more so than either of its coordinate branches, the judiciary is dependent upon public support for its mission in order to function effectively. As Walter Murphy explained in *Elements of Judicial Strategy*, "If prestige is one of the major sources of judicial power, it must follow that public opinion is one of the major limitations on the authority of the courts."[13] Absent the capacity to give force to its mandates, the courts must depend upon widespread acceptance of their legitimacy if their policies are to be taken seriously by other political actors as well as the American public. It is crucial, therefore, to explore the degree of trust that the public places in the court system. How do elites and the mass public evaluate the work of the courts? Do they have the kind of confidence in courts that is necessary to sustain the work of an independent judiciary within a democratic system?

Public Confidence

One of the great assets of the Supreme Court is the high esteem in which it is held by the American people. Surveys consistently show that the public places considerable trust in the Court. In fact, a 2006 Gallup Poll revealed that public esteem for the Court was at its highest level in several years, well above that of the Congress and the president.[14] The Annenberg data tell a similar tale. The vast majority of the mass public has either a fair amount or a great deal of confidence that the justices of the Supreme Court (75 percent)—and the judiciary more generally (79 percent)—are operating in the best interests of the American people.

These evaluations can be explained, at least in part, by education. Education provides the tools necessary to make sense of the Court, and this in turn produces greater support for the Supreme Court and the judiciary as a whole. So, for example, college graduates register significantly greater trust in the Court than those who did not graduate from high school. Partisanship and ideology also color the perceptions of the mass public; Republicans and conservatives hold the Court in somewhat higher esteem than Democrats and liberals. These differences are of degree, not kind, however. In the main, there is strong support for the Supreme Court across the political spectrum.

Notwithstanding such general support, it is important to bear in mind that neither the general public nor the legal community perceives the Court as totally free from subjectivity. Gerald N. Rosenberg notes that "Americans believe that the judicial system sometimes and perhaps often fails to provide the rule of law necessary for democracy. This is particularly the case with questions of equal access and bias."[15] So, despite the diffuse support for the institutional mission of the judicial branch, many Americans see specific limitations in its ability to perform effectively and fairly.

In addition to institutional support, confidence in the courts can also be seen at the individual level. What do Americans think of the individuals who sit on the Supreme Court? Citizens express a conviction that President Bush's nominees to the Court will make independent-minded decisions. Even Democrats, who are less sanguine than Republicans about Bush's picks for the Court, still express a strong belief in the independence of these justices. Because the Annenberg surveys were conducted prior to the nominations of Harriet Miers, John Roberts, and Samuel Alito, the responses to these questions reflect a diffuse confidence, unconditioned by any particular nominee.

However important public esteem may be, the support of the legal community is perhaps of greater relevance. Because lawyers themselves comprise the judiciary, the esteem in which judges are held by their colleagues in the legal profession serves as a check on the potential excesses of the judicial branch. At least since the early twentieth century, explains Kermit L. Hall, lawyers have recognized this connection; the late Roscoe Pound, dean of Harvard Law School, was one of the leading advocates of making judges responsible to the bar. "Roscoe Pound did not want judges free from all external influences, just political ones, and he preached consistently that judges should be accountable to the organized bar. By placing judges under the oversight of professionals, rather than naked public opinion, he insisted, an even-handed administration of justice was assured."[16]

Judged by that standard, the judicial branch is perceived as operating with a high degree of independence. Almost all lawyers (90 percent) surveyed believe that the Supreme Court specifically as well as the judicial system more generally can be trusted to make decisions that are in the best interests of the American people. Neither the president nor the Congress can muster even a majority of these elites to express the same degree of confidence that lawyers extend to the courts. Clearly, members of the legal community place the greatest faith in their own. More importantly, they provide the support that underwrites the independent decision making of judges.

Evaluation of Performance

Confidence in the Supreme Court is a prospective judgment, a belief about what the justices are likely to do in the future. How is the Court evaluated in retrospect? How do the mass public and elites assess the past performance of their judges? On the question of job performance, the Supreme Court gets reasonably high marks; some 40 percent rate the Court as "good" or "very good." The legal community is predictably more upbeat about the Supreme Court's performance. Lawyers see the Court in a highly favorable light—70 percent rate the Court as "good" or "very good"—and even more (77 percent) are impressed with the work of the judicial system as a whole. What is more, lawyers' judgments do not seem to be idiosyncratic to the particular time period during which they were surveyed. When asked to offer a more longitudinal perspective, most lawyers (55 percent) said that their opinion of the Supreme Court has remained the same over the last ten years, although more lawyers indicated that they had graded the Court down (34 percent) rather than up (10 percent) over the past decade.

For their part, the public at large offers similar responses, albeit in lesser degrees. Like the elites, a majority reported their evaluation of the Court as largely unchanged over the last decade, and those whose evaluations have declined pointed to the 2000 election as a factor that lowered their estimation of the Court.

Judgments of the Supreme Court's performance are necessarily made in light of the expectations that citizens have of the Court. So, how elites and the mass public evaluate the justices' policies will be guided by what they believe the Court has the capacity to do. If citizens have low expectations for the Supreme Court, they may judge even incremental policy changes as major initiatives. Conversely, those who have high hopes for the Court may end up being disappointed by anything less than a landmark ruling. How does the public view the Court's policymaking capacity and, in turn, how does it evaluate the Court's effectiveness?

In the eyes of most Americans, the Supreme Court has a sufficient amount of authority to carry out its responsibilities. As is explained in Chapter 4, a majority think that the justices have about the right amount of power. But what of those who concluded that the Court has too much authority? These Americans are apt to believe that the justices should show greater respect for the traditions of judicial restraint. Among those who think that the justices wield too much power, for example, a majority said that the Court ought to adhere closely to the intentions of the founding fathers. By contrast, most of those who think that the Court has adequate authority believe that the justices should try to apply the Constitution in light of the evolving needs of society. Consequently, one group may see a ruling from the Court as effective policy promulgated by an institution that is simply fulfilling its constitutional responsibilities, while another group may see that same ruling as a Court exceeding its mandate.

These tendencies within the mass public are only magnified among the legal community. Overwhelmingly, lawyers believe that the courts are entrusted with an appropriate level of authority. Regardless of the type of court—state or federal, trial or appellate—the vast majority of the legal profession see the judiciary as having the right amount of power. Elites have particular faith in the institutional capacities of the U.S. Supreme Court; 84 percent think that the Court's power is at the appropriate level.

Such high levels of confidence are belied by at least some research that suggests that the Supreme Court lacks the power to generate policy change. Most prominently, Gerald Rosenberg argues that the Court, acting on its own, is unable to direct the courts of public policy. Without support from either the elected branches or the public, the justices have enormous difficulty blazing a trail for others to follow. Part of the reason for this failure, Rosenberg suggests, is that the Supreme Court lacks the requisite powers that are entrusted instead to the Congress and the president.[17]

Despite their trust that the judicial system has sufficient authority, lawyers believe that many courts in the United States have an excessive workload. A slight majority (51 percent) says that the judicial system as a whole is generally overworked, and that some courts—state courts and federal trial courts—are under particular strain. None of this will be news to the judges and their staffs on these courts, many of whom have perennially voiced concerns about their excessive caseloads.

At the same time, lawyers do not believe that the federal appellate courts shoulder too heavy a burden. Fully 60 percent expressed the belief that the Supreme Court—which, after all, has a discretionary agenda—takes on about as much work as it can, and 20 percent believe that the justices could actually increase their workload. This judgment is scarcely surprising, given that the Court's plenary docket is almost half the size in 2006 that it was in the 1970s. Moreover several contemporary justices—including Stephen Breyer, Sandra Day O'Connor, Antonin Scalia, and William Rehnquist—found the time to write books while serving on the Court. A diminished docket and a seemingly adequate amount of leisure time would surely reinforce a belief that the Court should increase its workload.

Regardless of how hard they work, the justices do have the trust of their colleagues in the legal profession. Eighty percent of lawyers disagree—50 percent strongly so—with the suggestion that the justices even occasionally make decisions on issues that they do not fully understand. Nearly all lawyers believe that it is important for the justices to understand the lives of those who are affected by their decisions, and two out of three lawyers are confident that they do. Oddly enough, the Supreme Court as constituted in the first decade of the twenty-first century probably has less direct experience with the personal lives of the American public than at any time in its history. To be sure, the justices are highly qualified and collectively bring to the bench a wealth of appellate judicial experience. The experience in public life—service as state legislator, governor, senator, executive branch official, and so on—that has traditionally been present on the Court has been noticeably lacking for some time. Whatever perspective justices such as Hugo Black, Robert Jackson, Thurgood Marshall, Earl Warren, and Byron White may have brought to the Court, lawyers do not seem to believe that it is necessary for effective policymaking.

For most Americans, the Court may be a distant and abstract institution, but they nevertheless believe the choices the justices make have real implications for their lives. Like the members of the legal community, a large majority (75 percent) said that it is very important for the justices to have an understanding of the relationship between their decisions and the lives of those who are affected by them. Moreover, a sizable segment (62 percent) think that the justices understand this relationship to either a moderate or great extent. Overall, then, the mass public as well as elites believe that the Supreme Court has the time, resources, and expertise necessary to serve as a national policymaker.

Future Concerns for the Court

Like any institution, the Supreme Court continues to face new issues that test its mettle. How the Court and the rest of the judicial system will confront those challenges remains to be seen. Both lawyers and the lay public recognize the continual tension between judging on the one hand and the democratic process on the other. Thus, they perceive a number of challenges on the horizon.

Several issues that, in one way or another, concern the democratic accountability of the Supreme Court have been simmering and will no doubt continue to be a source of debate. There have been proposals to limit the amount of time that the justices can serve on the Supreme Court. Until 2005, the Court experienced one of its longest periods without a change in membership. Given increased life expectancy and the quality of health care, the justices can be expected to have very long tenures indeed. Are mandatory retirements necessary to keep the Court more in touch with the concerns of the citizens over which they exercise authority?

Most Americans (57 percent) believe that there should be mandatory retirement for the Court, and nearly half say that the age should more or less conform to the norms of American society—between the ages of sixty-five and seventy. Elites take a decidedly different view on the wisdom of this proposal, with nearly two-thirds opposing a legally imposed retirement. Forced to choose, however, lawyers suggest an older age, either between seventy-one and seventy-five (27 percent) or some age greater than seventy-five (35 percent). This reaction may indicate deference to the older justices serving on the Court at the time of the survey or, more likely, an appreciation of the time required to build the type of legal career that merits serious consideration for an appointment to the nation's highest court.

A related question that pertains to how the democratic branches should structure the judiciary concerns the comparatively low salaries of federal judges. The late chief justice Rehnquist for years lobbied Congress to increase the pay of federal judges, arguing that, without a competitive salary, the courts would be deprived of the most capable talent that could otherwise command a more substantial salary in private practice.

This proposal—as indeed any that aims to increase the pay of federal employees—generates an underwhelming response from the mass public. Only a quarter thinks that federal judges' salaries ought to be increased, even if only to keep up with inflation. About the same modest number believe that the inability of judicial salaries to keep pace with inflation constitutes an impediment to recruiting the most capable judges. The majority of the public (63 percent) instead says that the intangibles of authority and prestige compensate for the opportunity costs associated with forgoing income.

Among lawyers, two out of three do think that the salaries of judges should at least be pegged to the rate of inflation, but they are less certain about whether that salary should be made more comparable to salaries in the private sector. About half of the elites say that the intangible qualities of judicial service make up for any financial shortfall, but nearly as many (46 percent) claim that, absent a competitive salary, the potentially best judges will be unwilling to serve in the office.

Some argue that another way to demystify and democratize the Supreme Court is to allow television cameras into the Court chamber during oral arguments. Cameras are a pervasive presence in many of the nation's courts, and advocates believe that this openness has increased public awareness and appreciation of the work that judges do.

Historically, however, the justices have been quite camera shy, and the contemporary Court seems little different. Some justices, even the extremely camera-phobic Scalia, have allowed some of their public remarks to be televised, but the justices show no signs of permitting the television lens into the Court itself.

Despite the widespread broadcast of judicial proceedings, most Americans seem to share the justices' apprehensions. A majority (56 percent) would prefer that the camera be kept out of oral arguments, even though most (60 percent) concede that allowing cameras would promote a better understanding of the Supreme Court. Lawyers are largely undecided on this question, with 48 percent favoring cameras and 51 percent opposing them, and unlike the mass public, they have no clear agreement on whether televised oral arguments would be beneficial to society.

Another pluralistic force with which the Supreme Court will surely contend is the transmission of legal precedents from different parts of the world. As high national courts take on greater political significance, they will look to more established courts, such as the Supreme Court, for guidance in crafting the law. If national court rulings begin to take on an international character, there will be increasing opportunities for the justices to draw upon the judicial opinions of other countries. It is far from clear that the Court and its various publics are prepared to support such innovations. In *Roper v. Simmons* (2005), a decision invalidating the death penalty for juveniles, the majority referenced the laws and norms of several other countries on this question. Even though the Court explicitly indicated that it was in no way bound by the rules of other nations, the allusion to comparative legal values provoked not only a withering dissent from Justice Scalia but a good deal of public hand-wringing by various legal observers. When polled on the issue, lawyers reflect this general uncertainty: one-third said that the justices should rely upon comparative legal sources to a moderate or great extent; one-third said they should be used to a small extent; and one-third said they should not be used at all.

Conclusion

Americans see a lot of good in the Supreme Court. From the perspective of democratic government, that by itself is noteworthy. An institution that is not electorally accountable is supported in a whole variety of ways, not only by the legal community but by the mass public as well. A healthy majority of lawyers (60 percent) believe that the Court's involvement in policymaking helps, rather than hinders, the democratic system. And looking ahead, the public sees the Court's policies as having positive repercussions for the future: two out of three forecast that the decisions the Supreme Court makes today will benefit the next generation of Americans.

Elites and the mass public often understand the Court in quite different ways. The legal community has what is perhaps an idealized view of the Court's role. They have greater faith in its process of decision making, and they more often believe that the justices interpret the law without regard to political or strategic considerations. The mass public sometimes shares these perceptions of the legal community, but the public is not always as optimistic about the Court's capacity and independence.

Still, the public and elites have a good deal of confidence that the justices are motivated by a desire to promote responsible legal policy. Even if the Court remains comparatively isolated from democratic forces, Americans believe that an independent Supreme Court—one that is not beholden to any set of litigating interests—is actually a force of democratic government. By helping secure both substantive and procedural guarantees, the Supreme Court has earned a reputation as a necessary condition for representative government in the United States.

Notes

1. See Howard Gillman, *The Votes That Counted* (Chicago: University of Chicago Press, 2002).

2. James L. Gibson, Gregory A. Caldeira, and Lester Kenyatta Spence, "The Supreme Court and the U.S. Presidential Election of 2000: Wounds, Self-Inflicted or Otherwise?" *British Journal of Political Science* 33 (2003), 535–56.

3. Gregory A. Caldeira and Kevin McGuire, "What Americans Know about the Court and Why It Matters," in *The Judicial Branch*, ed. Kermit L. Hall and Kevin J. McGuire, Institutions of American Democracy (New York: Oxford University Press, 2005).

4. R. Jeffrey Smith and Michael Fletcher, "Bush Says Detainees Will Be Tried; He Confirms Existence of CIA Prisons," *Washington Post*, September 7, 2006, A1.

5. Press release, Annenberg Public Policy Center, University of Pennsylvania, August 31, 2006.

6. Michael X. Delli Carpini and Scott Keeter, *What Americans Know about Politics and Why It Matters* (New Haven, Conn.: Yale University Press, 1997).

7. Richard Morin, "Wapner v. Rehnquist: No Contest," *Washington Post*, June 23, 1989, A21.

8. See, for example, Walter F. Murphy, *Elements of Judicial Strategy* (Chicago: University of Chicago Press, 1964); Forrest Maltzman, James F. Spriggs II, and Paul J. Wahlbeck, *Crafting Law on the Supreme Court: The Collegial Games* (Cambridge: Cambridge University Press, 2000).

9. Mark Silverstein, *Judicious Choices: The New Politics of Supreme Court Confirmations*, rev. ed. (New York: Norton, 1997).

10. Lawrence Baum, *The Puzzle of Judicial Behavior* (Ann Arbor: University of Michigan Press, 1998); H. W. Perry Jr., *Deciding to Decide: Agenda Setting on the United States Supreme Court* (Cambridge, Mass.: Harvard University Press, 1991).

11. See, e.g., J. Mitchell Pickerell, "Leveraging Federalism: The Real Meaning of the Rehnquist Court's Federalism Jurisprudence for States," *Albany Law Review* 66, no. 3 (2002–3), 823–34.

12. Keith E. Whittington, "Judicial Review and Interpretation: Have the Courts Become Sovereign When Interpreting the Constitution?" in *The Judicial Branch*, ed. Hall and McGuire.

13. Walter F. Murphy, *Elements of Judicial Strategy* (Chicago: University of Chicago Press, 1964).

14. The Gallup Poll, "Supreme Court Approval Rating Best in Four Years," September 29, 2006, www.galluppoll.com/content/?ci=24802.

15. Gerald N. Rosenberg, "The Impact of Courts on American Life," in *The Judicial Branch*, ed. Hall and McGuire, 305.

16. Kermit L. Hall, "Judicial Independence and the Majoritarian Difficulty," in *The Judicial Branch*, ed. Hall and McGuire.

17. Gerald N. Rosenberg, *The Hollow Hope: Can Courts Bring About Social Change?* (Chicago: University of Chicago Press, 1991).

8

THE THREE BRANCHES
OF GOVERNMENT: COMPARATIVE
TRUST AND PERFORMANCE

Mark A. Peterson

An effective government predicated on separation-of-powers arrangements requires a reasonable and substantially shared understanding by
both public officials and the electorate of the underlying constitutional
principles and their policymaking implications. The survey data reported in
Chapter 4 offered some confidence that this minimal prerequisite for a healthy
democracy in the United States is being fulfilled. Although the least educated
among Americans revealed a disturbing lack of awareness of the founders' intentions and some of the rudimentary features of the U.S. government, most of the
public seemed to know and appreciate the purpose and qualities of the
Constitution's design. Perhaps even more significant, the survey findings did not
identify any profound differences between the general public and institutional
insiders on these core issues of American governance.

The subsequent chapters on the individual branches of government, however, presented results from the surveys that raise significant alarms about the
state of play in politics and policymaking in the first decade of the twenty-first
century. In particular, while there was no apparent divide between the public and
insiders, America was shown to display a yawning and persistent partisan schism
between Republicans and Democrats both in government and in the electorate.
Such partisan divisions—which go well beyond the expected policy disputes and
appear over claims of constitutional authority, the legitimacy of the "unilateral
executive," and the manner in which the legislature operates—may have disturbing implications for how well the national government can perform overall. In

the separation-of-powers setting they can frustrate the pursuit of consensus and compromise that are often necessary for policymaking, and foment rather than ameliorate confrontation and conflict. Indeed, the former House Republican majority leader Tom DeLay posed these effects as virtues, commenting as he ended his House career in June 2006, "It is not the principled partisan, however obnoxious he may seem to his opponents, who degrades our public debate, but the preening, self-styled statesman who elevates compromise to a first principle."[1] One would not expect to find such a statement in the *Federalist Papers*. Because institutional checks, mutual engagement, and even bargaining are so central to the American system conceived by the founders, such an adversarial, battle-ax form of political and policy contestation, which frequently risks generating more rhetorical heat than policy light, is, to borrow from commentator E. J. Dionne, "why Americans hate politics."[2] Pressing issues of concern to the public go unaddressed as neither side can achieve legislative victory on its terms alone, and there is insufficient willingness to find any potential for common ground.[3] The political juices of ideological opponents get flowing, the activist base of each party is rallied, but much of the electorate can end up alienated.[4]

The Annenberg surveys provide a unique opportunity to see how both the public and the respective institutional insiders judge, at roughly the same time, the comparative performance of the legislative, executive, and judicial branches of government in this politically contentious milieu. An effective democracy calls for at least a modest degree of confidence in its institutions expressed by both the public and elites. In addition, if one branch of government falters dramatically even while the others are well regarded, it would be difficult to sustain the policy-making capabilities of government and preserve the protective features of checks and balances. It is thus important to step back and assess the three branches, and their component parts, seeing how the public and the practitioners most familiar with them evaluate their overall capabilities and performance. As the data presented in this chapter will show, the assessments of neither the public nor insiders suggest the presence of an institutional crisis in American national government. Nor do they reveal, however, perceptions of an adept federal government, capable of taking action, uninhibited by either organized interests or a less-than-informed public, or free of superficial impulses in response to electoral incentives. Perhaps it is the paradox of modern American democracy that the institution most formally removed from electoral pressures and designed to be the least responsive to popular sentiment—the judiciary—enjoys, marginally, the most positive reviews.

Trust and Performance

Annenberg's collective surveys of the public and insiders allow for side-by-side evaluations of how much each branch can be trusted to "operate in the best interest of the public" and how well they perform their jobs within the governing framework. Our questions were posed with the intention of obtaining, as best we could, measures about the "generic" institutions, such as Congress as a legislature, rather than the particular assemblage of leaders and partisans that sat in the House and Senate at the time. It is unlikely, however, that respondents were able to divorce their judgments about these institutions from the incumbents and their actions at the time of the surveys, whether it was Congress with its Republican majorities, the presidency as represented by George W. Bush, or the Supreme Court under the leadership of then-Chief Justice William Rehnquist. Nonetheless, the surveys have the potential to signal whether the public, and the individuals who work in or directly with the institutions, have lost confidence in the three core institutions of American government.

Figure 1 presents summary results on the key issue of trust—a theme explored in depth in Chapter 3 and addressed individually for each branch in

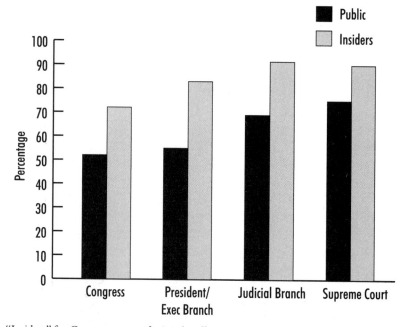

Note: "Insiders" for Congress are professional staff in House and Senate member offices; for executive branch they are senior career officials and political appointees in the administrations of Bill Clinton and George W. Bush; for the judicial branch and Supreme Court they are lawyers at the bar of the U.S. Court of Appeals or the Supreme Court. For the evaluation of the executive branch, the public was asked about the president, and the senior career officials and political appointees were asked about the executive branch. One percent or less of the respondents refused to answer the question.

Figure 1   Trust in Government Institutions (Percentage Reporting "Great Deal" or "Fair Amount" of Trust in Institutions to Operate in the Best Interest of the American People)

subsequent chapters. One can draw three important conclusions from this comparative assessment. First, at the time of the survey, around January 2005, a majority of the public (albeit a narrow one) believed that all three branches were worthy of either "a great deal" or "a fair amount" of trust (although more the latter than the former) that they "operate in the best interest of the American public." If these institutions of American democracy were truly vital and healthy, one might expect to see supermajorities of the public, instead of about a quarter or fewer, expressing a great deal of trust in them, but the crucial point here is that all garnered basic support from most Americans and none had profoundly lost the people's confidence.

At first these results suggest that popular trust in American national institutions, both individually and collectively, reveals a considerable amount of resiliency, having endured the contentious, polarized politics of the times. The earlier chapters described a litany of extraordinary actions and events that could have seriously eroded confidence: a slender 5 to 4 majority of the Supreme Court effectively determining the outcome of the presidential election of 2000, based on, at best, controversial reasoning; the emerging post-9/11 miasma of security policy both foreign and domestic, with setbacks and uncertainty in Iraq and unprecedented claims of presidential power; and internal dynamics in Congress that undermine its capacity to resolve issues of considerable national moment.

It is equally important to be reminded, however, that these surveys were completed by early 2005, before public opinion turned sour on Iraq as a result of mounting uncertainties about that conflict; prior to the Hurricane Katrina disaster; and well in advance of the indictment of the lobbyist Jack Abramoff, the guilty plea of Representative Randy "Duke" Cunningham, and the resignation of Representative Tom DeLay, the most potent recent symbols of accused or proven corruption in Congress. A later survey, administered in August 2006, may reveal the cumulative effect of these troubling events in American politics and policymaking. As shown in Figure 2, while the Supreme Court continued to hold the trust of the public, those who expressed "a great deal" or "a fair amount" of trust in either Congress or the president fell well below a majority of the public (18 percent indicated no trust at all in Congress, and fully 29 percent felt that way about the president).

A second conclusion to be drawn from Figure 1—perhaps not surprising but reassuring—is that the individuals who work in Congress and the executive branch, or who practice before the courts of the judicial branch, have considerably greater trust than the public (majorities of 75 percent to 91 percent) that these institutions work in the public's best interest. A cynic may suggest that these insiders are either delusional (given the events of the times) or untruthful, but it is also possible that the legislature, federal agencies, the Executive Office of the President, and the courts are staffed by innumerable hardworking individuals of

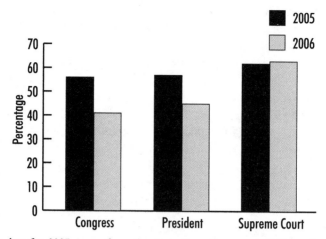

Note: The data for 2005 come from the Annenberg Congress and Executive Branch: Public Component survey, which was administered December 18, 2004, to January 18, 2005. The data for 2006 come from the Annenberg Judicial Independence survey, which was administered August 3–16, 2006. One percent or less of the respondents refused to answer the questions.

Figure 2   Change in Levels of Trust, 2005–2006 (Percentage Reporting "Great Deal" or "Fair Amount" of Trust in Government Institutions to Operate in the Best Interest of the American People)

principled motivation, and that the policy challenges they encounter derive from inherent issue complexity and legitimately competing perspectives and interests.[5] In support of this proposition, supermajorities of Clinton and Bush administration political appointees—individuals typically brought in from outside of government to lead departments and agencies for a few years, often with skepticism about government—reported that senior career civil servants were "very competent" (76 percent) and "very responsive . . . to the policy decisions of the president and his political appointees" (66 percent).[6]

Finally, both ironic and troubling for a democratic society, the judicial branch—the realm of public decision making at the national level the most (but clearly not entirely) removed from political conflict, electoral dynamics, and democratic norms[7]—earns the public's highest regard, while Congress—the institution the framers of the Constitution thought to be closest to the people and paramount in governing—is the least well regarded.[8] Although one would prefer that the legislature inspire more confidence than is apparent in results reported in Figures 1 and 2, it may well be that the courts are in greater need of the public's trust and respect. History has shown that Congress can legislate and even draw talent into its ranks without a surfeit of institutional trust expressed by the public. The credibility of the unelected judiciary, dependent as it is on others to accept its judgments—no matter how controversial—requires legitimacy built on the public's ultimate confidence in its procedures and personnel. Gregory Caldeira and Kevin McGuire argue that "judges who are not electorally accountable often behave as if they were. Despite the absence of formal democratic controls, federal judges seem to sense that, in order to ensure that their policies will be taken seriously by elected officials and those whom they represent, they cannot afford to ignore public sentiment."[9]

It may be too facile, but one could view trust as a determination of intention, and performance as a measure of follow-through, the demonstrated capacity to get the job done. As shown in Figure 3, according to the public, in this respect American institutions are not failing, but they are hardly worthy of accolades, whether the object of evaluation is the federal government as a whole or the individual branches and their constituent parts (with the reminder from Chapter 3, of course, that some members of the public are either incapable of or unwilling to distinguish effectively among them). Only a third to two-fifths of the public surveyed judges *any* feature of American national government to be doing either a "very good" or "good" job. Generally speaking, roughly half said that their job performance is "fair." About a fifth believe it is "poor." In this rendition of Lake Wobegon, all the institutions are below average. Once again, however, the judiciary and Supreme Court lead the pack (only 11 percent of the public think it is doing a poor job, half the percentage assigning that grade to the other branches).

Given the role of partisanship explored earlier in this volume, we should ask whether comparative perceptions of institutional performance are affected by the partisan or ideological lens through which individuals process the information they receive about government. Figure 4 presents the public's evaluations of each institution's performance broken down by the partisan identification of the respondents. Several results are worth noting. To start, in general there is relatively little variation in the assessments across these institutions provided by Republicans, Democrats, and Independents. All three types of respondents are neither profoundly dismissive of these governing institutions nor particularly impressed with how well they do their jobs.

In one significant respect, this lack of substantial variation is particularly surprising. From 1995 to 2006 Congress had unapologetic and aggressive Republican leadership. Except for a brief period with the Democrats holding a one-seat margin in the Senate, the first six years of the Bush administration enjoyed unified Republican government—a first since the initial two years of the Eisenhower administration (1953–54). Although full measures of President Bush's legislative success and impact in Congress were not available in 2006, one would have to go back to Lyndon Johnson's presidency to find a period when Congress provided the president with a higher percentage of victories on roll call votes, a higher percentage of wins on contested votes, or a higher average annual

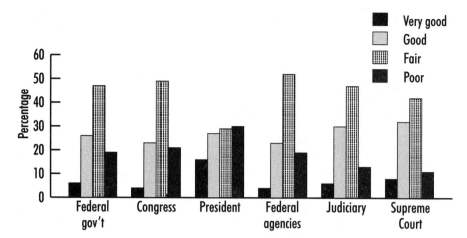

Note: With the exception of the question about "federal agencies," all responses come from the Annenberg Supreme Court: Public Component survey (administered March 17 to April 18, 2005). The question about federal agencies was worded somewhat differently and is taken from the Congress and Executive Branch: Public Component survey (administered December 18, 2004, to January 18, 2005). One percent or less of the respondents refused to answer the questions; "don't know" responses ranged from 1 percent for the president to 5 percent for the Supreme Court.

Figure 3   Public's Assessment of How Well Government Institutions Are Handling Their Jobs

level of support of the president's legislative positions by members of both chambers than occurred during Bush's first term.[10] And yet Republicans in the electorate were hardly more favorably disposed toward the legislature than Independents or Democrats. Roughly the same percentage rated the job Congress was doing as "fair," and only slightly more Republicans said it was doing a "very good" job. Democrats were somewhat more inclined to characterize it as "poor." Congress just could not get respect, even from the legislative majority's partisan constituency.

Unlike Congress, the president generates quite dramatic cross-partisan variation. So closely identified with the agendas, activities, and achievements or failures of the Oval Office, the chief executive is—not surprisingly—the most polarizing figure, generating at the time of the surveys both the highest and lowest ratings of job performance, as reflected in Figure 3. The distributions in Figure 4 anchor that polarization in the nation's partisan divide, as would be expected from the analysis in Chapter 6, which showed the stark differences between Republicans and Democrats in response to the unilateral approach to policymaking advanced by President Bush and his administration. In addition, in the 2004 election, "George Bush . . . was the most polarizing presidential candidate in modern political history and a much more polarizing candidate than he had been four years earlier."[11] It is thus not unexpected that in our surveys fielded shortly after

Figure 4   Public's Assessment of How Well Government Institutions Are Handling Their Jobs

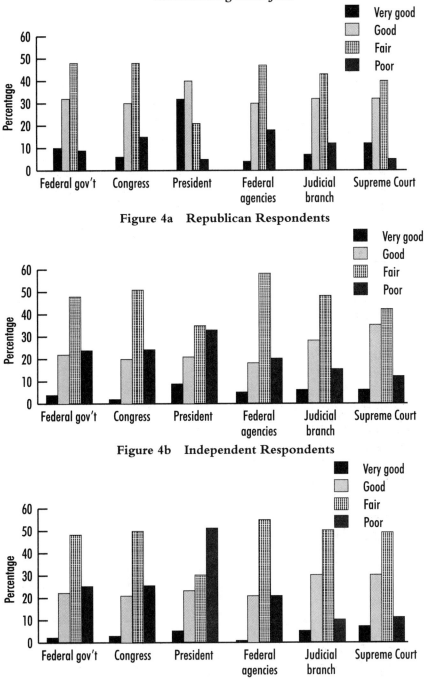

Figure 4a   Republican Respondents

Figure 4b   Independent Respondents

Figure 4c   Democratic Repondents

the election, a supermajority of Republicans indicated that the president was doing either a "very good" or "good" job, while more than half of the Democrats rated his performance as poor and only a handful thought it good or very good. As President Bush's job-performance ratings subsequently declined among the public after the Annenberg surveys were administered, the partisan and ideological polarization became even more pronounced. As shown in Figure 5, at a time when the president's overall approval rating was 33 percent in the Gallup Poll (April–May 2006), a huge majority of conservative Republicans (nearly eight in ten) continued to approve of the president's performance, and he held on to a bare majority of moderate and liberal Republicans. Very few Democrats (or even Independents), however, were favorable. Even among *conservative* Democrats, only 11 percent approved of the way President Bush was handling his job.

With so personalized an office, it is clearly impossible to separate in the eyes of the public the sitting president from the institution of the presidency. In addition, in an age of partisan polarization, those eyes are looking through very different lenses. Modern White House strategies for using internal polling to keep tabs on particular demographic and ideological groups and to target "narrowcasting" communication of messages to the president's political base—a practice carried out by the Bush administration and the president's reelection campaign with particular "sophistication and intensity"—contribute to this polarization.[12]

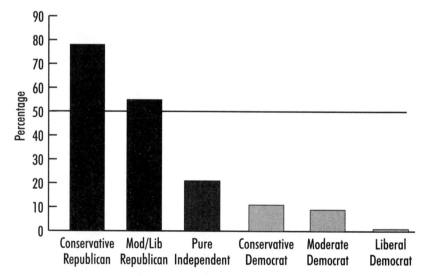

Source: Gallup News Service, "Liberal, Moderate Republicans Show Large Drop in Support for Bush," May 26, 2006.

Figure 5   Gallup Poll: President George W. Bush Job-Approval Rating (April–May 2006)

Constraints on Policymaking

One potential source of popular frustration with the performance of government would be the lack of policymaker responsiveness to serious policy issues.[13] As much as the public, as reported in Chapter 4, favors deliberation over hasty action, and seems to understand the barriers to dispatch imposed by the checks and balances in the policymaking process, stalemate and periods of intragovernment competition and conflict—even if due to institutional design and not malfeasance—could undermine confidence in American national institutions. Does the public realize just how challenging it can be to compel major policy actions or to motivate programmatic shifts in a government of decentralized power? People clearly recognize this issue. Figure 6 indicates that healthy majorities of the public concede that "significant policy change" is difficult for Congress, federal agencies, and even the president to accomplish. But, on average, only one in ten "strongly agree" with that assessment. Those who serve in the respective institutions, however, and reflect on the specific policy arenas in which they labor, are dramatically more emphatic about just how arduous it is to transcend the prevailing policy status quo. There is near consensus that Congress and the executive branch have difficulty making such changes. Congressional staffers and executive branch officials are four to five times as likely as the public to "strongly agree" with that proposition.

However self-serving this assessment may be for policymakers, possibly trying to excuse their own ineffectiveness, the contrasting perspectives on this issue may be among the most important for understanding divisions between the public and government officials about the role and capacity of American government constrained by the separation of powers. The public may be expecting more than politicians in this system can deliver. As noted in Chapter 4, Lloyd Cutler, White House counsel to Jimmy Carter, believed that the institutional constraints on policymaking created a problem serious enough to warrant a fundamental change in the structural design of the American government.

These policymaking challenges also offer additional impetus for the rise of the unilateral presidency described in Chapter 6. Conventional checks and balances may stand in the way of the significant and timely action deemed necessary by the president as defined by the president. Instead of formally rewriting the Constitution, as endorsed by Cutler, a president may follow the temptation, as George W. Bush did, to interpret the existing constitutional language as granting the chief executive the authority to act without the collaboration, consent, or even oversight of the legislative and judicial branches.[14] Bruce Fein, a Republican constitutional lawyer and former official in the Reagan Justice Department, argues that this approach to policymaking is ahistorical and runs counter to the founders' intentions. Commenting on Vice President Dick Cheney and his chief of staff David Addington, the individuals

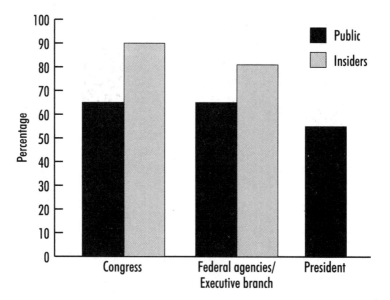

Note: Measures as phrased for the public: "It is hard for the president to take action that involves significant policy changes"; "It is hard for federal agencies to take action that involves significant policy changes"; and "It is hard for Congress to take action that involves significant policy changes." For insiders the wording is somewhat different: "Thinking about policymaking by [your department or agency/the executive branch; the House/Senate] in [policy area], how true is the following statement: 'Significant policy change (is/was) extremely difficult?'" Insiders were not asked about the president. One percent or fewer of the respondents refused to answer the questions.

Figure 6   It Is Difficult for Institutions to Make Significant Policy Change (Percentage Reporting "Strongly Agree" or "Agree")

most responsible for the administration's claims of expansive presidential power, Fein said,

> If you read the Federalist Papers, you can see how rich in history they are. . . . The Founders really understood the history of what people *did* with power, going back to the Greek and Roman and Biblical times. Our political heritage is to be skeptical of executive power, because, in particular, there was skepticism of King George III. But Cheney and Addington are not students of history. If they were, they'd know that the Founding Fathers would be shocked by what they've done.[15]

Further, emblematic of the Constitution's checks and balances, in its 2006 *Hamdan v. Rumsfeld* decision "the Supreme Court . . . methodically dismantled the legal framework" that Bush administration lawyers had crafted in support of the president's unilateral approach to identifying, labeling, holding, and trying suspected terrorists.[16] In the long run, popular success with a strategy that denies checks and balances—whether or not it is consistent with the founders' intentions or strictly constitutional—is likely to require that the public agrees with the president about the urgency of action, believes that the policy being pursued is appropriate to the task, and is convinced that extraordinary measures were made necessary by the president's opponents inappropriately exploiting constitutional impediments.

A central consequence of dispersed power in a system of separation of powers with checks and balances is the accessibility of many parts of government to both organized interests and the close attention of individual elected officials to their constituencies, however poorly informed the public may be about policy matters.[17] The bicameral legislature, including its structure of committees and subcommittees with long membership tenure and standing jurisdiction; the separation of the executive and legislative branches, with the federal agencies and their permanent civil servants constitutionally positioned between the president and Congress; the independent federal court system, providing access to alternative means for influencing policy and its implementation; and the electoral process, including frequent elections involving different constituencies for the House, Senate, and president, provide "special" interests with myriad portals to policymakers and elevate the political significance of any part of the electorate that is or could be mobilized in response to policy ideas and/or their fears about them.[18]

Figures 7 and 8 explore the extent to which the public and insiders perceive a threat to coherent policymaking caused by interest groups and an "uninformed public." Given the differences in wording between the public and insider survey questions, and in the questions the different surveys posed about the executive and Congress in contrast to those about the Supreme Court, one has to be careful in interpreting the data. With this caveat firmly in hand, a number of conclusions nonetheless seem warranted. To start, overall the public expresses more trepidation about the role of "special interests" and "an uninformed public" than do congressional staff, executive branch officials, or lawyers who regularly engage the federal courts, although the insiders' own concerns are not trivial. Second, consistent with the earlier assessments of trust and performance, and reflective of both the relative accessibility of the legislature to lobbyists and the focus of legislators on their constituencies, these negative influences are thought to have the most impact on Congress. In addition, there is some link between perceptions of the permeability of Capitol Hill to organized interests and views about the capacity of Congress to act. Among the public, people who believe that Congress is adversely affected by interest groups are somewhat more likely than those with a more benign perspective on groups to view significant policy change as difficult for Congress (72 percent to 58 percent).

Finally, while there are moderate differences between the public and insiders about the influence of narrow interests and an unaware public (especially

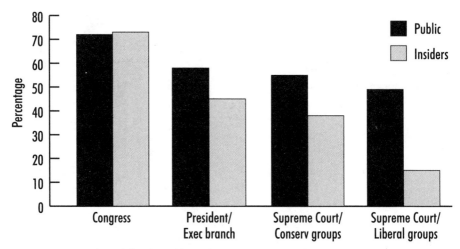

Note: Measure as phrased for the public: "The policy decisions that [institution/sector] makes are often negatively influenced by special interests," or "To what extent do you think the current Supreme Court is influenced by [conservative/liberal] interest groups when making [its] decisions?" (here reporting "great extent" or "moderate extent"). The public was asked about the president, not the executive branch. For insiders the wording is somewhat different: "Policies (are/were) distorted by pressure from special interests." For the Supreme Court, the question asked only about influence, not whether it was "distorting": "To what extent do you think the current Supreme Court is influenced by (conservative/liberal) interest groups when making [its] decisions?"

**Figure 7   Interest Groups Have a Negative Influence on Institutional
Policymaking and Influence Supreme Court Decision Making
(Percentage Responding "Strongly Agree" or "Agree")**

with regard to the influence of liberal organizations on the Supreme Court), their views fully converge about the effects on Congress. Supermajorities of each sense that groups distort congressional policymaking, and majorities of each suggest that an ignorant public is similarly disruptive. Although interest groups and parochial perspectives have ways to access the parliamentary governments of other nations,[19] the separation of powers in the United States creates conditions that make the legislative branch especially vulnerable to group penetration, giving organized interests institutional assets that make it easier for them to thwart policies that threaten their stakes and to promote legislative provisions that benefit their members.[20] The public also perceives that electoral pressures in the American system divert elected officials from due attention to the public interest. As shown in Figure 9, while survey respondents overwhelmingly indicated that Congress and the president *should* "do what they think is best for the country" instead of "what they think is most popular with voters," a majority of the public believed that these policymakers, in fact, actually end up being responsive to their perceptions of popular

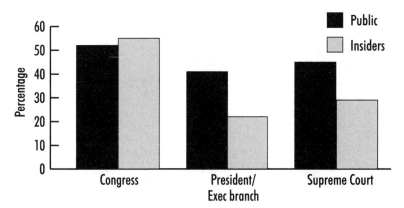

Note: Measure as phrased for the public: "The policy decisions that [Congress/president] makes are often negatively influenced by poorly informed citizens" or, more neutral for the Court, "To what extent do you think the current Supreme Court is influenced by public opinion when making [its] decisions?" (here reporting "great extent" or "moderate extent"). The public was asked about the president, not the executive branch. For insiders the wording is somewhat different: "Policies (are/were) distorted by pressure from poorly informed citizens" or, "To what extent do you think the current Supreme Court is influenced by public opinion when making [its] decisions?"

Figure 8   An Uninformed Public Distorts Institutional Policymaking, and Public Opinion Influences Supreme Court Decision Making (Percentage Responding "Strongly Agree" or "Agree")

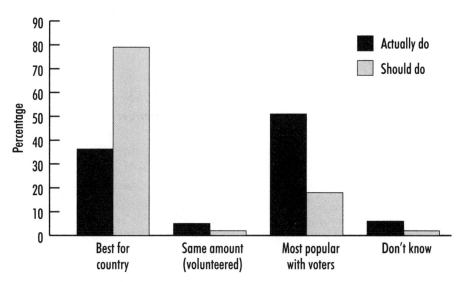

Figure 9   Public's Views of Whether the President and Congress Do What Is Best for the Country or Most Popular with Voters

preferences rather than to the nation's best interest (with only 5 percent volunteering that they do both equally).

We would generally expect both members of Congress and the president, elected by the people and regularly subject to polling, to take public opinion into consideration in some manner throughout their time in office. Elections require it and norms of democratic responsiveness and accountability further promote it. The question then becomes the one considered above—Does responsiveness to popular opinion take the form of enhancing democratic responsibility or having ill-informed opinion distort policy decision-making? For the judicial branch, the basic issue is whether public opinion has any influence at all. As noted earlier, the federal courts are constitutionally shielded from electoral politics and direct, immediate popular accountability, even though judicial scholars have found that the courts are nonetheless constrained from straying too far from what is acceptable to the public. As reported in Figure 9, neither the public nor the lawyer respondents in the Annenberg survey saw public opinion per se as a major force on the Supreme Court. Close to a majority of the public, however, believed that Supreme Court decisions are influenced by public opinion to a great or moderate extent, compared with only 29 percent of the lawyers practicing before major federal courts. Sixty-nine percent of them saw little or no influence. For the lawyers, this limited impact is another virtue of the separation of powers and the political autonomy it affords the Court. Rather than viewing such detachment from public opinion as "a troubling antidemocratic aspect of the Supreme Court," a position held by just 6 percent of the respondents, almost all—90 percent—considered it "a safeguard that helps ensure stability in our system of government." If public opinion is not influencing the Court's decision making, it is not distorting it.

Conclusion

The well-being of American institutions of democracy would be cast in doubt if the public and the insiders who have proximate experience with the three branches of government held fundamentally different views about the nature and performance of the executive, legislature, and judiciary. The survey results presented in Chapter 4 offered some assurance that the public, in general, and elites, in general, adhere to relatively consonant understandings of the separation of powers, the system of checks and balances, and their connotations for politics and policymaking. Here the results showed considerable congruence between the public and the insiders sampled in their assessments of how well the three branches of government are functioning and their sense of some of the potentially negative influences on the policymaking process.

Most differences between the appraisals provided by the public and the insiders are matters of degree or intensity, not direction. The three most significant disparities of this sort involve institutional capacity and performance. Those with experience working in or directly with the institutions of American government express markedly greater trust than the public that the governing institutions operate in the public's best interest. They also assert that pursuing significant change in policy is appreciably more difficult for Congress and the executive branch than the public perceives. Finally, despite those challenges, they are noticeably less likely than the public to conclude that the institutions are hobbled by the entreaties of special interests or the demands of an uninformed public.

Most disconcerting, perhaps, are actually two core points of agreement. First, both the public and the House and Senate legislative staff believe that Congress is particularly vulnerable to the undesirable influences of narrow special interests and a public poorly informed about policy issues. Second, both the public and the lawyers who practice before the federal courts of appeals and Supreme Court have more trust in the judicial branch and the Court than the public and the legislative and executive insiders have in the other institutions of government. Although the differences are not great, this is another instance of Congress once again receiving the lowest marks. When considering the vitality of the American democratic system, it cannot be comforting that the legislature—the institution the founders intended to be most in tune with the electorate—is the most disparaged by the public, while the judiciary—designed to be the most insulated from electoral pressures—is the most revered by the public. There is a long history of Congress, as an institution, not being particularly popular with the American people. As the congressional scholar Richard Fenno pointed out long ago, and surveys continue to show, people tend to love their own representative but hate Congress.[21] That dynamic is especially troubling when it occurs even in a period of unified government, with a Congress that has acted in reasonable concert with the president. The dysfunctional attributes of the contemporary legislature identified in Chapter 5 apparently diminish the confidence the public has in that institution.

The partisan differences brought into stark relief in Chapter 5 on Congress and Chapter 6 on the executive branch take on an interesting and surprising cast when viewed in the context of this chapter's comparison across the branches. As one would predict given the controversial rise of the unilateral presidency, taken to new heights by the Bush administration in the post-9/11 environment, the president—the recognizable embodiment for the public of the institution of the presidency—is the most partisanly polarizing figure in the public's assessment of the federal government, the executive branch, federal agencies, Congress, the judiciary, and the Supreme Court. What one might not have anticipated is the very limited degree to which partisanship matters in the public's appraisal of the legislative branch. Even though there was no mistaking the policy orientation of the Republican-led House and Senate, and despite the fact that Congress largely did the bidding of the president they so admired, Republicans appeared to be scarcely more enthusiastic about the legislature than Independents or even Democrats. For the public, the nation's governing institution that is most associated with democratic processes—frequent elections (at least in the House), relatively small constituencies, and the most open to direct public communication and influence—was evidently operating to the least satisfying effect, as far as the people are concerned. Staff inside the institution shared the worry (although it was most pronounced among those working for the minority Democratic opposition). Any future periods of divided government, especially if the pronounced ideological and partisan polarization continue, are only likely to exacerbate the situation.

As a citizen, one may extol individual presidents or hold them in contempt, but the president, elected by a national constituency, can—however self-servingly—lay claim to serving the national interest and astutely control the image and message conveyed by the chief executive's actions.[22] Buoyed by the mystique of the judicial process and the political asceticism of the judicial black robes, the courts can seem in the public's mind to rise above petty politics and adhere to the sanctity of the law.[23] Congress has no such redoubt. It is a microcosm of the society's divisions in values and politics, as well as a barometer of the maldistribution of economic and social power. The incentives of an open, accessible legislature built on single-member districts can bring out the worst in politics—parochialism, celebration of local or narrow interests over national imperatives, shortsightedness, partisan discord, and a premium placed on rhetoric over serious deliberation.[24] Such is the irony—and dilemma—of America's democratic institutions.

Notes

1. Carl Hulse, "Defiant to the End, DeLay Pats Himself on the Back and Bids the House a Torrid Goodbye," *New York Times,* June 9, 2006, 22.
2. E. J. Dionne, *Why Americans Hate Politics: The Death of the Democratic Process* (New York: Simon & Schuster, 1992).
3. Sarah A. Binder, *Stalemate: Causes and Consequences of Legislative Gridlock* (Washington, D.C.: Brookings Institution, 2003).
4. Morris P. Fiorina, with Samuel J. Abrams and Jeremy C. Pope, *Culture War? The Myth of a Polarized America,* 2nd ed. (New York: Pearson Longman, 2006).
5. This was my personal read on Congress when, in the early 1990s, as an American Political Science Association Congressional Fellow, I served as a legislative assistant for health policy for a prominent Democratic senator. These themes can also be seen in works such as Richard F. Fenno Jr., *The Emergence of a Senate Leader: Pete Domenici and the Reagan Budget* and *Learning to Legislate: The Senate Education of Arlen Specter* (both Washington, D.C.: CQ Press, 1991); and Paul Light, *Still Artful Work: The Continuing Politics of Social Security Reform,* 2nd ed. (New York: McGraw-Hill, 1995)

and Paul C. Light, *Forging Legislation* (New York: Norton, 1992).

6. For each measure, these were the highest categories in a four-level scale.

7. Kermit L. Hall, "Judicial Independence and the Majoritarian Difficulty," in *The Judicial Branch,* ed. Kermit L. Hall and Kevin T. McGuire, Institutions of American Democracy (New York: Oxford University Press, 2005).

8. Public approval of the federal courts may be more nuanced than the Annenberg survey results revealed. A 1998 survey of the public commissioned by the American Bar Association found a comparably high level of endorsement of the Supreme Court, with half of the respondents stating that they were "extremely or very confident" in it, but also showed more skepticism in other federal judges, in whom only 28 percent of the respondents had such confidence. Gerald N. Rosenberg, "The Impact of Courts on American Life," in *The Judicial Branch,* ed. Hall and McGuire, 304.

9. Gregory A. Caldeira and Kevin T. McGuire, "What Americans Know about the Courts and Why It Matters," in *The Judicial Branch,* ed. Hall and McGuire, 271.

10. Andrew Rudalevige, "The Executive Branch and the Legislative Process," in *The Executive Branch,* ed. Joel D. Aberbach and Mark A. Peterson, Institutions of American Democracy (New York: Oxford University Press, 2005), Table 1, 431.

11. Alan I. Abramowitz and Walter J. Stone, "The Bush Effect: Polarization, Turnout, and Activism in the 2004 Presidential Election," *Presidential Studies Quarterly* 36 (June 2006), 141.

12. Lawrence R. Jacobs, "Communicating from the White House: Presidential Narrowcasting and the National Interest," in *The Executive Branch,* ed. Aberbach and Peterson, 204.

13. Lawrence R. Jacobs and Robert Y. Shapiro, *Politicians Don't Pander: Political Manipulation and the Loss of Democratic Responsiveness* (Chicago: Chicago University Press, 2000).

14. Joel D. Aberbach and Mark A. Peterson, "Control and Accountability: Dilemmas of the Executive Branch," in their *The Executive Branch.* See also Jane Mayer, "Letter from Washington: The Hidden Power—The Legal Mind behind the White House's War on Terror," *New Yorker,* July 3, 2006, 44–55.

15. Quoted in Mayer, "Letter from Washington," 55; italics in original.

16. Adam Liptak, "The Court Enters the War, Loudly," *New York Times,* July 2, 2006, sec. 4, 1.

17. R. Kent Weaver and Bert A. Rockman, eds., *Do Institutions Matter? Government Capabilities in the United States and Abroad* (Washington, D.C.: Brookings Institution, 1993); R. Douglas Arnold, *The Logic of Congressional Action* (New Haven, Conn.: Yale University Press, 1992).

18. The perceived negative consequences of such interest group access are most forcefully explored in Theodore J. Lowi, *The End of Liberalism: Ideology, Policy, and the Crisis of Public Authority* (New York: Norton, 1969), and Mancur Olson, *The Rise and Decline of Nations* (New Haven, Conn.: Yale University Press, 1982).

19. R. Kent Weaver and Bert A. Rockman, "Assessing the Effects of Institutions," in their *Do Institutions Matter?*

20. See Scott H. Ainsworth, *Analyzing Interest Groups: Group Influence on People and Policies* (New York: Norton, 2002), especially chapter 5.

21. Richard F. Fenno, *Home Style: U.S. House Members in Their Districts* (Boston: Little, Brown, 1978).
22. Jacobs, "Communicating from the White House."
23. Walter F. Murphy, *Elements of Judicial Strategy* (Chicago: University of Chicago Press, 1964), chapter 2.
24. David R. Mayhew, *Congress: The Electoral Connection* (New Haven, Conn.: Yale University Press, 1974).

CONCLUSION

W e have argued in this volume that the central institutions of American democracy are going through difficult times and, in some important respects, falling short. Yet we need to keep that claim in perspective. Conflicts and uncertainties about these institutions, comparable to those we have examined here, have existed before in American politics. More than a half century ago the Pulitzer Prize–winning writer and journalist William Allen White indicted newspapers for veering "from their traditional position as leaders of public opinion to mere peddlers and purveyors of news."[1] White's attack was mild compared with that voiced by Thomas Jefferson, who declared that newspapers filled men's minds "with falsehoods and errors."[2]

When the Soviets in 1957 launched Sputnik, the first satellite to orbit the earth, the United States underwent a process of soul-searching that concluded, among other things, that American schools had failed to produce the level of science education required by a world engulfed by the cold war. Many Americans feared that the United States' disadvantage in education would enable the Soviet Union, as Premier Nikita Khrushchev later predicted, to "bury" us. An infusion of financial aid flowed to students from the resulting National Defense Education Act of 1958.

The first session of the 104th Congress, in 1995, was so polarized that the formal "taking down" process, by which the House registers disapproval of uncivil speech, was used more often than at any other time since 1946. Concern with the drop in comity prompted members on both sides of the aisle to hold a congressional retreat. If one looks into the historical darker corners of Congress's past one finds attempted shootings and actual canings occurring on the floor of the House and Senate. In the early twentieth century, both senators and representatives overturned dictatorial party leadership of the respective chambers.

The institution of the presidency has seen what a widely quoted, although apocryphal, "Chinese curse" referred to as "interesting times." In just over thirty years, one president, Richard Nixon, resigned office under the almost certain threat of impeachment and removal in the Watergate scandal. A second president, Ronald Reagan, endured investigation with some discussion of possible impeachment, as several White House officials went to prison for their involvement in the Iran-Contra affair. And a third president, Bill Clinton, was actually impeached by the House of Representatives, on charges of perjury and obstruction of justice stemming from his sexual relationship with a White House intern, and then managed to avoid conviction and removal from office in the Senate trial. As extraordinary as that might seem, more than a century before Nixon's case, Andrew Johnson survived a Senate impeachment trial by a single vote, in a case that mostly reflected conflict with northern Republicans over the post–Civil War Reconstruction. The threat of impeachment has not affected only the presidency. In the 1950s, roadways throughout the country were posted with billboards calling for the impeachment of Chief Justice Earl Warren on account of his leadership of an "activist" Supreme Court. Before getting too alarmed about the state of American democracy, we should reflect that the political system managed to come through all of these difficulties. A certain amount of tumult is normal in the politics and policymaking of the institutions of American democracy.

The State of the Institutions

The current period is nevertheless, at a minimum, one of exceptional institutional ferment and apparent vulnerability. To be sure, some of the institutions we have examined appear to be relatively free of serious institutional conflict. The most trusted of the branches of government is the judicial branch—among our five institutions, the one most insulated both from elections and from market forces. As Kevin T. McGuire shows in Chapter 7, both the public and the elites who deal directly with the courts—lawyers—have favorable views of the courts' methods, saying that they base decisions on legal and constitutional grounds, and offer generous assessments of their contribution to the political system. Although these findings suggest a stable, generally approved judicial branch, they are not encouraging in all respects. Most citizens see the courts as making decisions entirely on neutral constitutional and legal grounds—a view that overlooks the sharp differences between liberal and conservative judges, or between judges appointed by Democratic and Republican presidents. To some degree it appears that the public trusts the judicial branch because the citizenry holds an unrealistic conception of its decisions, perceived to be free of politics and ideology.

Nevertheless, widespread support for the judiciary provides at least one strong basis for stability in the American political system.

In addition, despite broad-based perceptions of failure, the public schools in most areas of the country appear to function relatively well. As Daniel Romer, Patrick E. Jamieson, and Bruce W. Hardy show in Chapter 1, most parents are satisfied with the schools that their children attend. People who take a dim view of the performance of the schools are likely to get their information about schools from the media—which have adopted a crisis rhetoric in reporting about education—rather than from direct contact. In fact, the schools' performance in teaching academic skills has improved substantially since the 1980s. And there is no evidence of declining effectiveness in educating capable citizens or in encouraging a long-term interest in public affairs. As we have seen, however, the absence of decline in education for citizenship does not imply that schools engaged in primary and secondary education are succeeding in producing citizens who understand the constitutional predicates of American government and can participate effectively or intelligently in decisions about political institutions.

The main concerns about the health of American democracy are about the three institutions at the core of the political process—the legislative branch, the executive branch, and the press. With respect to the legislative and executive branches, and the separation of powers between them, our principal finding is one of profound partisan conflict among the relevant elites—not only over policy, as we would always expect, but over basic rules of the game. In Congress, as Paul J. Quirk shows in Chapter 5, the Republican majorities of the 108th and 109th Congresses ran the House and even the normally consensus-oriented Senate in ways that alienated the Democratic minorities and often struck them as illegitimate. Rather than producing effective one-party government, moreover, the partisan Congress proved subject to gridlock. It was relatively incapable of deliberating carefully. And when Congress finally acted, it was highly responsive to special interests and prone to distributing pork. Neither Democratic nor Republican staff members gave high ratings to the resulting performance in policymaking.

In the executive branch, the partisan conflict has encumbered the working relationships between political appointees and civil servants, and between Democratic and Republican civil servants. Suspicions that Republican administrations have had about opposing views held by Democratic civil servants were actually warranted—certainly during the administration of President George W. Bush. Democratic civil servants opposed Republican claims about the appropriate power of, and deference to, the presidency. As Joel D. Aberbach writes in Chapter 6, the differences between Democrats and Republicans within the executive branch "go . . . to the heart of how the system should operate"—including questions such as whether the president can, on his own authority: take preemptive military action, cancel U.S. obligations under international treaties, deny information to Congress and the public, and nullify parts of statutes, among other things.[3] Republican executives have largely approved of presidential practices that, according to Democrats, have seriously violated the constitutionally dictated separation of powers.

Regarding the press, the issues for democracy concern the consequences of profound institutional transformation or, indeed, the replacement of old institutions with brand-new ones. The basic "landscape" of the press, as Kathleen Hall Jamieson, Bruce W. Hardy, and Daniel Romer write in Chapter 2, is being transformed by the arrival of new organizations and new forms of political information. Figures with no connection to conventional news organizations, such as the gossip-mongering conservative Internet blogger Matt Drudge and the liberal television comedian Jon Stewart, provide what constitutes news for many Americans. The Fox News Channel aggressively cultivates a conservative audience, with minimal pretense of objectivity. *Countdown* with Keith Olbermann on MSNBC tilts to the opposite side of the political divide.

At the same time, traditional journalism is under siege. The "detached" media are seen as biased by the public. And newspaper reading—the best predictor of citizens' level of information—is in decline. Elites in the legislative and executive branches find fault with the press, judging that it is not fulfilling its function to inform and that the information it provides is frequently misleading or exaggerated. Journalists themselves recognize that the press fails to clarify which side in political debate is more deceptive; that it focuses on political strategizing rather than the substantive issues that citizens need to understand; and that it increasingly emphasizes "lifestyle" information, with no relevance to politics or government. Underlying these practices, concentration of ownership in big conglomerates has exaggerated the pursuit of economic success at the cost of sacrificing journalistic values. It should come as no surprise that many adult Americans remain alarmingly ill-informed about the constitutional design of American government and the specifics of contemporary politics and policymaking.

We, the Uninformed and Divided

The sovereigns of American democracy are, as the very first words of the Constitution remind us, "We the people." In theory, it is the citizenry that must take ultimate responsibility for the condition of the institutions of American government, by insisting that officials manage them appropriately and, if necessary, by demanding reforms. This responsibility pertains as well to the press and the schools, as much as to the branches of government. As we close this volume, we take the long view and ask: Should we be concerned about the public's ignorance of basic civics information? What about the deep partisan divisions within the public, so often similar to the schism among the governing elite?

The chapters in this volume have repeatedly pointed out the public's deficiencies in civics knowledge. When asked in our 2006 Annenberg Judicial Independence survey if they could identify any of the three branches of government, a third of the respondents could not name any of them; another third could name one or two; and only the remaining one-third could correctly name all of the branches. According to the 2005 Annenberg Judicial Branch survey, 22 percent of the public believes that the Supreme Court cannot declare an act of Congress unconstitutional, and another 23 percent does not know whether or not the Court has this power. Just over half of the public, 55 percent, say the U.S. Supreme Court can declare an act of Congress unconstitutional. In the same survey, 57 percent said, reasonably, that the founders intended the president, Congress, and the Supreme Court to have different but equal powers; but 35 percent said that they intended each branch to have a lot of power but the president to have the final say—a formula for a very different political system and a perspective that makes it particularly difficult to hold presidents accountable for excessive claims of power.

Nor are Americans well versed in the functioning of the branches of government. Quizzed on basic rules, many are profoundly uninformed. Less than half the respondents (47 percent) in the Judicial Branch survey said that a 5–4 decision by the Supreme Court carries the same legal weight as a 9–0 ruling; one in four (23 percent) said that such a decision is referred to Congress for resolution, and another 16 percent said it is sent back to the lower courts. Fifty-three percent of the public in the 2006 Judicial Independence survey said that Supreme Court justices usually give written reasons for their decisions, while nearly as many (47 percent) either said they do not give such reasons or did not know if they give them.

In the uncertain times of the twenty-first century's opening decade, beyond the most-educated individuals, the public does not have a clear understanding of the separation of powers or judicial independence, a theme of Mark A. Peterson's Chapter 4. As we noted in the opening pages of this volume, only 53–58 percent say the president must follow a Supreme Court ruling. Over one-third (38 percent) of adults think it is okay for the president to ignore a Supreme Court ruling if the president believes the ruling will prevent him from protecting the country against terrorist attacks. Only 58 percent believe that if the president disagrees with a Supreme Court ruling, he should follow it anyway rather than do what he thinks is in the country's best interest. A bare majority (53 percent) holds that a president must follow a Supreme Court ruling even if he believes it will prevent him from protecting the country from terrorist attack. These findings are striking in that in recent memory—from the so-called Steel Seizure case in 1952 and the Nixon tapes case in 1974 to the *Hamdan v. Rumsfeld* decision in 2006—no president has defied a ruling of the Court.

Where the public has a shaky hold on the prerogatives of the Supreme Court, it has a clearer understanding of the presidential veto. Nearly three-fourths of respondents in the 2006 poll said that if a president disagrees with part of a bill, he should veto the bill rather than signing it and failing to enforce the disputed part. The schools, the press, or both, evidently have done a better job of explaining the presidential veto than they have the separation of powers or judicial review.

Citizens' lack of knowledge may be problematic if it leads them to support or accept encroachment on the constitutional prerogatives of one of the institutions of democracy. We find suggestions to that effect in our 2006 survey. Our analysis shows that knowledge and education decrease the beliefs held by the public that judges are motivated by self-interest, that they favor the more affluent members of society, and that they are overly affected by the political process. These three types of perceived judicial bias (self-interest, favoring the rich, and being too affected by the political process) are problematic because they are negatively associated with trust in courts. Trust in the courts is important because a drop in trust is associated with the beliefs that the president can ignore Supreme Court decisions, that the courts (both the Supreme Court and local courts) have too much power, and that judges should be impeached for unpopular rulings.[4]

To be sure, although the levels of knowledge about government that we and others have found are generally low, there is no reason to believe that they are lower than in past generations.[5] The more-educated survey respondents—those who have a college education—are far more likely than the less educated to understand and endorse the central tenets of the American constitutional system. As we noted earlier, respondents who lack a college education were as likely as not to embrace the unsupportable claim that the founders' intended to subordinate Congress and the judiciary and give the president "the final say." The existence of such misinformation about the nation's constitutional system among a substantial fraction of the public raises questions about the ability of the public to object to overreaching by the executive—especially in a time of an ongoing external threat from terrorists. It underlines the importance of civics education in high school. Education not only increases the likelihood that a person will be appropriately knowledgeable about constitutional issues; it also increases the likelihood that he or she will vote.

Apart from deficiencies of knowledge, we find a high level of ideological polarization between Democrats and Republicans in the electorate. Not only elites, but the public, too, are increasingly divided. Attack-based election campaigns reinforce the partisan dispositions of citizens who may be exposed mainly to partisan sources of news and political comment. Just before the November 2006 midterm elections, the Pew Research Center for the People and the Press released a survey that found that "the vast divide between voters who intend to vote Democratic and Republican . . . extends well beyond matters of opinion. These voters also see the world quite differently. For the vast majority of Republican voters—70%—the economy is doing well; most Democratic voters (74%) say the economy is doing only fair or poorly. Despite the rising American death toll in Iraq, 61% of GOP voters say things there are going at least fairly well. Eight in ten Democratic voters (81%), however, disagree."[6]

An Annenberg post-election survey in 2004 featured another facet of a polarized electorate. In that study Democrats seemed to uncritically embrace Senator John Kerry's attacks on the Republicans, regardless of their accuracy, while Republicans returned the favor by adopting even more deceptive attacks on the Democrats.[7] Given these figures, we are surprised when partisans actually agree with those of opposite ideological disposition about basic institutional issues—as they do, for example, in expressing high levels of trust in the Supreme Court and state courts, and in judging that a media outlet did a good job of investigating a scandal in journalism. Agreement seems to rise when the subject in question does not involve our most democratic institutions.

Lost in such a world may be both the disposition to engage in deliberation and any confidence that, in the clash of competing ideas, some on each side of the ideological divide remain open to persuasion, permitting the stronger ideas, buttressed by evidence, to ultimately prevail. Crushed in such a partisan world may be any ground hospitable to moderate positions.

Whether because of the deficiencies of media discourse and citizens' information or for other reasons, our analyses have also sometimes found problematic conflicts between the perceptions of the public and those of elites. Why, for example, do parents regard their children's public school as better than public schools in general? Again, Romer, Jamieson, and Hardy argue that the media's focus on crisis in the schools may account at least in part for this anomalous finding. Why do mainstream journalists believe that they correct major mistakes while the public holds that they do not? Whatever the reason, the difference in perception is problematic because public belief that the press does not live up to its ideals predicts a willingness to censor the press. Similarly, why do most citizens have a negative view of members of Congress collectively—regarding them as self-serving and often corrupt—and yet hold their own representatives in high esteem? Such attitudes helped produce popular support for legislative term limitations in the 1990s and could produce support for drastic, potentially harmful reforms in Congress that could further undermine its capacity for promoting expertise, deliberation, and accommodation of multiple legitimate interests. Observers of American institutions need to look out for potentially harmful conflicts between citizens' and elites' perceptions of those institutions.

The Future of a Divided Republic

Despite these concerns, we also should underscore signs of resilience in a system committed to democratic elections. Elections act as a check on excesses in the legislative and executive branch. In the past century in all but one midterm election in the second term of a president, the president's party has lost seats in Congress. The election of 2006 was no exception. The party out of power reclaims power in part by adjusting its positions to draw votes from a new majority alignment of the electorate. Importantly, in the 2006 midterm election, the Democrats successfully fielded candidates in key states who took moderate positions. Some candidates at the extreme of the Republican Party, including Pennsylvania senator Rick Santorum, lost their seats to these Democratic contenders. Reflecting the public's frustrations with the Iraq war, the uneven rewards of the economy, and the sheer volume of partisanship, in the 2006 election one-party rule gave way to divided government and with it higher levels of accountability between the legislative and executive branches, especially the president.

As worrisome as public ignorance of the constitutional system may seem, when given a set of choices that would have circumscribed the power of judges in 2006, voters just said no. In Colorado, voters defeated Amendment 40, which would have reduced the terms of state supreme court judges and courts of appeals judges to four years and limited their service to three terms.[8] By almost nine to one, in South Dakota voters rejected Constitutional Amendment E, which would have fined or jailed those who make judicial decisions that break rules formulated by a panel of thirteen grand jurors. The punishments could have been enforced for decisions made in past years.[9]

Sensing the mood of the electorate, in the run-up to the 2006 election even some representatives and senators in Congress within the president's own party sometimes stood up, though with varying levels of intensity and likely impact, for the prerogatives of the legislature. In response to concerns raised when President Bush signed a bill containing a ban on torture and then in a signing statement reserved the right to not carry out that provision, Republican senator Arlen Specter, then chair of the Senate Judiciary Committee, introduced legislation giving Congress standing to test such presidential statements in the Court.

Notwithstanding such resilience, however, a central question is whether the original constitutional structures of American government—in particular, the separation of powers and the independence of individual senators and representatives—remain viable for the future. In designing the constitutional system, the framers essentially ignored political parties, which they naively hoped would not develop. For much of American history, the party system has been fragmented and relatively incoherent—complicated by regional differences, especially about slavery and race. The nation's politics have now arrived at a condition in which political parties are increasingly coherent and, as a result, they are sharply divided and increasingly cohesive and disciplined. Thus the logical potential for parties either to nullify the separation of powers (in periods of unified party control of the branches) or else to infect it with exaggerated and destructive partisan conflict (in periods of divided control)—appear to be emerging as realities. The great question facing Americans, therefore, is whether to defend and seek to restore the traditional constitutional structures, or instead to accept that the basic conditions of party politics—the beliefs of politicians, their manner of conducting political campaigns, and the responses of voters—render those traditional structures essentially unworkable. The next question is whether real party government can be sustained in a system predicated on the separation of powers imbued with explicit checks and balances.

As he left the Constitutional Convention of 1787, Benjamin Franklin reportedly was asked by a passerby whether the effort had produced a democracy or a monarchy. In a reply as often recounted as any of the founders' statements, Franklin is said to have commented, "A republic, if you can keep it." Throughout the books of scholarly essays that several of us helped edit as part of the Institutions of American Democracy series, and here in this volume, we have asked how well the nation has indeed "kept" five basic institutions of American democracy: Congress, the presidency and the executive branch, the courts, the press, and the public schools. We have considered as well whether the times in which we find ourselves—with the policy challenges of war and terrorism, and the severity of the nation's political divisions—are critically different from prior periods. Those questions cannot yet be answered definitively. If Franklin could observe the nation's current state, he probably would no longer doubt that we can keep a republic, as opposed to reverting to a monarchy or other form of dictatorship. He might say that the institutions designed by the framers and the dynamics of twenty-first-century politics have given our generation, "a republic divided, if you can make it work."

Notes

1. Commission on Freedom of the Press, *A Free and Responsible Press: A General Report on Mass Communication: Newspapers, Radio, Motion Pictures, Magazines, and Books*, ed. Robert D. Leigh (Chicago: University of Chicago Press, 1947), 60.

2. Thomas Jefferson, *The Life and Selected Writings of Thomas Jefferson*, ed. Adrienne Koch and William Peden (New York: Random House, 1944), 581–82.

3. The Annenberg Institutions of Democracy survey data cover many, but not all, of these issues. Aside from those measures discussed in the text, the surveys asked respondents about suspending constitutional protections for individuals and about whether the president has a "broad right" to keep his communications with others on policy matters secret. Party identification was strongly related to answers to these questions, both at the elite level and among the general public.

4. See Kathleen Hall Jamieson and Michael Hennessy, "Public Information and the Courts," *Georgetown Law Review*, forthcoming.

5. Michael Delli Carpini and Scott Keeter, *What Americans Know about Politics and Why It Matters* (New Haven, Conn.: Yale University Press, 1997).

6. Pew Research Center for the People and the Press, "Profiling the Voters: Democrats and Republicans See Different Realities," Commentary, November 6, 2006, http://people-press.org.

7. Brooks Jackson and Kathleen Hall Jamieson, *Unspun: Finding Facts in a World of Disinformation* (New York: Random House, 2007).

8. Information from the Legislative Counsel of the Colorado General Assembly's *Analysis of the 2006 Ballot Proposals*.

9. Information from the *2006 Ballot Question Pamphlet* by the Office of South Dakota Secretary of State Chris Nelson.

APPENDIX
ANNENBERG SURVEYS

Annenberg Institutions of Democracy Surveys

1. Public Schools

The Annenberg Public Schools survey was conducted by telephone from January 24 to March 19, 2003. A total of 201 school administrators, 608 teachers, 800 parents, and 802 in the general population were interviewed. Fieldwork by ICR/International Communications Research, Media, Penn.

Margin of error = ±7% for school administrators
Margin of error = ±4% for teachers
Margin of error = ±4% for parents
Margin of error = ±4% for general public

2. Media

Prepared by Princeton Survey Research Associates International for the Annenberg Foundation Trust at Sunnylands and the Annenberg Public Policy Center

Public Component
N = 1,500 Adults 18 and older
Form A: N = 759
Form B: N = 741
Field dates: March 3, 2005, to April 5, 2005
Margin of error = ±3% for results based on full sample

Elite Component
N = 673 Journalists
Form A: N = 338

Form B: N = 335
Field dates: March 7, 2005, to May 2, 2005
Margin of error = ±4% for results based on full sample

3. Government

Prepared by Princeton Survey Research Associates International for the
Annenberg Foundation Trust at Sunnylands

General Public
N = 1,300 GP (with 210 African Americans, 330 Hispanics, and 283 18- to
29-year olds)
Field dates: August 19, 2003 to November 4, 2003
Margin of error = ±3% for results based on full sample

Presidential Appointees
N = 501 (with 104 in George W. Bush admin., 190 in Clinton admin., 132
in George H.W. Bush admin., 75 in second Reagan admin.)
Field dates: August 25, 2003, to November 10, 2003
Margin of error = ±4% for results based on full sample

4. Congress

Prepared by Princeton Survey Research Associates International for the Annenberg
Foundation Trust at Sunnylands and the Annenberg Public Policy Center

Congressional Staff Component
N = 182 Staff members in the House
N = 70 Staff members in the Senate
Total = 252 Congressional staff members
Field dates: August 4, 2004, to November 22, 2004 (House)
Field dates: August 10, 2004, to November 12, 2004 (Senate)
Margin of error = ±6% for results based on full sample

5. Executive Branch

SES and Political Appointees Component
Total = 787
N = 113 Bush presidential appointees
N = 152 Clinton presidential appointees
N = 444 Senior Executive Service (SES)
N = 33 Bush Executive Office of the President (EOP) career
N = 8 Bush Executive Office of the President (EOP) appointees
N = 37 Clinton Executive Office of the President (EOP) appointees
Field dates: August 3, 2004, to January 17, 2005
Margin of error = ±3% for results based on full sample

6. Congress and Executive Branch

Prepared by Princeton Survey Research Associates International for the Annenberg Foundation Trust at Sunnylands and the Annenberg Public Policy Center

Public Component
N = 1,500 Adults 18 and older
Form Split A: N = 746
Form Split B: N = 754
Form Split C: N = 601
Form Split D: N = 899
Form Split E: N = 504
Form Split F: N = 513
Form Split G: N = 767
Form Split H: N = 733
Field dates: December 18, 2004, to January 18, 2005
For results based on the full public samples, the margin of error is ±3.
Due to rounding, percentages may not add to 100.

House, Senate, and Executive Branch Triads
N = 92 Congressional committee staff members
Margin of error = ±10% for results based on congressional committee staff
           members
N = 203 Government officials and staff
Margin of error = ±7% for results based on government officials and staff
Total = 295
Field dates: December 27, 2004, to February 25, 2005

7. Judicial Branch

Prepared by Princeton Survey Research Associates International for the Annenberg Foundation Trust at Sunnylands and the Annenberg Public Policy Center

Public Component
May 24, 2005
N = 1,504 Adults 18 and older
Form A: N = 768
Form B: N = 736
Field dates: March 17, 2005, to April 18, 2005
Margin of error = ±3% for results based on full sample

Lawyer Component
Prepared by Princeton Survey Research Associates International for the Annenberg Foundation Trust at Sunnylands and the Annenberg Public Policy Center

N = 859 Lawyers admitted to practice before the Supreme Court or the courts of appeals

Form A: N = 423

Form B: N = 436

Field dates: March 18, 2005, to May 16, 2005

Margin of error = ±3% for results based on full sample

Judicial Independence

N = 1,002 Adults 18 and older

Field dates: August 3, 2006, to August 16, 2006

Margin of error = ±3% for results based on full sample

National Annenberg Election Survey

A complete description of the National Annenberg Election Survey (NAES) 2000 and 2004 can be found in Daniel Romer et al., *Capturing Campaign Dynamics: The National Annenberg Election Survey, 2000 and 2004* (Philadelphia: University of Pennsylvania Press, 2006).

Regression Analysis of Trust

Advanced statistical analysis shows that the public's level of trust in government rests on six main factors—government leadership, government performance, government power, understanding the public, political orientation, and age.

In this analysis, there are two measures of leadership—one scaled variable and one additional variable. The scaled variable is comprised of three questions: (1) whether federal officials are ethical and moral; (2) whether federal officials are trustworthy; and (3) whether presidents are honest with the American people. The other leadership variable asks the public about corruption in federal agencies.

Performance consists of one scaled variable and one additional variable. The scaled variable comprises four questions that ask the public how good a job the federal government does: (1) running its programs and services; (2) helping people who need assistance; (3) being fair in its decisions; and (4) spending its money wisely. The other variable asks which is the bigger problem with the federal government—having the wrong priorities, or having the right priorities but inefficiently run programs. Respondents who responded to both options (5 percent) were excluded from the analysis.

Power consists of two variables. First, the public is asked whether the federal government today has too much power, the federal government is using the right amount of power for meeting today's needs, or the federal government should use its powers more vigorously to promote the well-being of all segments

Regression Summary of Trust in Government

How much do you trust the federal government in Washington to operate in the best interests of the American people?		
N = 1,089		
	UNSTD. COEFF.	**STD. COEFF.**
Leadership		
Federal officials ethical and moral/Federal officials trustworthy/Presidents honest with American people	.117***	.228***
Corruption in federal agencies	−.068*	−.059*
Performance		
Running its programs and services/Helping people who need assistance/Being fair in its decisions/Spending its money wisely	.059***	.182***
Right priorities but runs programs inefficiently	−.193***	−.105***
Power		
Federal government has too much power	−.070**	−.067**
Maintain current level of services	−.038*	−.060*
High-level officials understand how public feels about important issues	.172***	.178***
Political party (Republican)	.145***	.130***
Self-reported knowledge of how government works	.055	.044
Demographics		
Age	.003**	.066**
Income	.001	.026
Race/ethnicity (white)	.037	.020
Education	.000	−.002
Gender (women)	−.034	−.019
(constant)	.843***	—
Adj. R²=.376***		
*p>.05; **p>.01; ***p>.001		

of society. Second, a commonly used measure of government power asks the following: if 1 represents someone who generally believes that, on the whole, federal government programs should be cut back greatly to reduce the power of government, and 6 represents someone who feels that government programs should be maintained to deal with important problems, where on the scale of 1 to 6 would you place yourself? This variable was recorded into a dichotomous variable—cut back programs (1–3) and maintain programs (4–6).

Beyond leadership, performance, and power, the regression analysis includes a question that asks the public how well they think high-level government officials understand what the public thinks about the issues facing the country, as well as political party affiliation (1 = Republican, 2 = Independent, 3 = Democrat). Also included in the analysis is a question that asks the public how much they say they know about how the federal government works. This variable was statistically insignificant and was excluded from the discussion.

Standard demographic variables were included in the analysis as well. Only age was a statistically significant factor in explaining trust in government.

INDEX

Index

Index

Index

Index